CONTENTS

Maps

Fo

Toronto

The complete guide, thoroughly up-to-date

Packed with details that will make your trip

The must-see sights, off and on the beaten path

What to see, what to skip

Vacation itineraries, walking tours, day trips

Smart lodging and dining options

Essential local dos and taboos

Transportation tips

Key contacts, savvy travel advice

When to go, what to pack

Clear, accurate, easy-to-use maps

Fodor's Travel Publications, Inc.
New York • Toronto • London • Sydney • Auckland
www.fodors.com

Fodor's Toronto

EDITOR: Linda Cabasin

Editorial Contributors: David Brown, Mike Filey, Liza Finlay, Deborah Kaufman, Terrence Moloney, Shawna Richer, Helayne Schiff, Sara Waxman

Editorial Production: Stacey Kulig

Maps: David Lindroth, *cartographer*; Steven Amsterdam, Bob Blake, *map editors*

Design: Fabrizio La Rocca, *creative director*; Guido Caroti, *associate art director*; Jolie Novak, *photo editor*

Production/Manufacturing: Robert B. Shields

Cover Photograph: Bob Krist

Copyright

Twelfth Edition

ISBN 0–679–00063–1

Special Sales

Fodor's Travel Publications are available at special discounts for bulk purchases for sales promotions or premiums. Special editions, including personalized covers, excerpts of existing guides, and corporate imprints, can be created in large quantities for special needs. For more information, contact your local bookseller or write to Special Markets, Fodor's Travel Publications, 201 East 50th Street, New York, NY 10022. Inquiries from Canada should be directed to your local Canadian bookseller or sent to Random House of Canada, Ltd., Marketing Department, 2775 Matheson Boulevard East, Mississauga, Ontario L4W 4P7. Inquiries from the United Kingdom should be sent to Fodor's Travel Publications, 20 Vauxhall Bridge Road, London SW1V 2SA, England.

PRINTED IN THE UNITED STATES OF AMERICA

10 9 8 7 6 5 4 3 2 1

ON THE ROAD WITH FODOR'S

WHEN I PLAN A VACATION, the first thing I do is cast around among my friends and colleagues to find someone who's just been where I'm going. That's because there's no substitute for a recommendation from a good friend who knows your tastes, your budget, and your circumstances, someone who's just been there. Unfortunately, such friends are few and far between. So it's nice to know that there's Fodor's *Toronto*.

In the first place, this book won't stay home when you hit the road. It will accompany you every step of the way, steering you away from wrong turns and wrong choices and never expecting a thing in return. Most important of all, it's written and assiduously updated by the kind of people you *would* hit up for travel tips if you knew them. They're as choosy as your pickiest friend, except they've probably seen a lot more of Toronto. In these pages, they don't send you chasing down every town and sight in Toronto but have instead selected the best ones, the ones that are worthy of your time and money. To make it easy for you to put it all together in the time you have, they've created itineraries and neighborhood walks that you can mix and match in a snap. Will this be the vacation of your dreams? We hope so.

About Our Writers

Our success in helping to make your trip the best of all possible vacations is a credit to the hard work of our extraordinary writers.

Mike Filey, updater of the Exploring and Side Trips chapters, brought a wealth of knowledge about Toronto to the task. The author of more than a dozen books about the city's history, he has also written a popular column for the *Sunday Sun,* "The Way We Were," for years. His enthusiasm for all aspects of his city, from its streetcars to its changing skyline, is evident in everything he writes.

Liza Finlay, who was in charge of the Shopping and Nightlife and the Arts chapters, is a journalist, communications expert, and self-confessed shopping addict.

The former managing editor of *Flare* (Canada's answer to *Vogue*), she now contributes to several Canadian magazines and newspapers covering social and lifestyle issues as well as entertainment. She lives in downtown Toronto with her golden retriever, whom she sheepishly admits to dressing in designer wear.

Allan Gould's *The Toronto Book,* a highly personal guide to his chosen city, first directed Fodor's attention to its author in the 1980s. Since then, in addition to writing the original and some previous updated versions of *Fodor's Toronto,* Gould has also written a book about the Stratford Festival with its founder, Tom Patterson, and anthologized Canadian humor. In all, he has written 24 books.

Terrence Moloney, who updated the Lodging chapter and the Gold Guide, cheerfully tracked down more good places to stay around town. He has a master's degree in classics from the University of Toronto. A contributor to Fodor's *Greece* and *Canada,* he has spent time in Toronto during his current legal studies.

Shawna Richer, updater of the Outdoor Activities and Sports chapter, is a sports reporter for *The Globe and Mail,* Canada's national newspaper. She lives in Toronto and writes mainly about professional football (she's fervent about the Canadian version of the game) but also covers baseball, basketball, and hockey.

Sara Waxman, who wrote the expanded Dining chapter and all the dining reviews in the Side Trips chapter, is the restaurant critic for the *Financial Post* and the *Toronto Sun.* Her witty, savvy reviews reveal an insider's knowledge of the trends of the city's fast-changing dining scene. She is the author of three best-selling cookbooks and a Toronto restaurant guide.

Connections

We're pleased that the American Society of Travel Agents continues to endorse Fodor's as its guidebook of choice. ASTA is the world's largest and most influential travel trade association, operating in more than 170 countries, with 27,000 members pledged to adhere to a strict code of ethics reflecting the Society's motto, "Integrity in Travel." ASTA shares Fodor's devotion to providing smart, honest travel information and advice to travelers, and we've long recommended that our readers—even those who have guidebooks and traveling friends—consult ASTA member agents for the experience and professionalism they bring to your vacation planning.

On Fodor's Web site (www.fodors.com), check out the new Resource Center, an online companion to the Gold Guide section of this book, complete with useful hot links to related sites. In our forums, you can also get lively advice from other travelers and more great tips from Fodor's experts worldwide.

How to Use This Book

Organization

Up front is the **Gold Guide,** an easy-to-use section arranged alphabetically by topic. Under each listing you'll find tips and information that will help you accomplish what you need to in Toronto. You'll also find addresses and telephone numbers of organizations and companies that offer destination-related services and detailed information and publications.

The first chapter in the guide, Destination: Toronto helps get you in the mood for your trip. New and Noteworthy cues you in on trends and happenings, What's Where gets you oriented, Pleasures and Pastimes describes the activities and sights that make Toronto unique, Great Itineraries lays out a selection of complete trips, Fodor's Choice showcases our top picks, and Festivals and Seasonal Events alerts you to special events you'll want to seek out.

The Exploring chapter is divided into neighborhood sections; each recommends a walking or driving tour and lists neighborhood sights alphabetically, including sights that are off the beaten path. The remaining chapters are arranged in alphabetical order by subject (dining, lodging, nightlife and the arts, outdoor activities and sports, shopping, and side trips).

Icons and Symbols

★ Our special recommendations
✕ Restaurant
🏨 Lodging establishment
🐤 Good for kids (rubber duck)
☞ Sends you to another section of the guide for more information

✉ Address
☎ Telephone number
🕐 Opening and closing times
💰 Admission prices (those we give apply to adults; substantially reduced fees are almost always available for children, students, and senior citizens)

Numbers in white and black circles ③ ❸ that appear on the maps, in the margins, and within the tours correspond to one another.

Credit Cards

The following abbreviations are used: **AE,** American Express; **D,** Discover; **DC,** Diners Club; **MC,** MasterCard; and **V,** Visa.

Currency

Unless otherwise noted, all prices, including those for dining and lodging, are given in Canadian dollars.

Don't Forget to Write

You can use this book in the confidence that all prices and opening times are based on information supplied to us at press time; Fodor's cannot accept responsibility for any errors. Time inevitably brings changes, so always confirm information when it matters—especially if you're making a detour to visit a specific place.

Were the restaurants we recommended as described? Did our hotel picks exceed your expectations? Did you find a museum we recommended a waste of time? Keeping a travel guide fresh and up-to-date is a big job, and we welcome your feedback, positive *and* negative. If you have complaints, we'll look into them and revise our entries when the facts warrant it. If you've discovered a special place that we haven't included, we'll pass the information along to our correspondents and have them check it out. So send us your thoughts via e-mail at editors@fodors.com (specifying the name of the book on the subject line) or on paper in care of the Toronto editor at Fodor's, 201 East 50th Street, New York, NY 10022. In the meantime, have a wonderful trip!

Karen Cure

Karen Cure
Editorial Director

Toronto Area Orientation

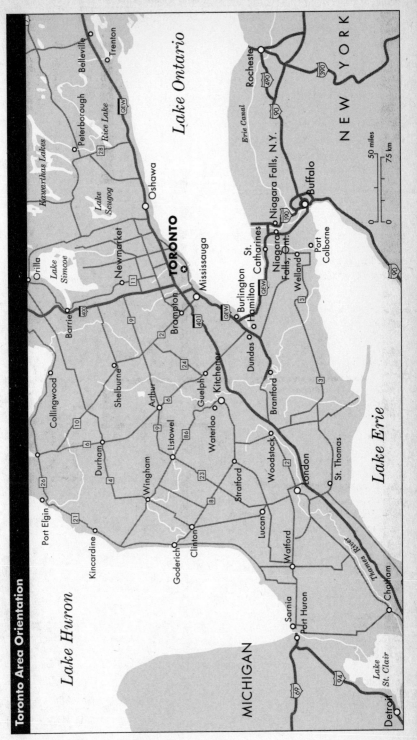

TTC Subway Routes

Subway Lines

———	Yonge–University
▪▪▪▪	Bloor–Danforth
═══	Scarborough LRT
▬▬▬	Harbourfront LRT
⊙	Transfer

McCowan
Scarborough Centre
Midland
Ellesmere
Kennedy
Warden
Victoria Park
Main Street
Woodbine
Coxwell
Greenwood
Donlands
Pape
Chester
Broadview
Castle Frank
Sherbourne

Lawrence East

Danforth Avenue

Finch
North York Centre
Sheppard
York Mills
Lawrence
Eglington
Davisville
St. Clair
Summerhill
Rosedale
Wellesley
College
Dundas
Queen
King

Yonge Street

St. George
Yonge-Bloor
Bay

University Avenue

Union
Queen's Quay
York Str.
Simcoe St.
Rees Str.
Spadina Ave.

Museum
Queen's Park
St. Patrick
Osgoode
St. Andrew

Spadina
Dupont

Downsview
Wilson
Yorkdale
Lawrence West
Glencairn
Eglington West
St. Clair West

Bathurst
Christie
Ossington

Bloor Street

Dufferin
Lansdowne
Dundas West
Keele
High Park
Runnymede
Jane
Old Mill
Royal York
Islington
Kipling

SMART TRAVEL TIPS A TO Z

Basic Information on Traveling in Toronto, Savvy Tips to Make Your Trip a Breeze, and Companies and Organizations to Contact

AIR TRAVEL

BOOKING YOUR FLIGHT

Price is just one factor to consider when booking a flight: frequency of service and even a carrier's safety record are often just as important. Major airlines offer the greatest number of departures. Smaller airlines—including regional and no-frills airlines—usually have a limited number of flights daily. On the other hand, so-called low-cost airlines usually are cheaper, and their fares impose fewer restrictions, such as advance-purchase requirements. Safety-wise, low-cost carriers as a group have a good history—about equal to that of major carriers.

When you book, **look for nonstop flights** and **remember that "direct" flights stop at least once.** Try to **avoid connecting flights,** which require a change of plane. Two airlines may jointly operate a connecting flight, so ask if your airline operates every segment—you may find that your preferred carrier flies you only part of the way. International flights on a country's flag carrier are almost always nonstop; U.S. airlines often fly direct.

Ask your airline if it offers electronic ticketing, which eliminates most paperwork. There's no ticket to pick up or misplace. In many airports you go directly to the gate and give the agent your confirmation number. There's no worry about waiting on line at the airport while precious minutes tick by.

CARRIERS

When flying internationally, you must usually choose between a domestic carrier, the national flag carrier of the country you are visiting, and a foreign carrier from a third country. You may, for example, choose to fly Air Canada to Toronto. National flag carriers have the greatest number of

nonstops. Domestic carriers may have better connections to your hometown and serve a greater number of gateway cities. Third-party carriers may have a price advantage.

➤ MAJOR AIRLINES: **Air Canada** (☎ 800/776–3000). **American Airlines** (☎ 800/433–7300). **Canadian International Airlines** (☎ 800/426–7000). **Continental** (☎ 800/231–0856 or 800/525–0280). **Delta** (☎ 800/221–1212). **Northwest** (☎ 800/225–2525). **TWA** (☎ 800/221–2000 or 800/892–4141). **United Airlines** (☎ 800/241–6522). **US Airways** (☎ 800/428–4322).

➤ SMALLER AIRLINES: A low-cost airline, **Canada 3000** (☎ 416/674–2661) flies between Toronto and major Canadian cities, such as Vancouver, Edmonton, and Winnipeg, as well as several cities in the United States, including Las Vegas and Orlando.

➤ FROM THE U.K.: **British Airways** (☎ 0345/222–111). **Canadian Airlines International** (☎ 0181/577–7722 or 0345/616–767 outside London).

CHECK IN & BOARDING

Airlines routinely overbook planes, assuming that not everyone with a ticket will show up, but sometimes everyone does. When that happens, airlines ask for volunteers to give up their seats. In return these volunteers usually get a certificate for a free flight and are rebooked on the next flight out. If there are not enough volunteers, the airline must choose who will be denied boarding. The first to get bumped are passengers who checked in late and those flying on discounted tickets, so **get to the gate and check in as early as possible,** especially during peak periods.

Although the trend on international flights is to drop reconfirmation requirements, many airlines still ask

THE GOLD GUIDE / SMART TRAVEL TIPS

you to reconfirm each leg of your international itinerary. Failure to do so may result in your reservation being canceled.

Always **bring a government-issued photo ID to the airport.** You may be asked to show it before you are allowed to check in; you will definitely be asked to show it if you have an electronic ticket.

CONSOLIDATORS

Consolidators buy tickets for scheduled international flights at reduced rates from the airlines, then sell them at prices that beat the best fare available directly from the airlines, usually without restrictions. Sometimes you can even get your money back if you need to return the ticket. Carefully read the fine print detailing penalties for changes and cancellations, and **confirm your consolidator reservation with the airline.**

➤ CONSOLIDATORS: **Cheap Tickets** (☎ 800/377–1000). **Discount Travel Network** (☎ 800/576–1600). **Unitravel** (☎ 800/325–2222). **Up & Away Travel** (☎ 212/889–2345). **World Travel Network** (☎ 800/ 409–6753).

CUTTING COSTS

The least-expensive airfares to Toronto are priced for round-trip travel and usually must be purchased in advance. It's smart to **call a number of airlines, and when you are quoted a good price, book it on the spot**—the same fare may not be available the next day. Airlines generally allow you to change your return date for a fee. If you don't use your ticket, you can apply the cost toward the purchase of a new ticket, again for a small charge. However, most low-fare tickets are nonrefundable. To get the lowest airfare, **check different routings.** Compare prices of flights to and from different airports if your destination or home city has more than one gateway. Also price off-peak flights, which may be significantly less expensive.

Travel agents, especially those who specialize in finding the lowest fares (☞ Discounts & Deals, *below*), can be especially helpful when booking a plane ticket. When you're quoted a price, **ask your agent if the price is likely to get any lower.** Good agents know the seasonal fluctuations of airfares and can usually anticipate a sale or fare war. However, waiting can be risky: The fare could go *up* as seats become scarce, and you may wait so long that your preferred flight sells out. A wait-and-see strategy works best if your plans are flexible. If you must arrive and depart on certain dates, don't delay.

ENJOYING THE FLIGHT

For better service, **fly smaller or regional carriers,** which often have higher passenger-satisfaction ratings. Sometimes you'll find leather seats, more legroom, and better food.

For more legroom, **request an emergency-aisle seat.** Don't sit in the row in front of the emergency aisle or in front of a bulkhead, where seats may not recline.

If you don't like airline food, **ask for special meals when booking.** These can be vegetarian, low-cholesterol, or kosher, for example.

FLYING TIMES

Flying time to Toronto is 1½ hours from New York and Chicago, 4½ hours from Los Angeles.

HOW TO COMPLAIN

If your baggage goes astray or your flight goes awry, complain right away. Most carriers require that you **file a claim immediately.**

➤ AIRLINE COMPLAINTS: U.S. Department of Transportation **Aviation Consumer Protection Division** (✉ C-75, Room 4107, Washington, DC 20590, ☎ 202/366–2220). **Federal Aviation Administration Consumer Hotline** (☎ 800/322–7873).

AIRPORTS & TRANSFERS

AIRPORTS

The major airport is **Lester B. Pearson International Airport.** A handful of flights—mostly domestic—also land at tiny **Toronto City Centre Airport** in the Toronto Islands, a brief ferry ride from downtown.

➤ AIRPORT INFORMATION: **Lester B. Pearson International Airport** (✉ Airport Rd., ☎ 416/247–7678).

Toronto City Centre Airport (✉ Centre Island, ☎ 416/203–2036).

TRANSFERS

Although Pearson International Airport is not far from the downtown area (about 32 km, or 20 mi), the drive can take well over an hour during Toronto's weekday rush hours (7–9 AM and 3:30–6:30 PM). Taxis and limos to a hotel or attraction near the lake can cost $40 or more. Airport cabs have fixed rates to different parts of the city. You must pay the full fare from the airport, but it is often possible to negotiate a lower fare from downtown, where airport cabs compete with regular city cabs. It is illegal for city cabs to pick up passengers at the airport, unless they are called—a time-consuming process, but sometimes worth the wait. Many airport and downtown hotels offer free buses to their locations from each of the airport's three terminals.

Express buses offered by PW (Pacific Western) Transportation Limited link the airport to three subway stops in the southwest (Islington) and north-central (Yorkdale; York Mills) areas of the city. Buses depart every 40 minutes from the airport, and from those subway points to the airport, beginning about 5 AM and ending around midnight; the cost is about $8 one-way, $12 round-trip.

Bus service to and from several downtown hotels (including the Westin Harbour Castle, Royal York, Holiday Inn on King, Toronto Marriott Eaton Centre, and the Delta Chelsea Inn) runs every 20 minutes, from about 5 AM to about 11 PM. Buses also stop at the Bus Terminal at Edward and Bay streets; the cost is approximately $12.50 one-way, $21.50 round-trip.

If you rent a car at the airport, ask for a street map of the city. Highway 427 runs south some 6 km (4 mi) to the lakeshore. Here you pick up the Queen Elizabeth Way east to the Gardiner Expressway, which runs east into the heart of downtown. If you take the QEW west, you'll find yourself swinging around Lake Ontario, toward Hamilton, Niagara-on-the-Lake, and Niagara Falls.

➤ TAXIS & SHUTTLES: PW (Pacific Western) Transportation Service (☎ 905/564–6333 automated; 905/564–3232 administration).

BIKE TRAVEL

BIKES IN FLIGHT

Most airlines will accommodate bikes as luggage, provided they are dismantled and put into a box. Call to see if your airline sells bike boxes (about $5; bike bags are at least $100) although you can often pick them up free at bike shops. International travelers can sometimes substitute a bike for a piece of checked luggage for free; otherwise, it will cost about $100. Domestic and Canadian airlines charge a $25–$50 fee.

BUS TRAVEL

Greyhound has regular bus service into Toronto from all over the United States. From Detroit, the trip takes six hours; from Buffalo, two to three hours; from Chicago and New York City, 11 hours. Buses arrive at 610 Bay Street, just above Dundas Street.

➤ BUS LINES: Greyhound (☎ 800/231–2222 in the U.S. or 416/367–8747). Metro Toronto Coach Information Centre (for other companies) (☎ 416/393–7911).

DISCOUNT PASSES

Five-fare tickets are available for $8. Visitors who plan to stay in Toronto for most or all of a calendar month should consider a Metropass, good for unlimited rides in one calendar month: $83 plus $3 extra for the photo identity card.

The Day Pass costs $6.50 and is good for unlimited travel for one person, weekdays after 9:30 AM, and all day Saturday. On Sunday and holidays, it's good for up to six persons (maximum two adults) for unlimited travel.

INFORMATION

You can call the Toronto Transit Commission (TTC) 7 AM–11:30 PM for information on public transit in the city.

➤ INFORMATION: TTC Information (☎ 416/393–4636 or 416/393–8663).

WITHIN TORONTO

All buses and streetcars (as well as subways) accept only exact change, tickets, or tokens. The single fare for buses, streetcars, and subway trains is $2. Paper transfers are free; pick one up at the time that you pay your fare.

Be sure to **pick up a free Ride Guide,** available in most subways. This handy guide, published annually by the Toronto Transit Commission (TTC), shows nearly every major place of interest in the city and how to reach it by public transit.

BUSINESS HOURS

Most retail stores are open Monday through Saturday 10–6 and may be open on Sunday (generally noon–5) as well. Downtown stores are usually open until 9 PM. Some shops are open Thursday and/or Friday evenings, too. Shopping malls tend to be open weekdays from 9 or 10 AM to 10 PM, Saturday from 9 AM to 6 PM, and Sunday from noon to 5 PM.

Banks are open Monday through Thursday from 10 to 5 and Friday from 10 to 6. Trust companies and some banks open as early as 8:30 AM and on Saturday as well, and some remain open as late as 8 PM.

CAMERAS & COMPUTERS

EQUIPMENT PRECAUTIONS

Always **keep your film, tape, or computer disks out of the sun.** Carry an extra supply of batteries, and **be prepared to turn on your camera, camcorder, or laptop** to prove to security personnel that the device is real. Always **ask for hand inspection of film,** which becomes clouded after successive exposure to airport X-ray machines, and **keep videotapes and computer disks away from metal detectors.**

➤ PHOTO HELP: **Kodak Information Center** (☎ 800/242–2424). *Kodak Guide to Shooting Great Travel Pictures,* available in bookstores or from Fodor's Travel Publications (☎ 800/533–6478; $16.50 plus $4 shipping).

CAR RENTAL

Rates in Toronto begin at $45 a day and $240 a week for an economy car with unlimited mileage. This does not include tax on car rentals, which is 14%.

➤ MAJOR AGENCIES: **Alamo** (☎ 800/522–9696, 0800/272–2000 in the U.K.). **Avis** (☎ 800/331–1084, 800/879–2847 in Canada, 008/225–533 in Australia). **Budget** (☎ 800/527–0700, 0800/181181 in the U.K.). **Dollar** (☎ 800/800–4000; 0990/565656 in the U.K., where it is known as Eurodollar). **Hertz** (☎ 800/654–3001, 800/263–0600 in Canada, 0345/555888 in the U.K., 03/9222–2523 in Australia, 03/358–6777 in New Zealand). **National InterRent** (☎ 800/227–3876; 0345/222525 in the U.K., where it is known as Europcar InterRent).

CUTTING COSTS

To get the best deal, **book through a travel agent who is willing to shop around.**

Also **ask your travel agent about a company's customer-service record.** How has the company responded to late plane arrivals and vehicle mishaps? Are there often lines at the rental counter? If you're traveling during a holiday period, does a confirmed reservation guarantee you a car?

Be sure to **look into wholesalers,** companies that do not own fleets but rent in bulk from those that do and often offer better rates than traditional car-rental operations. Prices are best during off-peak periods. Rentals booked through wholesalers must be paid for before you leave the United States.

➤ RENTAL WHOLESALERS: **Auto Europe** (☎ 207/842–2000 or 800/223–5555, FAX 800–235–6321). **Kemwel Holiday Autos** (☎ 914/835–5555 or 800/678–0678, FAX 914/835–5126).

INSURANCE

When driving a rented car you are generally responsible for any damage to or loss of the vehicle. You also are liable for any property damage or personal injury that you may cause while driving. Before you rent, **see what coverage you already have** under the terms of your personal auto-insurance policy and credit cards.

REQUIREMENTS

In Canada your own driver's license is acceptable.

SURCHARGES

Before you pick up a car in one city and leave it in another, **ask about drop-off charges or one-way service fees,** which can be substantial. Note, too, that some rental agencies charge extra if you return the car before the time specified in your contract. To avoid a hefty refueling fee, **fill the tank just before you turn in the car,** but be aware that gas stations near the rental outlet may overcharge.

CAR TRAVEL

AUTO CLUBS

➤ In Australia: **Australian Automobile Association** (☎ 06/247–7311).

➤ In Canada: **Canadian Automobile Association** (CAA, ☎ 613/247–0117).

➤ In New Zealand: **New Zealand Automobile Association** (☎ 09/377–4660).

➤ In the U.K.: **Automobile Association** (AA, ☎ 0990/500–600), **Royal Automobile Club** (RAC, ☎ 0990/722–722 for membership, 0345/121–345 for insurance).

➤ In the U.S.: **American Automobile Association** (☎ 800/564–6222).

➤ Breakdowns: The **CAA** (the Canadian version of AAA) has 24-hour road service (☎ 416/222–5222, 800/268–3750, or cellular *222 for all services).

FROM THE U.S.

Expect a slight wait at major border crossings. The wait at peak visiting times can be 30 minutes. If you can, avoid crossing on weekends and holidays at Detroit–Windsor and Buffalo–Fort Erie, when the wait can be even longer.

Highway 401, which reaches up to 16 lanes as it slashes across metropolitan Toronto from the airport on the west almost as far as the Toronto Zoo on the east, is the major link between Windsor, Ontario (and Detroit), and Montréal, Québec.

There are no tolls anywhere along it, but you should be warned: Between 6:30 and 9:30 each weekday morning and from 3:30 to 6:30 each afternoon, the 401 can become very crowded, even stop-and-go; plan your trip to avoid rush hours. A new toll highway, the 407, offers quicker travel; there are no toll booths, but a camera takes photographs of the license plates and bills the owner (if the system has the address). The 407 runs roughly parallel to the 401 for a 65-km (40-mi) stretch immediately north of Toronto.

If you're driving from Buffalo, New York, or Niagara Falls, take the Queen Elizabeth Way, which curves up along the western shore of Lake Ontario and eventually turns into the Gardiner Expressway, which flows right into the downtown core. Yonge Street, which divides the west side of Toronto from the east, begins at the lakefront and continues north for 1,612 km (1,000 mi).

RULES OF THE ROAD

Seat-belt use is mandatory in the province of Ontario. The law applies to everyone in the car, and that means infants as well. Fines can be stiff. Canada went metric some years ago, so gas is sold by the liter, and signs are in kilometers. The "100 kph" signs on highways are a warning not to go more than 60 mi per hour. The speed limit in most areas of the city is 50 kph (30 mph). Pedestrian crosswalks are sprinkled throughout the city, marked clearly by overhead signs and very large painted yellow Xs. Pedestrians have the right of way in these crosswalks; do exercise normal caution. Right turns on red lights are generally permitted, except where otherwise posted. You must come to a complete stop before making a right turn on red.

CHILDREN & TRAVEL

CHILDREN IN TORONTO

Be sure to plan ahead and **involve your youngsters** as you outline your trip. When packing, include things to keep them busy en route. On sightseeing days try to schedule activities of special interest to your children. If you are renting a car don't forget to

THE GOLD GUIDE / SMART TRAVEL TIPS

arrange for a car seat when you reserve.

➤ BABY-SITTING: **Active Home Services** (☎ 416/785–4818) has been around for a quarter-century, providing sitters as far west as Jane Street, a few miles east of the airport. There's a four-hour minimum reservation, day or night, and the service starts at $8 an hour. **Christopher Robin Services** (☎ 416/289–4430) covers all of metropolitan Toronto, with a five-hour daily and four-hour nightly minimum and costs $8 an hour. Also check *City Parent* (☞ *below*) for local agencies. It's free at libraries, bookstores, supermarkets, nursery schools, several banks, and even at many McDonald's restaurants.

➤ LOCAL INFORMATION: **City Parent** (✉ Metroland Printing, 467 Speers Rd., Oakville, Ontario L6K 3S4, ☎ 905/815–0017) is a superior monthly newspaper for parents, with listings of activities and resources.

FLYING

If your children are two or older, **ask about children's airfares.** As a general rule, infants under two not occupying a seat fly at greatly reduced fares or even for free.

In general the adult baggage allowance applies to children paying half or more of the adult fare. When booking, **ask about carry-on allowances for those traveling with infants.** In general, for babies charged 10% of the adult fare you are allowed one carry-on bag and a collapsible stroller, which may have to be checked; you may be limited to less if the flight is full.

Experts agree that it's a good idea to use safety seats aloft for children weighing less than 40 pounds. Airlines, however, can set their own policies: U.S. carriers allow FAA-approved models but usually require that you buy a ticket, even if your child would otherwise ride free, since the seats must be strapped into regular seats. Airline rules vary, so it's important to **check your airline's policy about using safety seats during takeoff and landing.** Safety seats cannot obstruct the movement of other passengers in the row, so get an appropriate seat assignment as early as possible.

When making your reservation, **request children's meals or a free-standing bassinet** if you need them; the latter are available only to those seated at the bulkhead, where there's enough legroom. Remember, however, that bulkhead seats may not have their own overhead bins, and there's no storage space in front of you—a major inconvenience.

HOTELS

Most hotels in Toronto allow children under a certain age to stay in their parents' room at no extra charge, but others charge them as extra adults; be sure to **ask about the cutoff age for children's discounts.**

➤ BEST CHOICES: **The Delta Chelsea Inn** (✉ 33 Gerrard St., Toronto, Ontario M5G 1Z4, ☎ 416/595–1975 or 800/243–5732) maintains a supervised Children's Creative Center and allows children under 18 to stay free with their parents. The **Inn on the Park** (✉ 1100 Eglinton Ave. E, Toronto, Ontario M3C 1H8, ☎ 416/444—2561) has a supervised children's program (summer only).

CONSULATES

➤ IN TORONTO: **Consulate General of the United States** (✉ 360 University Ave., north of Queen St., M56 1S4, ☎ 416/595–1700). **British Consulate General** (✉ 777 Bay St., at College St., M56 2G2, ☎ 416/593–1267).

CONSUMER PROTECTION

Whenever possible, **pay with a major credit card** so you can cancel payment or get reimbursed if there's a problem, provided that you can provide documentation. This is the best way to pay, whether you're buying travel arrangements before your trip or shopping at your destination.

If you're doing business with a particular company for the first time, **contact your local Better Business Bureau and the attorney general's offices** in your state and the company's home state, as well. Have any complaints been filed?

Finally, if you're buying a package or tour, always **consider travel insur-**

ance that includes default coverage (☞ Insurance, *below*).

➤ LOCAL BBBS: **Council of Better Business Bureaus** (⊠ 4200 Wilson Blvd., Suite 800, Arlington, VA 22203, ☎ 703/276–0100, ℻ 703/525–8277).

CUSTOMS & DUTIES

When shopping, **keep receipts** for all of your purchases. Upon reentering the country, **be ready to show customs officials what you've bought.** If you feel a duty is incorrect, appeal the assessment. If you object to the way your clearance was handled, get the inspector's badge number. In either case, first ask to see a supervisor, then write to the appropriate authorities, beginning with the port director at your point of entry.

IN CANADA

Clothing and personal items may be brought in without charge or restriction. American and British visitors may bring in the following items duty-free: 200 cigarettes, 50 cigars, 2 pounds of tobacco, and 40 ounces of alcohol; personal cars (for less than six months); boats or canoes; rifles and shotguns (but no handguns or automatic weapons); cameras, radios, sports equipment, and typewriters. Very rarely, deposit is sometimes required for trailers and household equipment (refunded upon return). If you are driving a rented car, be sure to keep the contract with you. Cats may enter freely, but dogs must have proof of a veterinary inspection to ensure that they are free of communicable diseases. Plant material must be declared and inspected.

IN AUSTRALIA

Australia residents who are 18 or older may bring back $A400 worth of souvenirs and gifts (including jewelry), 250 cigarettes or 250 grams of tobacco, and 1,125 ml of alcohol (including wine, beer, and spirits). Residents under 18 may bring back $A200 worth of goods.

➤ INFORMATION: **Australian Customs Service** (Regional Director, ⊠ Box 8, Sydney, NSW 2001, ☎ 02/9213–2000, ℻ 02/9213–4000).

IN NEW ZEALAND

Although greeted with a "Haere Mai" ("Welcome to New Zealand"), homeward-bound residents with goods to declare must present themselves for inspection. If you're 17 or older, you may bring back $700 worth of souvenirs and gifts. Your duty-free allowance also includes 4.5 liters of wine or beer; one 1,125-ml bottle of spirits; and either 200 cigarettes, 250 grams of tobacco, 50 cigars, or a combo of all three up to 250 grams.

➤ INFORMATION: **New Zealand Customs** (⊠ Custom House, 50 Anzac Ave., Box 29, Auckland, New Zealand, ☎ 09/359–6655, ☎ 09/309–2978).

IN THE U.K.

From countries outside the EU, including Canada, you may import, duty-free, 200 cigarettes or 50 cigars; 1 liter of spirits or 2 liters of fortified or sparkling wine or liqueurs; 2 liters of still table wine; 60 milliliters of perfume; 250 milliliters of toilet water; plus £136 worth of other goods, including gifts and souvenirs.

➤ INFORMATION: **HM Customs and Excise** (⊠ Dorset House, ⊠ Stamford St., London SE1 9NG, ☎ 0171/202–4227).

IN THE U.S.

U.S. residents may bring home $400 worth of foreign goods duty-free if they've been out of the country for at least 48 hours (and if they haven't used the $400 allowance or any part of it in the past 30 days).

U.S. residents 21 and older may bring back 1 liter of alcohol duty-free. In addition, regardless of your age, you are allowed 200 cigarettes and 100 non-Cuban cigars. Antiques, which the U.S. Customs Service defines as objects more than 100 years old, enter duty-free, as do original works of art done entirely by hand, including paintings, drawings, and sculptures.

You may also send packages home duty-free: up to $200 worth of goods for personal use, with a limit of one parcel per addressee per day (and no alcohol or tobacco products or perfume worth more than $5); label the package PERSONAL USE, and attach a

THE GOLD GUIDE / SMART TRAVEL TIPS

list of its contents and their retail value. Do not label the package UNSOLICITED GIFT, or your duty-free exemption will drop to $100. Mailed items do not affect your duty-free allowance on your return.

➤ INFORMATION: **U.S. Customs Service** (Inquiries, ✉ Box 7407, Washington, DC 20044, ☎ 202/927–6724; complaints, Office of Regulations and Rulings, ✉ 1301 Constitution Ave. NW, Washington, DC 20229; registration of equipment, Resource Management, ✉ 1301 Constitution Ave. NW, Washington, DC 20229, ☎ 202/927–0540).

DISABILITIES & ACCESSIBILITY

ACCESS IN TORONTO

For general information about transportation and buildings that are accessible to visitors with disabilities, call the city accessibility planner. Community Information Toronto provides information on various facilities, as well as social and health services for those with disabilities; it's open Monday–Friday from 8 AM to 10 PM, weekends and statutory holidays from 10 to 10.

➤ LOCAL INFORMATION: **City accessibility planner** (☎ 416/392–0496, weekdays 8–5). **Community Information Toronto** (☎ 416/392–0505).

MAKING RESERVATIONS

When discussing accessibility with an operator or reservations agent, **ask hard questions.** Are there any stairs, inside *or* out? Are there grab bars next to the toilet *and* in the shower/tub? How wide is the doorway to the room? To the bathroom? For the most extensive facilities meeting the latest legal specifications, **opt for newer accommodations,** which are more likely to have been designed with access in mind. Older buildings or ships may have more limited facilities. Be sure to **discuss your needs before booking.**

TRANSPORTATION

➤ LOCAL SERVICES: The **Toronto Transit Commission** (TTC; ☎ 416/393–4222, TTY 416/393–4555 for advance and same-day reservations; phone and TDD 416/481–2523 for routes and schedules; 416/393–4111

for customer service) offers a bus service, called Wheel-Trans, for people with disabilities who are unable to use regular public vehicles.

Transportation to and from Pearson International Airport is available for travelers with disabilities through **Wheel-Trans** (☎ 416/393–4111). Three limousine companies—**Aaroport, MacIntosh** (☎ 416/225–1555 for both), and **Airline Limousine** (☎ 905/676–3210)—operate, wheelchair-accessible vans. By prearrangement, people with disabilities can be picked up or dropped off at points in all three of the airport's terminals.

Greyhound/Trailways (☎ 800/752–4841) will carry a person with a disability along with one companion for the price of a single fare provided you book at least three days in advance. **Amtrak** (☎ 800/872–7245) requests 24-hour notice to provide Redcap service and special seats. Passengers with disabilities are entitled to a 25% discount on the normal discount coach fare; for best service, mention your disability when booking.

➤ COMPLAINTS: **Disability Rights Section** (✉ U.S. Department of Justice, Civil Rights Division, ✉ Box 66738, Washington, DC 20035–6738, ☎ 202/514–0301 or 800/514–0301, TTY 202/514–0383 or 800/514–0383, FAX 202/307–1198) for general complaints. **Aviation Consumer Protection Division** (☞ Air Travel, *above*) for airline-related problems. **Civil Rights Office** (✉ U.S. Department of Transportation, Departmental Office of Civil Rights, S-30, ✉ 400 7th St. SW, Room 10215, Washington, DC 20590, ☎ 202/366–4648, FAX 202/366–9371) for problems with surface transportation.

TRAVEL AGENCIES & TOUR OPERATORS

As a whole, the travel industry has become more aware of the needs of travelers with disabilities. In the U.S., the Americans with Disabilities Act requires that travel firms serve the needs of all travelers. Note, though, that some agencies and operators specialize in making travel arrangements for individuals and groups with disabilities.

➤ TRAVELERS WITH MOBILITY PROBLEMS: **Access Adventures** (✉ 206 Chestnut Ridge Rd., Rochester, NY 14624, ☎ 716/889–9096) is run by a former physical-rehabilitation counselor. **Accessible Journeys** (✉ 35 W. Sellers Ave., Ridley Park, PA 19078, ☎ 610/521–0339 or 800/846–4537, FAX 610/521–6959) runs escorted tours exclusively for travelers with mobility impairments. **CareVacations** (✉ 5019 49th Ave., Suite 102, Leduc, Alberta T9E 6T5, ☎ 403/986–6404, 800/648–1116 in Canada) has group tours and is especially helpful with cruise vacations. **Flying Wheels Travel** (✉ 143 W. Bridge St., Box 382, Owatonna, MN 55060, ☎ 507/451–5005 or 800/535–6790, FAX 507/451–1685) is a travel agency specializing in customized tours and itineraries worldwide. **Hinsdale Travel Service** (✉ 201 E. Ogden Ave., Suite 100, Hinsdale, IL 60521, ☎ 630/325–1335) is a travel agency that benefits from the advice of wheelchair traveler Janice Perkins.

➤ TRAVELERS WITH DEVELOPMENTAL DISABILITIES: **Sprout** (✉ 893 Amsterdam Ave., New York, NY 10025, ☎ 212/222–9575 or 888/222–9575, FAX 212/222–9768).

DISCOUNTS & DEALS

Be a smart shopper and **compare all your options** before making any choice. A plane ticket bought with a promotional coupon may not be cheaper than the least expensive fare from a discount ticket agency. For high-price travel purchases, such as packages or tours, keep in mind that what you get is just as important as what you save. Just because something is cheap doesn't mean it's a bargain.

CLUBS & COUPONS

Many companies sell discounts in the form of travel clubs and coupon books, but these cost money. You must use participating advertisers to get a deal, and only after you recoup the initial membership cost or book price do you begin to save. If you plan to use the club or coupons frequently, you may save consider-

ably. Before signing up, find out what discounts you get for free.

➤ DISCOUNT CLUBS: **Entertainment Travel Editions** (✉ 2125 Butterfield Rd., Troy, MI 48084, ☎ 800/445–4137; $20–$51, depending on destination). **Great American Traveler** (✉ Box 27965, Salt Lake City, UT 84127, ☎ 801/974–3033 or 800/548–2812; $49.95 per year). **Moment's Notice Discount Travel Club** (✉ 7301 New Utrecht Ave., Brooklyn, NY 11204, ☎ 718/234–6295; $25 per year, single or family). **Privilege Card International** (✉ 237 E. Front St., Youngstown, OH 44503, ☎ 330/746–5211 or 800/236–9732; $74.95 per year). **Sears's Mature Outlook** (✉ Box 9390, Des Moines, IA 50306, ☎ 800/336–6330; $19.95 per year). **Travelers Advantage** (✉ CUC Travel Service, ✉ 3033 S. Parker Rd., Suite 1000, Aurora, CO 80014, ☎ 800/548–1116 or 800/648–4037; $59.95 per year, single or family). **Worldwide Discount Travel Club** (✉ 1674 Meridian Ave., Miami Beach, FL 33139, ☎ 305/534–2082; $50 per year family, $40 single).

CREDIT CARD BENEFITS

When you use your credit card to make travel purchases you may get free travel-accident insurance, collision-damage insurance, and medical or legal assistance, depending on the card and the bank that issued it. American Express, MasterCard, and Visa provide one or more of these services, so **get a copy of your credit card's travel benefits policy.** If you are a member of an auto club, always **ask hotel and car rental reservations agents about auto club discounts.** Some clubs offer additional discounts on tours, cruises, and admission to attractions.

DISCOUNT RESERVATIONS

To save money, **look into discount-reservations services** with toll-free numbers, which use their buying power to get a better price on hotels, airline tickets, even car rentals. When booking a room, always **call the hotel's local toll-free number** (if one is available) rather than the central reservations number—you'll often get a better price. Always ask about special packages or corporate rates.

When shopping for the best deal on hotels and car rentals, **look for guaranteed exchange rates,** which protect you against a falling dollar. With your rate locked in, you won't pay more, even if the price goes up in the local currency.

➤ AIRLINE TICKETS: ☎ **800/FLY–4–LESS.** ☎ **800/FLY–ASAP.**

➤ HOTEL ROOMS: **RMC Travel** (☎ 800/245–5738).

PACKAGE DEALS

Packages and guided tours can save you money, but don't confuse the two. When you buy a package, your travel remains independent, just as though you had planned and booked the trip yourself. Fly/drive packages, which combine airfare and car rental, are often a good deal. In cities, ask the local visitor's bureau about hotel packages. These often include tickets to major museum exhibits and other special events.

ELECTRICITY

The electrical current is the same as in the United States: 110 volts, 60 cycles.

EMERGENCIES

➤ DOCTORS & DENTISTS: Check the Yellow Pages or ask at your hotel desk. **Medvisit Doctors House Call Service** (☎ 416/631–3000). **Academy of Dentistry** (☎ 416/967–5649).

➤ EMERGENCIES: **Police** and **ambulance** (☎ 911).

➤ LATE-NIGHT PHARMACIES: **Shoppers Drug Mart** (✉ 700 Bay St., ☎ 416/979–2424; ✉ 2500 Hurontario St., Mississauga ☎ 905/896–2500). **Pharma Plus Drugmart** (✉ Church St. and Wellesley Ave., ☎ 416/924–7760). Call **Shoppers Drug Mart** (☎ 800/363–1020 for the 24-hr location nearest you).

➤ PET CARE: **Veterinary Emergency Clinic** (✉ 1180 Danforth Ave., ☎ 416/465–3501) is open Monday–Thursday 7 PM–8 AM, Friday 7 PM–Monday 8 AM, and 24 hours on holidays.

➤ POISON INFORMATION: Call the **Poison Information Center at the Hospital for Sick Children** (✉ University Ave., north of Dundas St., ☎ 416/813–5900, 800/268–9017, or TTY 416/597–0215 for people with hearing impairments).

GAY & LESBIAN TRAVEL

The heart of the gay and lesbian community is near Church and Wellesley streets, just a few blocks east and north of Eaton Centre (or east and south of Bloor and Yonge streets). Gay and lesbian travelers tend to find Toronto a relatively safe and welcoming destination. Lesbian and Gay Pride Day takes place on the last Sunday of June each year, usually attended by more than 100,000 people. The most popular gay beach in the Toronto area is Hanlan's Point, at the northwest tip of the Toronto Islands.

Pick up a free copy of *XTRA!*, a biweekly newspaper for the gay and lesbian community, available on the streets around the Church–Wellesley area. Or call the newspaper for other locations nearer you and for a current list of local events and meeting places. Also consult the Pink Pages, an annual reference directory (found in various bookstores and bars) for Toronto's gay and lesbian community, and other free newspapers such as *Icon* or *Fab*.

➤ LOCAL RESOURCES: **XTRA!** (✉ 491 Church St., Suite 200, Toronto, Ontario M4Y 2C6, ☎ 416/925–6665; $2) can send you a copy before your trip. *XTRA!* runs a **Gay Community Information Line** (☎ 416/925–9872). The **519 Community Centre** (✉ 519 Church St., ☎ 416/392–6874) can provide information about events, bars, and more.

➤ GAY- AND LESBIAN-FRIENDLY TRAVEL AGENCIES: **Corniche Travel** (✉ 8721 Sunset Blvd., Suite 200, West Hollywood, CA 90069, ☎ 310/854–6000 or 800/429–8747, FAX 310/659–7441). **Islanders Kennedy Travel** (✉ 183 W. 10th St., New York, NY 10014, ☎ 212/242–3222 or 800/988–1181, FAX 212/929–8530). **Now Voyager** (✉ 4406 18th St., San Francisco, CA 94114, ☎ 415/626–1169 or 800/255–6951, FAX 415/626–8626). **Yellowbrick Road** (✉ 1500 W. Balmoral Ave., Chicago, IL 60640, ☎ 773/561–

1800 or 800/642–2488, FAX 773/
561–4497). **Skylink Travel and Tour**
(✉ 3577 Moorland Ave., Santa Rosa,
CA 95407, ☎ 707/585–8355 or
800/225–5759, FAX 707/584–5637),
serving lesbian travelers.

HEALTH

MEDICAL PLANS

No one plans to get sick while traveling, but it happens, so **consider
signing up with a medical-assistance
company.** Members get doctor referrals, emergency evacuation or repa-
triation, 24-hour telephone hot lines
for medical consultation, cash for
emergencies, and other personal and
legal assistance. Coverage varies by
plan, so **review the benefits of each
carefully.**

➤ MEDICAL-ASSISTANCE COMPANIES:
International SOS Assistance (✉
8 Neshaminy Interplex, Suite 207,
Trevose, PA 19053, ☎ 215/245–
4707 or 800/523–6586, FAX 215/
244–9617; ✉ 12 Chemin Riant-
bosson, 1217 Meyrin 1, Geneva,
Switzerland, ☎ 4122/785–6464,
FAX 4122/785–6424; ✉ 10 Anson
Rd., 14-07/08 International Plaza,
Singapore 079903, ☎ 65/226–3936,
FAX 65/226–3937).

HOLIDAYS

The main civic and national holidays
observed in Toronto are New Year's
Day, Good Friday (April 2), Easter
Monday (April 5), Victoria Day (third
Monday in May), Canada Day (July
1), Civic Holiday Day (also known as
the Bank Holiday or Simcoe Day; first
Monday in August), Labour Day
(first Monday in September), Thanksgiving (second Monday in October),
Remembrance Day (November 11),
Christmas, and Boxing Day (December 26.) Although banks, schools, and
government offices close for national
holidays, many stores remain open.

INSURANCE

Travel insurance is the best way to
protect yourself against financial loss.
The most useful plan is a comprehensive policy that includes coverage for
trip cancellation and interruption,
default, trip delay, and medical expenses (with a waiver for preexisting
conditions).

Without insurance, you will lose all
or most of your money if you cancel
your trip, regardless of the reason.
Default insurance covers you if your
tour operator, airline, or cruise line
goes out of business. Trip-delay
covers unforeseen expenses that you
may incur due to bad weather or
mechanical delays. It's important to
compare the fine print regarding trip-
delay coverage when comparing
policies.

For overseas travel, one of the most
important components of travel
insurance is its medical coverage.
Supplemental health insurance will
pick up the cost of your medical bills
should you get sick or injured while
traveling. U.S. residents should note
that Medicare generally does not
cover health-care costs outside the
United States, nor do many privately
issued policies. Residents of the
United Kingdom can buy an annual
travel-insurance policy valid for most
vacations taken during the year in
which the coverage is purchased. If
you are pregnant or have a preexisting condition, make sure you're
covered. British citizens should buy
extra medical coverage when traveling overseas, according to the Association of British Insurers. Australian
travelers should buy travel insurance,
including extra medical coverage,
whenever they go abroad, according
to the Insurance Council of Australia.

Always **buy travel insurance directly
from the insurance company;** if you
buy it from a cruise line, airline, or
tour operator that goes out of business you probably will not be covered
for the agency or operator's default, a
major risk. Before you make any
purchase, **review your existing health
and home-owner's policies** to find out
whether they cover expenses incurred
while traveling.

➤ TRAVEL INSURERS: In the U.S.,
Access America (✉ 6600 W. Broad
St., Richmond, VA 23230, ☎ 804/
285–3300 or 800/284–8300). **Travel
Guard International** (✉ 1145 Clark
St., Stevens Point, WI 54481, ☎ 715/
345–0505 or 800/826–1300). In
Canada, **Mutual of Omaha** (✉
Travel Division, ✉ 500 University
Ave., Toronto, Ontario M5G 1V8,

☏ 416/598–4083, 800/268–8825 in Canada).

➤ INSURANCE INFORMATION: In the U.K., **Association of British Insurers** (✉ 51 Gresham St., London EC2V 7HQ, ☏ 0171/600–3333). In Australia, the **Insurance Council of Australia** (☏ 613/9614–1077, FAX 613/9614–7924).

LANGUAGE

Canada is a bilingual country in that it has two official languages, French and English. Road signs, for example, carry both languages. But Toronto is the Anglophone center of Canada, which means that 99% of the people living here will speak to you in English.

LODGING

APARTMENT & VILLA RENTALS

If you want a home base that's roomy enough for a family and comes with cooking facilities, **consider a furnished rental.** These can save you money, especially if you're traveling with a large group of people. Home-exchange directories list rentals (often second homes owned by prospective house swappers), and some services search for a house or apartment for you (even a castle if that's your fancy) and handle the paperwork. Some send an illustrated catalog; others send photographs only of specific properties, sometimes at a charge. Up-front registration fees may apply.

➤ RENTAL AGENTS: **Property Rentals International** (✉ 1008 Mansfield Crossing Rd., Richmond, VA 23236, ☏ 804/378–6054 or 800/220–3332, FAX 804/379–2073).

HOSTELS

No matter what your age, you can **save on lodging costs by staying at hostels.** In some 5,000 locations in more than 70 countries around the world, Hostelling International (HI), the umbrella group for a number of national youth hostel associations, offers single-sex, dorm-style beds and, at many hostels, "couples" rooms and family accommodations. Membership in any HI national hostel association, open to travelers of all ages, allows you to stay in HI-affiliated hostels at member rates (one-year membership is about $25 for adults; hostels run about $10–$25 per night). Members also have priority if the hostel is full; they're eligible for discounts around the world, even on rail and bus travel in some countries.

➤ HOSTEL ORGANIZATIONS: **Hostelling International—American Youth Hostels** (✉ 733 15th St. NW, Suite 840, Washington, DC 20005, ☏ 202/783–6161, FAX 202/783–6171). **Hostelling International—Canada** (✉ 400-205 Catherine St., Ottawa, Ontario K2P 1C3, ☏ 613/237–7884, FAX 613/237–7868). **Youth Hostel Association of England and Wales** (✉ Trevelyan House, ✉ 8 St. Stephen's Hill, St. Albans, Hertfordshire AL1 2DY, ☏ 01727/855215 or 01727/845047, FAX 01727/844126); membership in the U.S. $25, in Canada C$26.75, in the U.K. £9.30).

MAIL

In Canada you can **buy stamps at the post office or from automatic vending machines** in most hotel lobbies, railway stations, airports, bus terminals, many retail outlets, and some newsstands. If you're sending mail to Canada, **be sure to include the postal code** (six digits and letters). Following are postal abbreviations for provinces and territories: Alberta, AB; British Columbia, BC; Manitoba, MB; New Brunswick, NB; Newfoundland and Labrador, NF; Northwest Territories, NT; Nova Scotia, NS; Ontario, ON; Prince Edward Island, PE; Québec, PQ; Saskatchewan, SK; Yukon, YT.

POSTAL RATES

Within Canada, postcards and letters up to 30 grams cost 45¢; between 31 grams and 50 grams, the cost is 71¢ and between 51 grams and 100 grams the cost is 90¢. Letters and postcards to the United States cost 52¢ for up to 30 grams, 77¢ for between 31 and 50 grams, and $1.17 for up to 100 grams. Prices include GST (Goods and Services Tax).

International mail and postcards run 90¢ for up to 20 grams, $1.37 for between 21 and 50 grams, and $2.25 for between 51 and 100 grams.

RECEIVING MAIL

Mail may be sent to you care of General Delivery, Toronto Adelaide Post Office, 36 Adelaide Street East, Toronto, Ontario M5C 1J0.

➤ SERVICES: American Express clients—cardholders and those who purchase traveler's checks or travel services—may pick up mail (with proper ID) without charge at **American Express** (⊠ 50 Bloor St. W (concourse level), ☎ 416/967–3411).

MONEY

COSTS

Throughout this guide, unless otherwise stated, prices are quoted in Canadian dollars.

It's true that the U.S. dollar is worth some 30% to 40% more than the Canadian dollar, but goods and services are priced slightly higher in Canada than in the United States. In Toronto, a can of Coke costs about $1–$1.25; a taxi, as soon as the meter is turned on, $2.50; a movie, about $9; and a glass of beer in a bar, about $4.

CREDIT & DEBIT CARDS

Should you use a credit card or a debit card when traveling? Both have benefits. A credit card allows you to delay payment and gives you certain rights as a consumer (☞ Consumer Protection, *above*). A debit card, also known as a check card, deducts funds directly from your checking account and helps you stay within your budget. When you want to rent a car, though, you may still need an old-fashioned credit card. Although you can always *pay* for your car with a debit card, some agencies will not allow you to *reserve* a car with a debit card.

Otherwise, the two types of plastic are virtually the same. Both will get you cash advances at ATMs worldwide if your card is properly programmed with your personal identification number (PIN). Both offer excellent, wholesale exchange rates. And both protect you against unauthorized use if the card is lost or stolen. Your liability is limited to $50, as long as you report the card missing.

Credit card expenditures in Canada will show up on your bill with the Canadian amount from the date of purchase, converted to your local currency on the day the charge reaches your bank.

➤ ATM LOCATIONS: **Cirrus** (☎ 800/424–7787). **Plus** (☎ 800/843–7587) for locations in the U.S. and Canada, or visit your local bank.

➤ REPORTING LOST CARDS: To report lost or stolen credit cards, call the following toll-free numbers: **American Express** (☎ 800/327–2177); **Diners Club** (☎ 800/234–6377); **Discover Card** (☎ 800/347–2683); **Master Card** (☎ 800/307–7309); and **Visa** (☎ 800/847–2911).

CURRENCY

The units of currency in Canada are the Canadian dollar (C$) and the cent, in almost the same denominations as U.S. currency, with bills beginning at $5. At press time, the exchange rate was fluctuating at about C$1.38 to U.S. $1 and C$2.35 to £1. The $1 and $2 bill are no longer used; they have been replaced by $1 and $2 coins (known as a "loonie," because of the loon that appears on the coin, and a "toonie," respectively).

EXCHANGING MONEY

For the most favorable rates, **change money through banks.** Although fees charged for ATM transactions may be higher abroad than at home, Cirrus and Plus exchange rates are excellent, because they are based on wholesale rates offered only by major banks. You won't do as well at exchange booths in airports or rail and bus stations, in hotels, in restaurants, or in stores, although you may find their hours more convenient. To avoid lines at airport exchange booths, **get a bit of local currency before you leave home.**

➤ EXCHANGE SERVICES: **Chase *Currency To Go*** (☎ 800/935–9935; 935–9935 in NY, NJ, and CT). **International Currency Express** (☎ 888/842–0880 on the East Coast, 888/278–6628 on the West Coast). **Thomas Cook Currency Services** (☎ 800/287–7362 for telephone orders and retail locations).

SMART TRAVEL TIPS / THE GOLD GUIDE

➤ LOCAL EXCHANGES: **Thomas Cook Currency Services** (✉ 10 King St. E, near Yonge St., ☎ 416/863–1611; ✉ Manulife Centre, 55 Bloor St. W, at Bay St., ☎ 416/961–9822; ✉ 9 Bloor St. W, ☎ 416/923–6549; ✉ Sheraton Centre hotel lobby, 123 Queen St. W, across from the New City Hall, ☎ 416/363–4867; ✉ Yorkdale Pl., ☎ 416/789–1827; ✉ International Plaza lobby, 655 Dixon Rd., near the airport, ☎ 416/247–4600).

TRAVELER'S CHECKS

Do you need traveler's checks? It depends on where you're headed. If you're going to rural areas and small towns, go with cash; traveler's checks are best used in cities. Lost or stolen checks can usually be replaced within 24 hours. To ensure a speedy refund, buy your own traveler's checks—don't let someone else pay for them: irregularities like this can cause delays. The person who bought the checks should make the call to request a refund.

PACKING

LUGGAGE

How many carry-on bags you can bring with you is up to the airline. Most allow two, but the limit is often reduced to one on certain flights. Gate agents will take excess baggage—including bags they deem oversize—from you as you board and add it to checked luggage. To avoid this situation, make sure that everything you carry aboard will fit under your seat. Also, get to the gate early, and request a seat at the back of the plane; you'll probably board first, while the overhead bins are still empty. Since big, bulky baggage attracts the attention of gate agents and flight attendants on a busy flight, make sure your carry-on is really a carry-on. Finally, a carry-on that's long and narrow is more likely to remain unnoticed than one that's wide and squarish.

If you are flying internationally, note that baggage allowances may be determined not by piece but by weight—generally 88 pounds (40 kilograms) in first class, 66 pounds (30 kilograms) in business class, and 44 pounds (20 kilograms) in economy.

Airline liability for baggage is limited to $1,250 per person on flights within the United States. On international flights it amounts to $9.07 per pound or $20 per kilogram for checked baggage (roughly $640 per 70-pound bag) and $400 per passenger for unchecked baggage. You can buy additional coverage at check-in for about $10 per $1,000 of coverage, but it excludes a rather extensive list of items, shown on your airline ticket.

Before departure, **itemize your bags' contents** and their worth, and label the bags with your name, address, and phone number. (If you use your home address, cover it so that potential thieves can't see it readily.) Inside each bag, **pack a copy of your itinerary.** At check-in, **make sure that each bag is correctly tagged** with the destination airport's three-letter code. If your bags arrive damaged or fail to arrive at all, file a written report with the airline before leaving the airport.

PACKING LIST

You may want to **pack light** because airport porters and baggage trolleys are scarce and airline luggage restrictions are tight. What you pack depends more on the time of year than on any specific dress code. For winter, you'll need your warmest clothes, in many layers, and waterproof boots. In summer, loose-fitting, casual clothing will see you through both day and evening events. Women should pack a sweater or shawl for summer evenings, which can get cool, and for restaurants that run their air conditioners full blast. Men will need a jacket and tie for the better restaurants and many of the night spots. Jeans are as popular in Toronto as they are elsewhere and are perfectly acceptable for sightseeing and informal dining. Be sure to **bring comfortable walking shoes.** Consider packing a bathing suit for your hotel pool.

In your carry-on luggage **bring an extra pair of eyeglasses or contact lenses** and **enough of any medication you take** to last the entire trip. You may also want your doctor to write a spare prescription using the drug's generic name, since brand names may vary from country to country. **Never put prescription drugs or valuables in**

luggage to be checked. To avoid customs delays, carry medications in their original packaging. And don't forget to copy down and carry addresses of offices that handle refunds of lost traveler's checks.

PASSPORTS & VISAS

When traveling internationally, **carry a passport even if you don't need one** (it's always the best form of ID) and **make two photocopies of the data page** (one for someone at home and another for you, carried separately from your passport). If you lose your passport, promptly call the nearest embassy or consulate and the local police.

ENTERING CANADA

Citizens and other legal residents of the United States do not need a passport or a visa to enter Canada, but proof of citizenship (a birth certificate, naturalization certificate, valid passport, or "green card") and proof of identity will probably be requested, so be prepared. Photo IDs are strongly preferred. Note that a driver's license is not sufficient on its own. U.S. residents entering Canada from a third country must have a valid passport, naturalization certificate, or "green card."

Citizens of the United Kingdom need only a valid passport to enter Canada for stays of up to six months.

PASSPORT OFFICES

The best time to apply for a passport or to renew is during the fall and winter. Before any trip, be sure to check your passport's expiration date and, if necessary, renew it as soon as possible. (Some countries won't allow you to enter on a passport that's due to expire in six months or less.)

➤ AUSTRALIAN CITIZENS: **Australian Passport Office** (☎ 13/1232).

➤ NEW ZEALAND CITIZENS: **New Zealand Passport Office** (☎ 04/494–0700 for information on how to apply, 0800/727–776 for information on applications already submitted).

➤ U.K. CITIZENS: **London Passport Office** (☎ 0990/21010), for fees and documentation requirements and to request an emergency passport.

SENIOR-CITIZEN TRAVEL

To qualify for age-related discounts, **mention your senior-citizen status up front** when booking hotel reservations (not when checking out) and before you're seated in restaurants (not when paying the bill). Note that discounts may be limited to certain menus, days, or hours. When renting a car, **ask about promotional car-rental discounts,** which can be cheaper than senior-citizen rates.

➤ EDUCATIONAL PROGRAMS: **Elderhostel** (✉ 75 Federal St., 3rd Floor, Boston, MA 02110, ☎ 617/426–8056).

SIGHTSEEING TOURS

➤ ORIENTATION TOURS: Toronto Harbour and Islands Boat Tours are provided by **Boat Tours International** (☎ 416/364–2412) on sleek touring boats. Boats leave from the Queen's Quay Terminal daily from early May through mid-October, noon–5; tours leave as late as 7 in summer. Other boats depart from the Harbour Castle Westin. The fare is $9.95.

Executive Coach Services (☎ 416/740–3339; $25) runs, year round, a two-hour "Greater Toronto City Tour" in a minibus. The company picks up from most city hotels. (It also runs daily tours to Niagara Falls: $90.)

Gray Line Sightseeing Bus Tours (☎ 416/594–3310) has tours from April through November. Tours start at the bus terminal (✉ 610 Bay St., north of Dundas St.) and include trips of several lengths around the city and to Niagara Falls; cost is $25–$99.

Olde Town Toronto Tours (☎ 416/798–2424) has hop-on, hop-off tours on London double-decker buses and turn-of-the-century trolleys. Both take you around the city on a two-hour loop and cost $25; your ticket is good for 24 hours, so you can get on and off. Tours leave every 15 minutes in summer, every two hours in winter. The company also has tours to Niagara Falls.

Toronto Tours (☎ 416/869–1372) runs one-hour boat tours of the Toronto harborfront from mid-

April through late October; fare is about $15.

➤ SPECIAL-INTEREST TOURS: **Antours** (☎ 416/424–4403) provides several tours of Stratford and Niagara-on-the-Lake, which include lunch and tickets to major performances at the Shakespeare or Shaw Festival, and of the Ontario countryside.

The **Bruce Trail Association** (☎ 416/690–4453) arranges day and overnight hikes around Toronto and environs.

Call of the Wild (☎ 416/200–9453) leads guided trips of different lengths—dogsledding and cross-country skiing in winter, canoeing and hiking in summer—in Algonquin Park and other areas in southern Ontario. Prices include transportation from Toronto.

Great Lakes Schooner Company (☎ 416/260–6355) lets you see Toronto's skyline from the open deck of the tall ship Challenge, among other excursions. Tours start in early May and end in September and cost about $13–$17, depending on length.

Heritage Toronto (☎ 416/392–6827, ext. 265) has free guided walking tours on weekends and occasional holiday Mondays from mid-April to early October. They last 1½ to two hours and cover one neighborhood or topic, such as the historic theater block.

The world-class **Royal Ontario Museum** (☎ 416/586–5514) offers Romwalk, with such tours as "Citadels of Wealth" and "Cabbagetown" among the 11 offered. They usually take place Wednesday and Saturday and some include afternoon tea. Tours start in early June and run until late September; there is a nominal fee for tours that include afternoon tea.

Sculpture in Toronto (☎ 416/537–3627) explores the works of world-famous Canadian and international artists. The tour includes a visit to SkyDome, with its fine sculpture collection.

Toronto Field Naturalists (☎ 416/968–6255) schedules about 150 guided tours during the year, each focusing on some aspect of physical nature (geology, wildflowers) and with starting points accessible by public transit.

Tourism Toronto (☎ 416/203–2500 or 800/363–1990) can provide information about a variety of special-interest tours.

STUDENT TRAVEL

TRAVEL AGENCIES

To save money, **look into deals available through student-oriented travel agencies.** To qualify you'll need a bona fide student ID card. Members of international student groups are also eligible.

➤ STUDENT IDs & SERVICES: **Council on International Educational Exchange** (✉ CIEE; ✉ 205 E. 42nd St., 14th Floor, New York, NY 10017, ☎ 212/822–2600 or 888/268–6245, FAX 212/822–2699), for mail orders only, in the United States. **Travel Cuts** (✉ 187 College St., Toronto, Ontario M5T 1P7, ☎ 416/979–2406 or 800/667–2887) in Canada.

➤ STUDENT TOURS: **Contiki Holidays** (✉ 300 Plaza Alicante, Suite 900, Garden Grove, CA 92840, ☎ 714/740–0808 or 800/266–8454, FAX 714/740–2034).

SUBWAY AND STREETCAR TRAVEL

The Toronto Transit Commission (TTC) operates a system that is safe, clean, and trustworthy. One fare plus a transfer wherever you enter the system permits continuous travel on several different vehicles to make a single trip. At press time, the adult single fare for buses, streetcars, and subway trains was $2 in exact change or one ticket/token. For information on discount passes and routes, *see* Bus Travel, *above.*

There are two subway lines, with 60 stations along the way: the Bloor/Danforth line, which crosses Toronto about 5 km (3 mi) north of the lakefront, from east to west, and the Yonge/University line, which loops north and south, like a giant "U," with the bottom of the "U" at Union

Station. A light rapid transit (LRT) line extends service to Harbourfront along Queen's Quay. Tokens and tickets are sold in each subway station and at hundreds of convenience stores. All vehicles accept tickets, tokens, or exact change, **but buy tickets and tokens before you board,** as drivers make no sales.

Subway trains stop running at 2 AM, but the Toronto Transit Commission runs bus service from 1 to 5:30 AM on Bloor and Yonge streets, and as far north as Steeles. Streetcars on major routes run for 24 hours, including lines on King Street, Queen Street, and College Street. Other streetcar lines run along Spadina Avenue and Dundas Street. All of them, especially the King line, are interesting rides with frequent service. Riding the city's streetcars is a great way to **capture the flavor of the city,** since you pass through many neighborhoods.

From Union Station you can walk underground to many hotels, including the Royal York, Toronto Hilton, and Sheraton Centre—a real boon in inclement weather.

TAXES

AIRPORT

In most cases, your airport departure tax will already have been included in your ticket purchase price.

GST AND PROVINCIAL

Visitors should **bear in mind the national 7% Goods and Services Tax** (alias "the GST") on virtually every transaction in Canada except for the purchase of basic groceries. In addition, Ontario has an 8% retail sales tax. Toronto has a 5% tax for accommodations, but the provincial tax does not apply to lodging.

You can **get a GST refund on purchases taken out of the country and on short-term accommodations** (but not on food, drink, tobacco, car or motor-home rentals, or transportation); rebate forms, which must be submitted within 60 days of leaving Canada, may be obtained from certain retailers, duty-free shops, customs officials, or from Revenue

Canada. Instant cash rebates up to a maximum of $500 are provided by some duty-free shops when leaving Canada, and most provinces do not tax goods that are shipped directly by the vendor to the purchaser's home. Always **save your original receipts** from stores and hotels, and **be sure the name and address of the establishment is shown on the receipt.** Original receipts are not returned. The amount of eligible goods and services on which you paid GST must total at least $200, and each receipt must be at least $50 before taxes.

➤ INFORMATION: **Revenue Canada** (✉ Visitor Rebate Program, Summerside Tax Centre, Summerside, Prince Edward Island C1N 6C6, ☎ 902/432–5608 or 800/668–4748 in Canada).

TAXIS

The meter begins at $2.50, and each .235 km (.145 mi) is 25¢—as is each passenger in excess of four. The waiting time "while under engagement" is 25¢ for every 33 seconds—and in a traffic jam, this could add up. Still, it's possible to take a cab across downtown Toronto for $8–$9.

➤ COMPANIES: **Beck** (☎ 416/751–5555). **Co-op** (☎ 416/504–2667). **Diamond** (☎ 416/366–6868). **Metro** (☎ 416/504–8294). For more information, call the **Metro Licensing Commission** (☎ 416/392–3000).

TELEPHONES

COUNTRY CODES

The country code for Canada is 1.

DIRECTORY & OPERATOR INFORMATION

For directory assistance in Canada, dial the area code followed by 555–1212; dial 1 before the area code if the area code is not the same as the one you are calling from.

INTERNATIONAL CALLS

If you're dialing Canada from the United States, dial 1 plus the area code and telephone number. If you're dialing the United States from Canada, dial 1 plus the area code and telephone number.

To call Great Britain, Australia, or New Zealand from Canada, dial 011 followed by the appropriate country code and the city code and number. The country codes are 44 for Great Britain, 61 for Australia, and 64 for New Zealand. To dial Canada from these countries, you should be able to dial 001 followed by the area code and telephone number.

LOCAL CALLS

For local calls, simply dial the number. No area code is needed.

LONG-DISTANCE CALLS

To dial another province or an area of the same province that has a different area code, dial 1 followed by the area code and number.

Competitive long-distance carriers make calling within the United States and Canada relatively convenient and let you avoid hotel surcharges. By dialing an 800 number, you can get connected to the long-distance company of your choice.

➤ LONG-DISTANCE CARRIERS: **AT&T** (☎ 800/225–5288). **MCI** (☎ 800/888–8000). **Sprint** (☎ 800/366–2255).

PUBLIC PHONES

Pay phones work as they do in the United States. Drop 25¢ in the slot and dial the number. There are no problems dialing direct to the United States; U.S. telephone credit cards are accepted. Almost all pay phones will also accept prepaid telephone cards which can be readily purchased from convenience stores.

TIPPING

Tips and service are not usually added to a bill in Toronto. In restaurants, 15% of the pre-tax subtotal bill is what most waiters and waitresses expect. A tip of 10% to 15% is usually in order for taxi drivers. Porters and doormen should get around $1 a bag in most hotels (more in luxury hotels). For maid service, $2 for the first night and $1 per day thereafter is customary.

American money is always welcome (a U.S. $1 tip is worth about C$1.38), so **don't worry if you run out of Canadian money.**

TOUR OPERATORS

Buying a prepackaged tour or independent vacation can make your trip to Toronto less expensive and more hassle-free. Because everything is prearranged, you'll spend less time planning.

Operators that handle several hundred thousand travelers per year can use their purchasing power to give you a good price. Their high volume may also indicate financial stability. But some small companies provide more personalized service; because they tend to specialize, they may also be more knowledgeable about a given area.

BOOKING WITH AN AGENT

Travel agents are excellent resources. In fact, large operators accept bookings made only through travel agents. But it's a good idea to **collect brochures from several agencies,** because some agents' suggestions may be influenced by relationships with tour and package firms that reward them for volume sales. If you have a special interest, **find an agent with expertise in that area;** ASTA (☞ Travel Agencies, *below*) has a database of specialists worldwide.

Make sure your travel agent knows the accommodations and other services. Ask about the hotel's location, room size, beds, and whether it has a pool, room service, or programs for children, if you care about these. Has your agent been there in person or sent others you can contact?

Do some homework on your own, too: Local tourism boards can provide information about lesser-known and small-niche operators, some of which may sell only direct.

BUYER BEWARE

Each year consumers are stranded or lose their money when tour operators—even very large ones with excellent reputations—go out of business. So **check out the operator.** Find out how long the company has been in business, and ask several travel agents about its reputation. If the package or tour you are considering is priced lower than in your wildest dreams, **be skeptical.** Try to

book with a company that has a consumer-protection program. If the operator has such a program, you'll find information about it in the company's brochure. If the operator you are considering does not offer some kind of consumer protection, then ask for references from satisfied customers.

In the U.S., members of the National Tour Association and United States Tour Operators Association are required to set aside funds to cover your payments and travel arrangements in case the company defaults. It's also a good idea to choose a company that participates in the American Society of Travel Agent's Tour Operator Program (TOP). This gives you a forum if there are any disputes between you and your tour operator; ASTA will act as mediator.

➤ TOUR-OPERATOR RECOMMENDATIONS: **American Society of Travel Agents** (☞ Travel Agencies, *below*). **National Tour Association** (✉ NTA, ✉ 546 E. Main St., Lexington, KY 40508, ☎ 606/226–4444 or 800/755–8687). **United States Tour Operators Association** (✉ USTOA, ✉ 342 Madison Ave., Suite 1522, New York, NY 10173, ☎ 212/599–6599 or 800/468–7862, FAX 212/599–6744).

COSTS

The more your package or tour includes, the better you can predict the ultimate cost of your vacation. Make sure you know exactly what is covered, and **beware of hidden costs.** Are taxes, tips, and service charges included? Transfers and baggage handling? Entertainment and excursions? These can add up.

Prices for packages and tours are usually quoted per person, based on two sharing a room. If traveling solo, you may be required to pay the full double-occupancy rate. Some operators eliminate this surcharge if you agree to be matched with a roommate of the same sex, even if one is not found by departure time.

GROUP TOURS

Among companies that sell tours to Toronto, the following have a proven reputation and offer plenty of options. The classifications used below represent different price categories. The key difference is usually in accommodations, which run from budget to better, and better-yet to best.

➤ DELUXE: **Globus** (✉ 5301 S. Federal Circle, Littleton, CO 80123-2980, ☎ 303/797–2800 or 800/221–0090, FAX 303/347–2080). **Maupintour** (✉ 1515 St. Andrews Dr., Lawrence, KS 66047, ☎ 785/843–1211 or 800/255–4266, FAX 785/843–8351). **Tauck Tours** (✉ Box 5027, 276 Post Rd. W, Westport, CT 06881-5027, ☎ 203/226–6911 or 800/468–2825, FAX 203/221–6866).

➤ FIRST-CLASS: **Caravan Tours** (✉ 401 N. Michigan Ave., Chicago, IL 60611, ☎ 312/321–9800 or 800/227–2826, FAX 312/321–9845). **Collette Tours** (✉ 162 Middle St., Pawtucket, RI 02860, ☎ 401/728–3805 or 800/340–5158, FAX 401/728–4745). **Mayflower Tours** (✉ Box 490, 1225 Warren Ave., Downers Grove, IL 60515, ☎ 708/960–3430 or 800/323–7064).

➤ BUDGET: **Cosmos** (☞ Globus, *above*).

PACKAGES

Like group tours, independent vacation packages are available from major tour operators and airlines. The companies listed below offer packages in a broad price range.

➤ AIR/HOTEL: **Air Canada's Canada** (☎ 800/774–8993). **Delta Vacations** (☎ 800/872–7786). **US Airways Vacations** (☎ 800/455–0123).

➤ RAIL/HOTEL: **Amtrak Vacations** (☎ 800/321–8684).

➤ FROM THE U.K.: **British Airways Holidays** (✉ Astral Towers, Betts Way, London Rd., Crawley, West Sussex RH10 2XA, ☎ 01293/723191). **Key to America** (✉ 1–3 Station Rd., Ashford, Middlesex TW15 2UW, ☎ 01784/248777). **Kuoni Travel** (✉ Kuoni House, Dorking, Surrey RH5 4AZ, ☎ 01306/740500).

THEME TRIPS

➤ PERFORMING ARTS: **Keith Prowse Tours** (✉ 234 W. 44th St., No. 1000, New York, NY 10036, ☎ 212/398–1430 or 800/669–8687, FAX 212/302–4251).

THE GOLD GUIDE / SMART TRAVEL TIPS

THE GOLD GUIDE / SMART TRAVEL TIPS

➤ SPAS: **Spa-Finders** (✉ 91 5th Ave., No. 301, New York, NY 10003-3039, ☎ 212/924–6800 or 800/255–7727).

➤ TENNIS: **Championship Tennis Tours** (✉ 8040 E. Morgan Trail No. 12, Scottsdale, AZ 85258, ☎ 602/443–9499 or 800/468–3664, FAX 602/443–8982).

TRAIN TRAVEL

Amtrak runs a daily train to Toronto from Chicago (a 12-hour trip) and another from New York City (12 hours). Canada's Via Rail runs trains to most major cities in Canada, and travel along the Windsor–Québec City corridor is particularly well served. Substantial discounts are available on Via Rail if you book at least five days in advance. Amtrak and Via Rail operate from Union Station on Front Street between Bay and York streets. You can walk underground to a number of hotels from the station. There is a cab stand outside the main entrance of the station.

➤ INFORMATION: **Amtrak** (☎ 800/872–7245). **Via Rail** (☎ 416/366–8411 or 800/561–3949).

TRAVEL AGENCIES

A good travel agent puts your needs first. Look for an agency that has been in business at least five years, emphasizes customer service, and has someone on staff who specializes in your destination. In addition, **make sure the agency belongs to a professional trade organization,** such as ASTA in the United States. If your travel agency is also acting as your tour operator, *see* Buyer Beware in Tour Operators, *above*).

➤ LOCAL AGENT REFERRALS: **American Society of Travel Agents** (ASTA, ☎ 800/965–2782 24-hr hot line, FAX 703/684–8319). **Association of Canadian Travel Agents** (✉ Suite 201, 1729 Bank St., Ottawa, Ontario K1V 7Z5, ☎ 613/521–0474, FAX 613/521–0805). **Association of British Travel Agents** (✉ 55–57 Newman St., London W1P 4AH, ☎ 0171/637–2444, FAX 0171/637–0713). **Australian Federation of Travel Agents** (☎ 02/9264–3299). **Travel**

Agents' Association of New Zealand (☎ 04/499–0104).

TRAVEL GEAR

Travel catalogs specialize in useful items, such as compact alarm clocks and travel irons, that can **save space when packing.**

➤ CATALOGS: **Magellan's** (☎ 800/962–4943, FAX 805/568–5406). **Orvis Travel** (☎ 800/541–3541, FAX 540/343–7053). **TravelSmith** (☎ 800/950–1600, FAX 800/950–1656).

VISITOR INFORMATION

TOURIST INFORMATION

➤ IN THE U.S. AND CANADA: **Tourism Toronto** (✉ 207 Queen's Quay W, Suite 590, Toronto, Ontario M5J 1A7, ☎ 800/363–1990 or 416/203–2500). **Tourism Ontario** (✉ 1 Concord Gate Pl., 9th Floor, Don Mills, Ontario M3C 3N6, ☎ 800/668–2746).

➤ IN THE U.K.: **Visit Canada Centre** (✉ 62–65 Trafalgar Square, London WC2 5DT, ☎ 0891/715000; calls cost 49p per minute peak rate or 39p per minute cheap rate).

U.S. GOVERNMENT

Government agencies can be an excellent source of inexpensive travel information. When planning your trip, **find out what government materials are available.**

➤ PAMPHLETS: **Consumer Information Center** (✉ Consumer Information Catalogue, Pueblo, CO 81009, ☎ 719/948–3334 or 888/878–3256) for a free catalog that includes travel titles.

WEB SITES

Do **check out the World Wide Web** when you're planning. You'll find everything fromup-to-date weather forecasts to virtual tours of famous cities. Fodor's Web site, www.fodors.com, is a great place to start. There are also many sites with information particularly useful for Toronto, a few of which follow.

➤ WEB SITES: **www.travelinx.com** provides information about Toronto and the province of Ontario; **www.tourism-toronto.com,** the site of Tourism Toronto, covers special events, dining, and lodging, and even has a special guide for women travelers; **www.city.toronto.on.ca,** the site of the City of Toronto, has helpful material about everything from local politics to public transit; **www.toronto-life.com,** the site of the monthly magazine *Toronto Life,* lists the latest art and nightlife events and carries information about dining, shopping, and more; **www.toronto.com** has links to the *Toronto Star* and information about topics including sports and dining out.

WHEN TO GO

The weather can often fall below freezing from late November into March and can be brutal in January and February. That simple fact alone may repel some people but also attract skiing and skating enthusiasts. In the often-bleak winter months, underground shopping concourses allow you to walk through much of the downtown area and avoid the cold.

Some of the best theater, ballet, opera, and concerts take place between September and May; both the Stratford and Shaw festivals, in venues each about a 90-minute drive from Toronto, are in full swing from mid-April or May to October. Toronto has year-round engagements of major theater productions.

Toronto is most pleasant to walk around and simply enjoy from late spring through early fall, when there are outdoor concerts and open-air dining—and the entire city seems to come to life. On the other hand, some hotels drop their prices up to 50% in the off-season, particularly December and January.

CLIMATE

Toronto's climate can be harsh in December, January, and February, and sometimes March and late November. Prolonged snowfalls rarely come to the northern shores of Lake Ontario, and many a December and January snowfall soon melts away. Spring can be brief, and a (hot) summer can last through much of June, July, and August, even September. The gorgeous autumn colors are seen best just north of the city and throughout the myriad parks; temperatures are moderate at this time.

Lake Ontario often cools the city air in summer and warms it in winter. The airport, therefore, being some distance from the lake, will be warmer in the summer than downtown and colder in the winter.

➤ FORECASTS: **Weather Channel Connection** (☎ 900/932–8437), 95¢ per minute from a Touch-Tone phone.

Climate in Toronto

The following are average daily maximum and minimum temperatures for Toronto.

Jan.	30F	– 1C	May	63F	17C	Sept.	69F	21C
	16	– 9		44	7		51	11
Feb.	30F	– 1C	June	73F	23C	Oct.	56F	13C
	15	– 9		54	12		40	4
Mar.	37F	3C	July	79F	26C	Nov.	43F	6
	23	– 5		59	15		31	– 1
Apr.	50F	10C	Aug.	77F	25C	Dec.	33F	1C
	34	1		58	14		21	– 6

THE GOLD GUIDE / SMART TRAVEL TIPS

1 Destination: Toronto

AN AMAZING METAMORPHOSIS

A POPULAR JOKE in the neighboring province of Québec between the wars went "First prize, one week in Toronto. Second prize, two weeks in Toronto. Third prize, three weeks in Toronto." And who could blame them for laughing? Toronto was a deadly city right into the 1950s, at which time its half million citizens used to rush off to Detroit (a four-hour drive to the southwest) and Buffalo (90 minutes to the south, around Lake Ontario) for a good time. Today, of course, the rush is in the opposite direction, for hundreds of reasons that are sprinkled through this book.

What has happened in so short a period? And why was no one surprised (in Toronto, at least) when various participants at the 1982 International Conference on Urban Design, held in Toronto, ran around spouting such superlatives as "This is the most livable city in North America" and "It is an example of how a city could grow"?

Toronto's excitement is partially explained by its ethnic diversity. Nearly two-thirds of the 4.3 million residents who now live in the Greater Toronto area were born and raised somewhere else. And that somewhere else was often very far away.

Nearly 500,000 Italians give Toronto one of the largest Italian communities outside Italy. It is also the home of the largest Chinese community in Canada and the largest Portuguese community in North America. The city hosts close to 150,000 Jews, nearly as many Muslims, and tens of thousands of Germans, joined by Greeks, Hungarians, East Indians, West Indians, Vietnamese, Maltese, South Americans, Ukrainians—more than 80 ethnic groups in all, speaking more than 80 different languages. Certainly, it's a city worthy of inviting the United Nations to consider moving here from Manhattan.

While the assimilation of these various cultures into the overall fabric of the city is ongoing, several ethnic neighborhoods have become attractions on their own for locals and visitors. These include Kensington Market (west of Spadina Avenue between College and Dundas), Chinatown (around the Spadina Avenue and Dundas Street intersection), Greektown (Danforth Avenue between Chester and Jones), Little Italy (College Street between Euclid and Shaw), Corso Italia (St. Clair Avenue West between Lansdowne and Westmount), Little Poland (Roncesvalles Avenue between King and Dundas), Portugal Village (Dundas Street West, west of Bathurst), Indian Bazaar (Gerrard Street between Coxwell and Greenwood), and Koreatown (Bloor Street West between Bathurst and Christie).

What this immigration has meant to Toronto is the rather rapid creation of a vibrant mix of cultures that has echoes of turn-of-the-century New York City—but without the slums, crowding, disease, and tensions. Toronto undoubtedly would have had this, too, had Canada been decent and wise enough to open its gates wide back then, as the Yanks did. (This fact the city continues to bemoan and tried to atone for by accepting more "boat people" in the 1970s than any other country in the world. Yet, there are still tensions over large-scale immigration to this day.)

Still, to give to its burgeoning ethnic population all, or even most, of the credit for Toronto's becoming a cosmopolitan, world-class city in just a few decades would not be totally correct. Much of the thanks must be given to the so-called dour Scots who set up the banks, built the churches, and created the kind of solid base for commerce, culture, and community that would come to such a healthy fruition in the three decades following World War II. The historian William Kilbourn wrote, "Once, Toronto the Good was embodied by the masters of the Orange Order: defenders of abstinence, Protestantism, and the British race . . . My own childhood was pure British colonial . . . But I know I couldn't stand living in that kind of Toronto now. Instead, I think of my two Italian grandsons and my Chilean granddaughter, and of this city as a welcoming and exciting place for them, and I celebrate my non-WASP home."

TORONTO'S SUCCESS can also be credited to thoughtful and sensitive government actions, such as the limits that the city council set in the 1970s on the number and size of new buildings, and the decision by the Ontario government to put a stop to a major (Spadina) expressway, which would have slashed like a knife through many precious, long-standing neighborhoods. At the same time, metropolitan Toronto has encouraged urban renewal, and many of the city's building projects have mixed low-rent housing with luxury condos, restaurants, offices, and businesses. Somehow, Toronto has managed to avoid the situation in many North American cities, where the middle class has fled to the suburbs, taking their taxes and children with them. On the contrary, one can see tens of thousands of young couples eagerly moving back to the same areas in the heart of the city where they grew up, and where they know that they will have fine schools for their kids and a healthy community to live in.

Like most major cities, Toronto has its share of problems. However, since late 1995 low interest rates have helped improve both the job market and the housing sector, which in turn has resulted in a remarkable 36% increase in house building. The vacancy rate on rental housing remains low, and the average resale cost of a home in the metropolitan area is approaching $222,000 (in Canadian dollars). These prices are lower than they were in the late 1980s, but the city remains a very expensive place to live.

Nevertheless, the city that once united Canadians from the Atlantic to the Pacific in a shared hatred of Toronto's sanctimoniousness now tends to draw their collective envy at how well the place works. Some critics insist that Toronto remains too smug (well, yes); too regulated (would they prefer chaos?); too provincial (actually, it's municipal; Ontario is provincial); too prim and proper (would they rather be mugged?); too young (as a major city, perhaps, but it was hardly born yesterday).

Montrealers—a quite different culture of primarily French-speaking Catholics—still joke that "Toronto is a city where people go around saying 'Thank God it's Monday.' " To this day, indeed, Torontonians seem to actually enjoy working, and they appear to lack the ability to enjoy themselves doing anything else. But with the prices of houses, who can afford not to work? And as for "having a good time," there have never been more fine restaurants, theaters, movie houses, concerts, and bars to enjoy oneself in—even on Sunday!

That's Toronto, in a nutshell: Clean. Safe. Orderly. Yet somehow dynamic and exciting. Groucho Marx sang an old vaudeville tune back in 1917 that went "It's better to run to Toronto/Than to stay in a place you don't wanta." And he was right. Eight decades later, we can honestly change the words to "It's best that you run to Toronto/There's no better place that you'd wanta."

NEW AND NOTEWORTHY

Americans traveling to Toronto (and anywhere else in Canada) will benefit from the favorable **exchange rate,** which means that dollars go further even with higher Canadian taxes. Following the trend of the past few years, the exchange rate (fall 1998) was about US$1 to C$1.38.

Toronto's waterfront has become one of its most popular areas, and the city continues to work on developing even more attractions there. The new **Music Garden,** beyond the west end of Harbourfront Centre, was developed by cellist Yo-Yo Ma and garden designer Julie Moir Messervy. Six landscaped areas interpret different movements of J. S. Bach's *Cello Suite No. 1.* A major museum event was the opening in mid-1998 of **The Pier,** a waterfront interpretive center at Harbourfront Centre that has displays showing the history of the city's waterfront as well as classes on boatbuilding and seafaring skills.

The Royal Ontario Museum (ROM), long a favorite of children for its Bat Cave, Discovery Centre, and Dinosaur Collection, has leased space to the new **Children's Own Museum (COM).** The museum is for younger kids and holds intriguing areas such as a workshop, a main street, and an attic.

To keep up with the past, many of Toronto's **historic properties** undergo continuous renovation. In the next few years, Fort York, a relic of the 1812–14 war, will see barracks and block house restorations, while Spadina House, a local magnate's mansion, is scheduled to produce a new living history display of its Depression-era kitchen.

There's plenty of building going on in the city. In 1999 a new waterfront sports arena, the **Air Canada Centre,** will become home to both the city's NBA Raptors basketball team and the NHL's Maple Leaf hockey team. The **Canadian Opera Company** is planning to build a new opera house downtown, to open in 2000.

The streetcar is alive and well in the city with the recently opened **Spadina Light Rail Transit** (a glorified term for the good old streetcar) line, connecting busy Union Station with the Bloor/Danforth east–west subway line.

WHAT'S WHERE

Old Toronto

The first settlements have mostly been obliterated in this earliest part of town, just north of the waterfront, but several public buildings from the 19th century remain. A visually exciting streetscape results from the mix of old buildings, new buildings, and old buildings restored for new uses. The area's draws include the Hockey Hall of Fame and Museum, the lively St. Lawrence Market, and the Hummingbird and St. Lawrence cultural centers.

The Financial District

West of Old Toronto, Bay Street is where the financial and legal power in Canada is focused. It's home to many imposing skyscrapers in various early and late-20th-century styles as well as to a couple of lovely miniparks and the Design Exchange (the former Toronto Stock Exchange). You'll find most of the major live theaters in or near this area, too.

The Waterfront

Toronto is bordered by Lake Ontario, and after decades of neglect the city has turned its waterfront into a major asset.

This most southerly area of the city includes lots of opportunities for outdoor activities and amusements, making it ideal for visitors with children. Among the attractions along the waterfront are Ontario Place, CN Tower, SkyDome, Fort York, and Harbourfront Centre, a cultural and recreation center. Just a 15-minute ferryboat ride across Toronto Bay is the best-kept secret of them all, the Toronto Islands.

Along Dundas and Queen Streets

This north-central core area is interesting for the vibrant street life of Kensington Market, Chinatown, and Nathan Phillips Square (the park in front of New City Hall). Cultural interests can be fulfilled by the Art Gallery of Ontario, many commercial galleries, and two restored historical homes. Shoppers flock to the mammoth Eaton Centre and fashionable Queen Street West with its black-garbed young habitués.

Around Queen's Park

Just west of the Dundas and Queen streets area, the Ontario provincial legislature and the main campus of the University of Toronto occupy prime central real estate. The area is liberally scattered with parks and lawns as well as libraries and museums, including the city's most famous, the Royal Ontario Museum. On the northern edge of this area is Yorkville, filled with restaurants and elegant, upscale stores and boutiques, and the Annex, an artsy neighborhood. To the west is Little Italy, with restaurants and cafés along College Street that have made it one of the coolest scenes in town.

Cabbagetown

This architecturally diverse area on the eastern edge of the central core, once the home of poor WASPS, has been restored by middle-class home owners. The streets hold some of the city's loveliest homes from the late-19th and early 20th centuries. The term Cabbagetown, though originally applied to an area farther south, comes from the fact that many of the poor residents grew cabbages on their lawns to feed the family or to sell in hopes of earning a few pennies.

Forest Hill and Beyond

Leafy streets and multimillion dollar homes dominate this midtown neighborhood, northwest of the central core. Those who want to see how the other half lived can visit Spadina, a 19th-century mansion, and even visit a fantasy castle, Casa Loma.

Southwest Toronto

Huge and lovely High Park is the highlight here, but West Indian, German, Polish, and Ukrainian enclaves attract those hungering for homemade sausage, roti, and other ethnic treats.

Northwest Toronto

This primarily residential area holds a thriving Italian community; Paramount Canada's Wonderland, a theme park; Kortright Centre, an attractive conservation center with hiking trails and aquariums; and Black Creek Pioneer Village, which recreates a mid-19th-century community. A bit farther out, in the town of Kleinburg, is the outstanding McMichael Canadian Art Collection.

Northeast Toronto

Most people visit this suburban section of town for the outstanding Toronto Zoo, but the many parks and ravines are also a draw.

Southeast Toronto

The southeastern area of the city is popular for its colorful ethnic neighborhoods, especially Greektown, which is centered around Danforth Avenue (called simply The Danforth). It also includes waterfront parks and The Beaches, an ideal place for a boardwalk stroll and some shopping.

PLEASURES AND PASTIMES

Dining

The city's dining scene has flourished in the late '90s, providing a huge variety of choices. Formal establishments and even steak houses are thriving, but not at the expense of the many new bistros, tapas bars, and noodle bars. After each of Toronto's immigration waves, an intriguing new batch of restaurants open. In the last half century, Toronto has been introduced to everything from Hungar-

ian schnitzel after the 1956 revolution to Vietnamese and other Southeast Asian cuisines in the 1970s and beyond. Italian restaurants dominate the city's dining scene, reflecting the locals' long-term passion for this cuisine in all its regional variations, but you can also choose from an abundance of excellent Chinese, French, Greek, Indian, Indonesian, Japanese, Korean, Latin, Thai, seafood, vegetarian, creative contemporary, and, of course, Canadian fare. The wine lists of the finest restaurants include, in addition to international selections, excellent regional wines, while local microbrews provide wonderful accompaniments to more casual meals. If you're visiting in summer, do as the locals do and dine alfresco, a cherished Toronto pastime.

Ethnic Neighborhoods

You can tour the world in Toronto, where you'll encounter markets, clothes, music, newspapers, cuisines, and customs from around the universe. If you walk around long enough, you'll hear everything from Hindi to Greek. You can pick up a sari on Gerrard Street East, purchase Chinese herbal medicine on Dundas Street, and browse for French books on Queen Street West. The West Indian community holds a summer festival, Caribana, that draws hundreds of thousands of people. Many of the immigrants who originally settled Toronto's ethnic enclaves have moved to the suburbs, but others have taken their places and kept the old traditions alive.

Lodging

Toronto offers an array of places to lay your head that is commensurate with a city of its size and sophistication. Although it isn't strong on historic lodgings or bed-and-breakfasts, there are some notable exceptions, and chain hotels have reliable properties in convenient locations around town. The First Nations inhabitants who came up with the name Toronto, or "place of meetings," certainly had foresight: Conventions book huge blocks of hotel rooms year-round. This can mean annoying lobby bustle, but it also tends to ensure that properties in this competitive town have plenty of amenities and high levels of service. The emphasis on business also means that rates sometimes go down drastically on the weekends; many hotels have special packages for couples and families, too.

Parks and Ravines

When Toronto was first settled, it not only had a fine natural port, but also sat at the mouth of two rivers and a handful of streams. While these small streams have either dried up or been covered over by urban development, their valleys and ravines have been retained by the city as parkland. Many parks offer dirt, cinder, or asphalt paths for bikers and joggers. High Park, west of downtown, is lovely, and miniparks throughout the urban core afford good views, public sculpture, historical plaques, and, of course, benches for resting tired feet.

Shopping

From haute couture to ethnic markets, Toronto has retail options for every purse and personal taste. Megamalls like the Eaton Centre vie with intimate boutiques on Bloor Street West and in the Yorkville area for shoppers' attention. Unique areas to explore include the St. Lawrence and Kensington markets; funky Queen Street West, with its street-smart shops; Chinatown and Spadina Avenue, loaded with bargains; Queen Street East, with a treasure trove of vintage and antiques stores; and Queen's Quay Terminal, a delightful converted warehouse on the waterfront (the Harbourfront Antiques Market is nearby, too).

Spectator Sports

Toronto has venues for American favorites like baseball (the Toronto Blue Jays) and basketball (the Toronto Raptors), as well as for other spectator sports that have a stronger following in Europe. Ice hockey is a national mania; children start out as soon as they're old enough to toddle around on skates, move to league play when they're around 10, and generally keep going as long as their knees hold out. Maple Leaf tickets are a scarce commodity in this town. Amateur leagues sometimes play at 2 AM because there's so much competition for ice time. For a free look at nonprofessional enthusiasts, check out any park with a skating rink on a bright winter's day. American fans may want to sample Canadian football at an Argonauts' game; the play is faster and (locals say) more exciting.

GREAT ITINERARIES

To see and experience all that is Toronto, you should plan a stay of at least a week (preferably during the spring, summer, or fall; winters can be bitter). If you're here for a short period, you need to plan carefully so you don't miss the must-see sights. The following suggested itineraries will help you structure your visit efficiently, and the neighborhood sections in Chapter 2 have more information about individual sights. These itineraries don't include the side trips in Chapter 8, so you'd need to adjust your plans to include them.

If You Have 1 Day

The four structures that have become the icons of modern Toronto are grouped close enough together that they can all be visited on a single (very busy) day. Start at the ultramodern **New City Hall** at Queen and Bay streets; then cross the street and explore its quaint predecessor, Old City Hall, from the turn of the century. Walk south on Bay Street through the heart of the financial district, with its handsome skyscrapers; head west on Front Street to the spectacular **CN Tower.** It's not hard to find—just look up at the world's tallest freestanding structure. From the tower's indoor and outdoor observation decks, the city lies spread out before you. Take a lunch break in the tower's 360 Revolving Restaurant.

Continue your day with a visit to the tower's neighbor to the west, the spectacular **SkyDome,** home of the Toronto Blue Jays baseball team and the Toronto Argonauts of the Canadian Football League. Provided the facility is not in use, you can take a guided tour, complete with a film showing how the retractable roof works. Leaving SkyDome, walk or take a taxi south to Queen's Quay Terminal, part of **Harbourfront Centre,** the city's lakefront cultural and recreational center. There's plenty to do along Queen's Quay, from shopping to visiting The Pier, a maritime museum. You can spend a comfortable evening strolling along the city's waterfront. The streetcar running along the center of Queen's Quay (make sure the sign in front says Union) will take you back uptown to Union subway station.

If You Have 3 Days

Visit the classic tourist sights described above on your first day and prepare for a mix of culture, shopping, and relaxation for the next two days. Spend the morning of Day 2 exploring the original **Chinatown** laid out west along Dundas Street behind the new City Hall all the way over to the "new" Chinatown in and around the busy Spadina Avenue/Dundas Street intersection. You'll be near the sights and smells of colorful **Kensington Market,** too. Walk south on Spadina to Queen Street West (five short blocks) and make a left to check out a funky, stylish new shopping district. You'll find restaurants and cafés here, too. Continue walking east, past the new and old City Halls (visited on Day 1) and on a little farther to the the 300 or so shops of **Eaton Centre,** at Yonge Street. Even people who don't like to shop may be tempted. The Bay, the nation's oldest oldest retailer, is on the south side of Queen Street. Eaton Centre has plenty of places to eat. If you want to skip Eaton Centre or just take a quick look, you can spend the afternoon at the **Art Gallery of Ontario** (at Dundas and McCaul streets), with its outstanding Henry Moore collection; you can eat here, too. In the evening, pick your favorite ethnic cuisine and head to one of the city's excellent restaurants.

On Day 3, continue your shopping explorations along Bloor Street West, dubbed by some as Toronto's 5th Avenue, between Yonge Street and Avenue Road. Don't forget to explore nearby **Yorkville,** just to the north, where modern chrome-and-glass-encased shops give way to streets of boutiques nestled within restored former Victorian residences. Your next stop is the nearby **Royal Ontario Museum,** at Bloor Street and Queen's Park. Treasures from the worlds of art, archaeology, and science fill this museum; plan to spend two to four hours here. To relax a bit in the afternoon, you have two options. The first is to take the subway south on Yonge and walk to the docks at the foot of Bay Street and Queen's Quay to catch a ferry to the serene **Toronto Islands;** the view of the city skyline is an added plus. You can also travel 6 km (4

mi) due west of Bloor and Yonge streets (take the subway west to the High Park station and walk south) to large, lovely **High Park.** In the evening, take in a show or a concert; Toronto is a great city for theater and music.

If You Have 5 Days

Follow the itineraries above for your first three days, and venture a bit farther afield on Day 4. You can head in either of two directions to see a number of sights that are accessible by public transportation but are more easily reached by car. The first choices—great family options—are the **Ontario Science Centre,** with its engaging exhibits and demonstrations, and the sprawling **Toronto Zoo.** You could truly spend a good day at either, so plan your time and don't be distracted if you want to see both. The science center is 11 km (7 mi) northeast of downtown; the zoo is 35 km (22 mi) northeast. The other choice for Day 4 is to head north of downtown and visit **Black Creek Pioneer Village,** a living history museum dedicated to 19th-century life, and the **McMichael Canadian Art Collection,** an outstanding museum with works by Canadian and First Nations artists. The art museum is set on 100 wooded acres. Black Creek Pioneer village is 20 km (12 mi) north of downtown; the McMichael is 30 km (19 mi) north. When you're back downtown in the evening, look for a place where you can dine alfresco—patio dining, as the locals say— or head to hip College Street in **Little Italy.**

On Day 5, you can choose to roam some special neighborhoods in Toronto—even explore the world. Purchase a TTC Day Pass, which allows unlimited use of transit vehicles after 9:30 AM and is available at subway stations. Some areas to the east of downtown are **The Beaches,** a great place to stroll the lakefront and shop, and **The Danforth,** with its Greek and other restaurants. West of The Danforth is **Cabbagetown,** with its handsome 19th-century homes. Other choices (northwest of downtown) are the arty **Annex** community and a number of Italian neighborhoods, including the suddenly hot strip of **Little Italy** on College Street from Euclid to Grace Street as well as the area around St. Clair Avenue West from Bathurst Street to Dufferin Street. You'll find intriguing eateries everywhere.

FODOR'S CHOICE

No two people will agree on what makes a perfect vacation, but it's fun and helpful to know what others think. We hope you'll have a chance to experience some of Fodor's choices yourself while visiting Toronto. For detailed information about each entry, refer to the appropriate chapters in this guidebook.

Cultural Highlights

★ **Art Gallery of Ontario.** Among a stellar array of art, the Henry Moore collection—the world's largest public holding of the sculptor's work—stands out.

★ **The National Ballet of Canada.** The dancers of this supremely professional company are always on their toes, whether they're performing their own work or imported classics.

★ **Royal Ontario Museum.** The museum that has been called Canada's "single greatest cultural asset" is particularly strong in ceramics and Chinese and Nubian art.

★ **The Shaw Festival.** GBS and his contemporaries hold forth for half a year in lovely Niagara-on-the-Lake.

★ **The Stratford Festival.** The play's the thing in Stratford from May to October; the rest of the year is spent preparing for the onslaught of Shakespeare fans.

Dining

★ **Centro.** The chefs here set city standards of excellence with a sophisticated menu that incorporates French-Mediterranean influences and regional ingredients. $$$$

★ **Truffles.** Set beyond wrought-iron gates, this is one of the country's best restaurants, in a suitably chic setting. Admirers swear by such dishes as poached and braised veal tournedos. $$$$

★ **Lai Wah Heen.** Silver serving dishes and formal service complement the creative 100-dish menu. For lunch, try the superb dim sum. $$$–$$$$

★ **Splendido.** Entertainment types crowd this au courant eatery with its excellent contemporary Italian cuisine. Come for a nightcap just to check out the scene. $$$–$$$$

★ **Rodney's Oyster Bar.** Showbiz and agency types flock to this basement raw bar for oceanic delights. Choices other than the array of oysters include soft-shell steamers, quahogs, and oyster slapjack chowder. $$–$$$$

★ **Grano.** Homemade gnocchi and ravioli shine at a friendly Italian restaurant with a large selection of antipasti and entrées. $$–$$$

★ **Herbs.** A deceptively plain menu changes with the season but always hosts a wealth of French-inspired delights. The room is lovely, too. $$–$$$

★ **Verona.** A good-value Italian eatery serves up elegant dishes such as pan-seared sea scallops on truffled asparagus spears with champagne cream. $$

Lodging

★ **Four Seasons Toronto.** The most exclusive property in town, it usually tops all the "best hotel" lists. A great location, top-notch service, afternoon tea—what could be more civilized? $$$$

★ **Inter-Continental Toronto.** The Inter-Continental offers spacious, nicely decorated rooms within walking distance of the city's best museum and of its toniest shops. $$$$

★ **Le Royal Meridien King Edward.** This downtown grande dame reflects the elegance of its 1903 opening date. Gentility and attention to detail are the rule here. $$$–$$$$

★ **Palmerston Inn Bed & Breakfast.** Floral-pattern linens and antiques fill the room of this 1906 Georgian mansion. You can stroll to hip College Street or busy Bloor Street. $–$$

★ **Neill-Wycik College-Hotel.** You get more than you might expect at this budget, dorm-style lodging: pleasant rooms plus a panoramic view from the roof deck. $

Natural Attractions

★ **Edward's Gardens.** Manicured lawns bordered by a profusion of flowers bring out the horticultural hordes in fine weather.

★ **High Park.** Close to the heart of urban Toronto lies a large oasis for fishing, bird-watching, and other rural activities. This is one of the loveliest in North America.

★ **Lake Ontario.** Toronto's watery border changes with the seasons, sporting frozen waves near the edges in winter and recreational vessels in summer, but you can depend on it for glorious sunsets year-round.

★ **Niagara Falls.** Pages of print have been devoted to Canada's world-famous cascades, but it's hard to capture the awesome phenomenon in words. You'll need to experience Niagara for yourself.

Nightlife

★ **ChaChaCha.** Latin dance clubs are hot in Toronto, and you can tap those stilettos on the stainless-steel dance floor of this Copacabana of the '90s.

★ **The Docks.** Want a basketball court or a pool as well as billiards and a dance floor? This entertainment center has it all, plus skyline views from its outdoor terrace.

★ **The Madison Avenue Pub.** An arty crowd enjoys the local ale, darts, and, in summer, outdoor patio of three connected town houses near the University of Toronto.

★ **The Rivoli.** Cutting-edge performance art, comedy improv, new music, and hip poetry draw black-clad intellectuals to this club.

★ **Second City.** Many *Saturday Night Live* regulars got their start at the Toronto offshoot of the famed Chicago comedy club; Mike Myers is one alum. The talent is still going strong in Second City's new theater on Blue Jays Way.

★ **Top O'The Senator.** All that jazz and a smokey, old-fashioned room—what more could retro romantics want?

Shopping

★ **Ashley China.** We don't know how William Ashley manages to secure such low prices on fine china and crystal, but we appreciate his passing them along to us.

★ **Eaton Centre.** It's big (300 stores) and it's crowded, but this downtown mall is also an architectural stunner. You'll find fashions, food, and films here—as well as a flock of Fiberglas Canada geese.

★ **Kensington Market.** Kosher pickles and Polish kielbasas mingle with Caribbean roti and Indian kebabs at this outdoor market, which will have you salivating when you get within sniffing distance.

★ **St. Lawrence Market.** Toronto's first city hall now serves citizens a daily array of delectables. There's also a Saturday-morning farmers' market.

★ **Yorkville.** The equivalent of New York's Madison Avenue, it's home to tony, one-of-a-kind boutiques, many of them set in old town houses.

FESTIVALS AND SEASONAL EVENTS

Top seasonal events in Toronto include the Caravan celebrations in June, Caribana in July, the Toronto International Film Festival in September, and the city's New Year's Eve Party. Telephone numbers are given for a number of events; for further details about others, contact Tourism Toronto (☎ 416/203–2500 or 800/363–1990).

MID-JAN.➤ The **Toronto International Boat Show** (☎ 416/591–6772) draws throngs of would-be and actual sailors to Exhibition Place to ogle state-of-the-art nautical toys.

MID-MAR.➤ **Toronto Sportsmen's Show** (☎ 416/695–0311) attracts the field-and-stream set to Exhibition Place, where the latest outdoor gear is displayed.

MID-APR.–OCT.➤ **Shaw Festival** (☎ 416/690–7301 or 905/468–2172), which presents plays by the contemporaries of the British curmudgeon as well as those of GBS himself, begins in Niagara-on the-Lake and continues through October.

MID-MAY–OCT.➤ **Stratford Festival** (☎ 416/364–8355 or 800/567–1600),

a theater festival featuring the best in classical and contemporary repertoire, with a special emphasis on the works of William Shakespeare, opens in Stratford and continues into October.

JUNE➤ **Gay & Lesbian Pride Week** (☎ 416/927–7433) includes cultural and political programs and a parade.

MID-JUNE➤ **Metro Toronto International Caravan** (☎ 416/977–0466) provides a 10-day tour of the world; at booths in the town's various ethnic communities, locals eat their way around the globe while attending performances of everything from Indonesian puppets to North African belly dancers.

MID-JUNE➤ **NorthbyNortheast** (☎ 416/469–0986), aka N×NE, is a three-day sound fest and conference showcasing new pop, rock, and world music.

LATE JUNE➤ **The du Maurier Jazz Festival** (☎ 416/363–5200) has featured such greats as Sarah Vaughan, Miles Davis, Dizzy Gillespie, and Branford Marsalis over the years.

EARLY JULY➤ **The Mariposa Festival** (☎ 416/979–9886) is the longest-running folk festival in North America; it takes place in Bracebridge, a pretty little town several hours north of Toronto. The legendary Pete Seeger

and Canadians Joni Mitchell and Gordon Lightfoot have appeared in past years.

JULY➤ **Caribana** (☎ 416/465–4884) is a 10-day cultural showcase with Caribbean music, dance, and arts put on by the West Indian communities; more than 500,000 people watch the events. One highlight is a spectacular parade of some 5,000 brightly dressed revelers.

MID-JULY➤ The **Molson Indy Toronto** (☎ 416/872–4639), one of the major events in the CART racing season, is held over a three-day period at the city's Exhibition Place. Besides races, there are themed attractions and a consumer and trade show with racing merchandise and auto-related displays.

MID-AUG.–EARLY SEPT.➤ **Canadian National Exhibition** (☎ 416/393–6000), the biggest fair in the country, has rides, entertainment, displays, and just about anything else you can think of. It's held (as it has been since 1879) at its namesake grounds on the Lake Ontario waterfront.

EARLY–MID-SEPT.➤ **The Toronto International Film Festival** (☎ 416/967–7371) brings together cinematographers and film stars from many countries. Film buffs can view more than a hundred new and classic films during the event.

LATE OCT.➤ **The International Festival of Authors** (☎ 416/973–4760) at Harbourfront Centre brings in major writers from around the world—Saul Bellow, Jan Morris, and Thomas Keneally have all participated. This is one of Toronto's major cultural experiences.

EARLY NOV.➤ **Royal Agricultural Winter Fair** (☎ 416/393–6400), held annually since 1922 at Exhibition Place, is North America's most prestigious agricultural fair; it showcases a multitude of related events as well as a commercial trade show and the International Royal Horse Show.

EARLY NOV.–MID-DEC.➤ **One of a Kind Christmas-Canadian Craft Show and Sale** offers excellent quality crafts from around the country, just in time to buy gifts for you-know-what.

MID-NOV.➤ **The Santa Claus Parade,** an annual city favorite since 1905, cruises downtown Toronto.

DEC. 31➤ **New Year's Eve at City Hall** is thrown in Nathan Phillips Square. **First Night Toronto, Celebration of the Arts** (☎ 416/362–3692), a popular "no-booze," family-oriented celebration, takes place in many locations all over downtown Toronto.

2 Exploring Toronto

You'll experience Toronto's mix of cultures in its myriad attractions, which range from the alternately staid and innovative architecture of its abundant bank buildings to the sensual overload of its ethnic markets. High-tone temples of art satisfy the most devoted culture lovers—the Royal Ontario Museum, for example, is one of the best museums in North America—while fun spots such as the CN Tower, Eaton Centre and Harbourfront Centre keep the seriously frivolous occupied.

Updated by
Mike Filey

CANADA'S CENTER OF CULTURE, commerce, and communications—"New York, as run by the Swiss," as Peter Ustinov once put it—Toronto has enough people and enough money to support a critical mass for each of many special interests. This means that it's easy to find attractions here to satisfy every taste, whether it be for historic buildings, science museums, or waterfront parks.

The city officially became Toronto on March 6, 1834, but its roots are much more ancient than that. A Frenchman named Etienne Brûlé was sent into the not-yet-Canadian wilderness in the early 1600s by the famous explorer Samuel de Champlain to see what he could discover. And he discovered plenty: the river and portage routes from the St. Lawrence to Lake Huron, possibly Lakes Superior and Michigan, and, eventually, Lake Ontario. Of course the local people of the First Nations had known about these places for centuries; they had long ago named the area between the Humber and Don rivers Toronto, believed to mean "a place of meetings." It was later a busy village named Teiaiagon, then the site of a French trading post and, in 1793, a British town named York (if the British hadn't won the Seven Years' War in the late 1700s, you would be reading this in translation from the French), and finally the city we know today, which once again took the original name of Toronto.

The city followed the usual history of colonial towns of the last century: It was invaded by the Americans in 1812; there were several devastating fires; there was a rebellion in 1837; and there was a slow but steady growth of white Anglo-Saxon Protestants, from about 9,000 in the 1830s to well over 500,000 before the outbreak of World War II, at which time they outnumbered the non-WASPs by five to two. In the last five decades, Toronto has metamorphosed into a great world city, where colorful ethnic enclaves mix with imposing banks and government buildings—making this a wonderful town to explore.

The most recent alteration to the municipal setup occurred in January 1998, when the six communities that formerly made up the Municipality of Metropolitan Toronto (which itself was created in 1953 to help alleviate growing pains faced by the community with the rapid increase in immigration following the end of World War II) became one large, so-called "megacity" under the name City of Toronto. Visitors, however, will still find reminders of those five cities and one borough from the pre-megacity era (Toronto, Etobicoke, North York, Scarborough, York, and East York, respectively) on shop signs, as part of postal addresses, and in the names of subway stations and newly established Civic Service Centres.

The boundaries of what Torontonians consider downtown, where you'll find most of the sights in this chapter, are subject to debate, but everyone agrees on the southern cutoff: Lake Ontario and the Toronto Islands. (Unless you're peering out from the top of one of the city's many high-rises, you'll have to take that fact on faith: Until the early 1970s, the city pretty much ignored and obscured its lakeshore.) The other coordinates of the rectangle that comprise the city core are Bathurst Street on the west, Parliament Street on the east, and Eglinton Avenue north. Beyond these borders—to the southeast, southwest, northeast, and northwest—are numerous sights that make excellent morning, afternoon, or full-day excursions on their own. An ideal way to get a sense of the city's layout is from an observation deck of the CN Tower on a clear day; it's especially lovely at sunset.

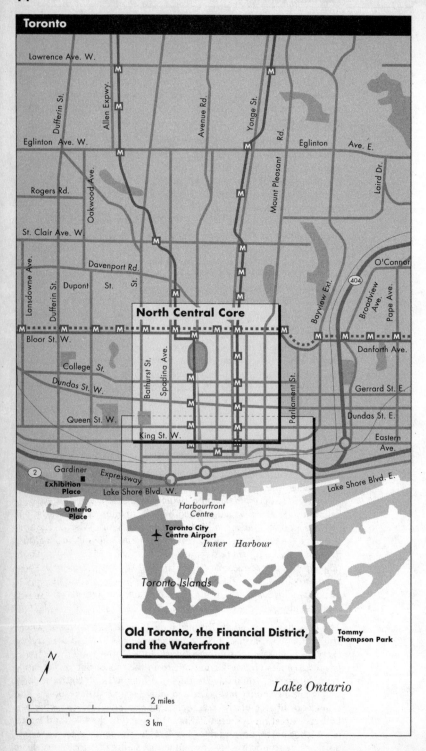

Toronto

Lawrence Ave. W.

Dufferin St.
Allen Expwy.
Avenue Rd.
Yonge St.
Mount Pleasant Rd.

Eglinton Ave. W.
Eglinton Ave. E.
Laird Dr.

Rogers Rd.
Oakwood Ave.

St. Clair Ave. W.

Lansdowne Ave.
Dufferin St.

Davenport Rd.
O'Connor

Dupont St. St.
Bayview Ext.
Broadview Ave.
Pape Ave.
404

Bloor St. W.
Danforth Ave.

North Central Core

Bathurst St.
Spadina Ave.
Parliament St.

College St.

Dundas St. W.
Gerrard St. E.

Queen St. W.
Dundas St. E.

King St. W.
Eastern Ave.

Gardiner Expressway
2
Exhibition Place
Lake Shore Blvd. W.
Lake Shore Blvd. E.

Ontario Place

Harbourfront Centre

Toronto City Centre Airport
Inner Harbour

Toronto Islands

Old Toronto, the Financial District, and the Waterfront
Tommy Thompson Park

N

Lake Ontario

0   2 miles
0   3 km

Most city streets are organized on a grid system: With some exceptions, street numbers start at zero from the lake and increase as you go north. On the east–west axis, Yonge Street, Toronto's main thoroughfare, is the dividing line: You can expect higher numbers the farther away you get from Yonge.

A tip: Traffic is dense and parking expensive within the city core. If you have a car with you, leave it at the hotel and save it for excursions, either to outlying attractions or to towns like Stratford. In the city, use the excellent Toronto Transit System (TTC) or taxis to reach, return, and move between sights.

OLD TORONTO

In this district, running from Yonge Street east to Parliament Street and from King Street south to the lake, Toronto got its start as the village of York in 1793. In 1834, the year the little community was "erected" into a city, the area, described as a ward, was renamed in honor of Canada's patron saint, St. Lawrence, whose name you'll see over and over again. A pleasing natural disorder now prevails in this neighborhood, which blends old and new buildings, residential and commercial space. You can move in a few blocks past the huge canopy of the 1960s-era Hummingbird Centre, where crowds throng for a ballet, to converted late-19th-/early 20th-century warehouses hosting an array of modern stores, to a hall operating continuously as a market since the early 19th century.

Numbers in the text and in the margin correspond to points of interest on the Old Toronto, the Financial District, and the Waterfront map.

A Good Walk

Start your tour at the northwest corner of Yonge and Front streets, where the **Hockey Hall of Fame and Museum** ① is housed in a decommissioned branch of the Bank of Montréal. After having your fill of hockey's golden moments, turn left and walk a short block north on Yonge to Wellington and turn left again. Walk less than half the block, then enter the modern new skyscraper where you'll find the former 15 Wellington Street West, the oldest building on this walk. The elegant Greek Revival–style bank was one of the earliest (1845) projects of William Thomas, the talented architect who also designed the St. Lawrence Hall (☞ *below*). Return to, and cross, Yonge Street, then go another short block north to Colborne, where on the right you'll see the former **Trader's Bank** ②, one of the city's first skyscrapers. From here, go one block north to King, turn right, and walk one short block to Victoria Street. Across Victoria is the beautiful King Edward Hotel (☞ Chapter 4), a 1903 structure by E. J. Lennox, who also designed Old City Hall, Massey Hall, and Casa Loma.

A little farther to the east, on the northeast corner of King and Church, the impressive Anglican **St. James Cathedral** ③ holds sway. Directly south of the church is the Toronto Sculpture Garden, a small landscaped area with sculpture and waterfall displays. Now head north one block on Church to Adelaide; two blocks to the east (look for the flags and postal drop box) you'll find **Toronto's First Post Office** ④, where you can transact your 20th-century postal business using 19th-century implements. Return 1½ block west to Jarvis; one block south at King is the elegant **St. Lawrence Hall** ⑤. Continue south one block on Jarvis to **St. Lawrence Market** ⑥; you're now on Front Street again, and from here it's three blocks west to the **Flatiron Building** ⑦. As you continue west from here on Front to your starting point, Yonge Street, you'll pass the St. Lawrence Centre and the Hummingbird Centre, two large municipally owned the-

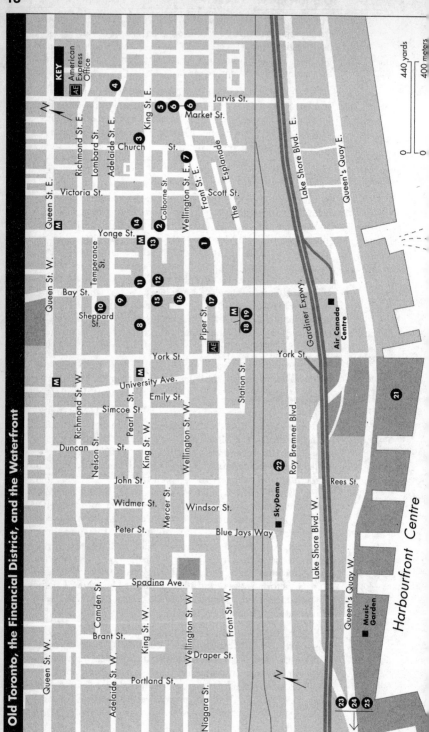

Old Toronto, the Financial District, and the Waterfront

KEY
AE American Express Office

Jarvis St.
Market St.
King St. E.
Richmond St. E.
Lombard St.
Adelaide St. E.
Church St.
Esplanade
The
Scott St.
Wellington St. E.
Front St. E.
Colborne St.
Victoria St.
Queen St. E.
Yonge St.
Temperance St.
Bay St.
Sheppard St.
Piper St.
York St.
Station St.
University Ave.
Emily St.
Simcoe St.
Pearl St.
King St. W.
Wellington St. W.
Richmond St. W.
Nelson St.
Duncan St.
John St.
Widmer St.
Mercer St.
Windsor St.
Peter St.
Blue Jays Way
Spadina Ave.
Camden St.
Brant St.
King St. W.
Wellington St. W.
Front St. W.
Draper St.
Adelaide St. W.
Queen St. W.
Portland St.
Niagara St.
Queen's Quay W.
Queen's Quay E.
Lake Shore Blvd. E.
Gardiner Expwy.
Roy Bremner Blvd.
Rees St.
Lake Shore Blvd. W.
York St.

Air Canada Centre
SkyDome
Music Garden
Harbourfront Centre

440 yards
400 meters

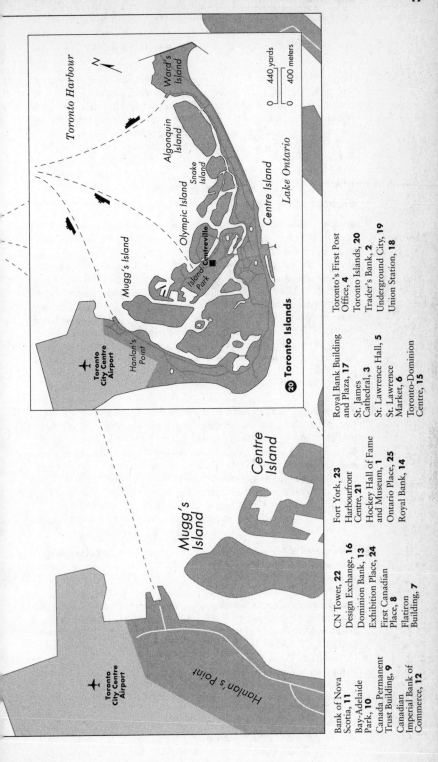

Toronto Harbour

Ward's Island

Algonquin Island

Olympic Island

Snake Island

Centre Island

Lake Ontario

Mugg's Island

Hanlan's Point

Toronto City Centre Airport

Island Centreville Park

0   440 yards
0   400 meters

20 Toronto Islands

Centre Island

Mugg's Island

Hanlan's Point

Toronto City Centre Airport

Bank of Nova Scotia, **11**
Bay-Adelaide Park, **10**
Canada Permanent Trust Building, **9**
Canadian Imperial Bank of Commerce, **12**

CN Tower, **22**
Design Exchange, **16**
Dominion Bank, **13**
Exhibition Place, **24**
First Canadian Place, **8**
Flatiron Building, **7**

Fort York, **23**
Harbourfront Centre, **21**
Hockey Hall of Fame and Museum, **1**
Ontario Place, **25**
Royal Bank, **14**

Royal Bank Building and Plaza, **17**
St. James Cathedral, **3**
St. Lawrence Hall, **5**
St. Lawrence Market, **6**
Toronto-Dominion Centre, **15**

Toronto's First Post Office, **4**
Toronto Islands, **20**
Trader's Bank, **2**
Underground City, **19**
Union Station, **18**

aters that serve as venues for everything from ballet to public debates (☞ Chapter 5). The Hummingbird opened as the O'Keefe Centre in 1960 and featured the world premiere of the musical *Camelot*.

TIMING

This walk will take from 45 minutes for the buildings alone to a half day to include time at the hockey museum, market, post office, and cathedral. If you add the adjacent Cabbagetown or Financial District to your tour, you could easily spend an interesting full day in the area. For those out to photograph scenic cityscapes, one of the best views is that of the Flatiron building in the early morning or late afternoon, with the building is framed by the sunlit skyscrapers behind it. If you want to watch or photograph the farmers setting out their wares at the St. Lawrence Market, you should arrive as early as 5 AM on Saturday.

Sights to See

OFF THE BEATEN PATH

ENOCH TURNER SCHOOLHOUSE – This small red-and-yellow brick building is a reminder that free public education began only in the mid-19th century. Back in the 1840s, Toronto parents paid two-thirds of teachers' salaries, and the government picked up the rest of the tab. When the Ontario legislature authorized cities to provide free schools paid for by property taxes in 1848, the Toronto City Council balked and closed every public school in town. A brewer named Enoch Turner, outraged by the reactionary policy of the city elders, created Toronto's first free educational institution. Three years later, the politicians relented and absorbed the Enoch Turner Schoolhouse into the public school system of Toronto. The schoolhouse is seven blocks east of Church Street, off King Street East. ⊠ *106 Trinity St.,* ☎ *416/863-0010.* ☐ *Free.* ☼ *Weekdays 9:30 AM–4:30 PM, but call ahead since it's sometimes booked for private events.*

❼ Flatiron Building. With similarly shaped relatives in wedge-shape lots all over North America, the building on the triangle of Wellington, Scott, and Front streets was erected in 1892 as the head office of the Gooderham and Worts distilling company and still hosts important offices today. You may wish to take a ride in its original elevator. On the back of the building, a witty trompe l'oeil mural by Derek Besant is drawn around the windows of the structure. Depicting even larger windows (they actually replicate the windows of the building on the south side of Front Street), it looks as though the whole thing has been tacked up on the wall and is peeling off. ⊠ *Front St. between Church and Scott Sts.*

❶ Hockey Hall of Fame and Museum. Even if you're not a hockey fan, it's worth a trip here to see this shrine to Canada's favorite sport. Relocated to a larger, beautifully ornate building in 1993, the museum has everything from the original Stanley Cup, donated in 1893, to displays of goalie masks, skate and stick collections, jerseys of the great players, video displays of big games, a copy of the Montréal Canadiens' locker room, and chairs from the old Madison Square Garden in New York City. The details of the 1885 building, a former Bank of Montréal branch designed by architects Darling & Curry, have been lovingly preserved: Note the richly carved Ohio stone and the Hermes figure supporting the chimney near the back of the building. ⊠ *30 Yonge St.,* ☎ *416/360-7765.* ☐ *$8.75.* ☼ *Mon.–Wed. 9–6, Thurs.–Fri. 9 AM–9:30 PM, Sat. 9–6, Sun. 10–6.*

NEED A BREAK?

BCE Place (⊠ Between Front and Wellington, Yonge and Bay Sts.), a modern office and retail complex cleverly designed to incorporate the Bank of Montréal building and other older structures under a glass roof, is not only one of the most impressive architectural spaces in Toronto—it's also a pleasant place to sit and enjoy a coffee and baguette. The BCE stands for Bell Canada Enterprises.

❸ **St. James Cathedral.** Even if bank towers dwarf it now, this Anglican church with noble Gothic spires has the tallest steeple in Canada. Its illuminated spire clock once guided ships into the harbor, which used to be much closer to the church (everything south of Front Street is landfill). This is the fourth St. James Cathedral on this site; the third one burned down in the Great Fire of 1849. As part of the church's bicentennial in 1997, a new peal of 12 bells was installed. Visitors to the corner most Sundays 30 minutes before the 11 AM service will be rewarded with a glorious concert. Other concerts are held throughout the year. ⊠ *Northeast corner of Church and King Sts.,* ☎ *416/364–7865.*

❺ **St. Lawrence Hall.** Standing on the site of Toronto's first city hall, the St. Lawrence Hall, built 1850–51, demonstrates Renaissance Revival architecture at its finest. Erected originally for musical performances and balls, this is where Jenny Lind sang, where antislavery demonstrations were held, and where P. T. Barnum first presented the midget Tom Thumb. Take time to admire both the exterior of this architectural gem, now used for special events. ⊠ *157 King St. E.*

❻ **St. Lawrence Market.** Built in 1844 as Toronto's first true city hall (for the first 10 years of the city's existence politicians were forced to use the former town hall up the street), the building now has an exhibition hall upstairs, the Market Gallery, where the council chambers once stood. The building continues to serve the citizens of the city, although in a more delicious fashion—as a food market, which began growing up around the city hall at the turn of the century. Renovated in 1978, the market is renowned for its wide range of foods, from kiwi fruit to Ontario cheddar, from homemade bread to conch meat. Its four dozen or so stalls are an ideal place to buy lunch fixings for a picnic or for excursions to the zoo, Canada's Wonderland, or the nearby Toronto Islands—where the excellence of the attractions doesn't guarantee the excellence of the cuisine. The plain brick building across Front Street, on the north side, is open only on Saturday morning as a farmer's market; it's a cornucopia of fine produce from the farms just north of Toronto. ⊠ *Corner of Front and Jarvis Sts.* ⊙ *North building: Sat. starting at 4 AM for farmer's market; south building, with permanent stalls: Tues.–Sat. roughly 10 AM–5 PM.*

🐣 ❹ **Toronto's First Post Office.** Dating from 1833, when Toronto was still the British colony called Upper Canada, this working post office continues to operate using quill pens, ink pots, and sealing wax. Its exhibits include examples of 1820s and 1830s letters. It costs $1 to write an old-fashioned letter and affix current postage on it. ⊠ *260 Adelaide St. E,* ☎ *416/865–1833.* 🕮 *Free.* ⊙ *Weekdays 9–4, weekends 10–4.*

❷ **Trader's Bank.** It's fun to see the turn-of-the-century equivalent of the CN Tower: At 15 stories, this was the first "skyscraper" of the city when it went up in 1905–06, complete with an observation deck. The construction of a high-rise next door to the north (at 69 Yonge Street) helped turn the intersection of Yonge and Colborne into a grouping of the tallest buildings in North America outside Manhattan. After more than 75 years, the building is still owned by Canadian Pacific, the largest private employer in Canada (planes, trains, hotels, and more). ⊠ *67 Yonge St.*

THE FINANCIAL DISTRICT

Those striking, often magnificent high-rises that form the greatest part of Toronto's skyline are banks, banks, and banks. Every one of the major banks of Canada, which are far wealthier and more powerful than most of their U.S. counterparts, has its headquarters in downtown Toronto, between University Avenue and Yonge Street. The fact that many of the older properties have now been included on the city's Inventory of Buildings of Architectural and Historical Importance proves Toronto is making a concerted effort to preserve its history. Only two cheers, though: There was massive destruction of great 19th-century buildings throughout earlier parts of this century.

The most interesting aspect of a Financial District walk is the architectural variety of the skyscrapers, temples to steel construction and the money that paid for them. You'll notice that many banks have more than one building named for them: This reflects the new ethic of recycling and reusing adequate old buildings even if corporate pride requires the building of a fancier, more up-to-date headquarters. Most of the towers have bank branches, restaurants, and retail outlets on their ground floors and are also connected to the Underground City of shops and tunnels, so you have many easy choices for a snack or to change money along the way.

Numbers in the text and in the margin correspond to points of interest on the Old Toronto, the Financial District, and the Waterfront map.

A Good Walk

Start the tour at the St. Andrew TTC station on the northeast corner of University and King. Walk one short block east on King past York Street, where you'll see the huge **First Canadian Place** ⑧ complex, which includes the **Toronto Stock Exchange.** Leave First Canadian Place by the Adelaide Street exit and proceed half a block east on Adelaide to the corner of Bay Street to the **Canada Permanent Trust Building** ⑨ and the **Bay-Adelaide Park** ⑩, tucked in from the street. From here, head one block south on Bay Street to King where, on the northeast corner, you'll see the **Bank of Nova Scotia** ⑪, with the Scotia Tower just to the east. Cross King to the **Canadian Imperial Bank of Commerce** ⑫ buildings, with their distinct architectural styles, and then go half a block east to Yonge Street, where on the southwest corner of Yonge and King you'll come to the **Dominion Bank** ⑬. At the northeast corner of the same intersection is the original **Royal Bank** ⑭ building.

Now walk back west along King Street to Bay, where the **Toronto-Dominion Centre (TD Centre)** ⑮ resides. It's a block south on Bay Street to the **Design Exchange** ⑯, the wonderful Art Deco building which housed the old Toronto Stock Exchange. Continue south on Bay Street for less than a block to reach the modern **Royal Bank Building and Plaza** ⑰; **Union Station** ⑱, where the trains of the national, intercity, and Toronto transit system meet, is just across Front Street from here. You can descend from Union Station into Toronto's vast **Underground City** ⑲, a warren worthy of its own tour.

TIMING

The walk outlined encompasses a little more than 1½ km (1 mi). Stock Market Place at the Toronto Stock Exchange and the Design Center exhibits take about 45 minutes each and, if you come from noon to 2 during the summer, you might catch a concert. Taking into account stops for the TSE and Design Exchange and a snack and/or concert, the tour should run two–three hours. This area is adjacent to Old Toronto, and the two tours together would fill a pleasant day.

Sights to See

⑪ **Bank of Nova Scotia.** Built between 1949 and 1951 and partially replaced by the ScotiaBank Tower just to the east, this bank features sculptural panels inspired by Greek mythology above its large windows. In the lobby, bas reliefs symbolize four regions of Canada; look up to see a brightly colored gilded plaster ceiling. Other interesting details include the original stainless-steel-and-glass stairway with marine motifs and the marble counters and floors. The north wall relief depicts some of the industries and enterprises financed by the bank. ⊠ *44 King St. W, northeast corner of King and Bay Sts.*

🔟 **Bay-Adelaide Park.** Originally designed to be a plaza for a building that fell victim to the early 1990s recession, the park was nevertheless completed in 1993 as an homage to those who worked on it. The multistory indoor-outdoor space includes a water sculpture, a monument dedicated to construction workers, and a tropical plant collection. ⊠ *Yonge St. between Richmond and Adelaide Sts.*

❾ **Canada Permanent Trust Building.** Built in the Roaring '20s, just before the 1929 stock-market crash, this skyscraper was designed in New York wedding cake–style. Look up at the ornate stone carvings that grace both the lower and top stories, where stylized faces peer down to the street below. You can walk through the imposing vaulted entrance with its polished brass doors; even the elevator doors in the foyer are embossed. The spacious banking hall has a vaulted ceiling, marble walls and pillars, and a marble floor with mosaic borders. Those were the days—or so the builders thought. ⊠ *320 Bay St., just south of Adelaide St.*

⑫ **Canadian Imperial Bank of Commerce.** The first of the "twin" Bank of Commerce buildings went up in the two years following the stock-market crash of 1929, but hard times didn't mean stinting on details: The stunning interior has marble floors, limestone walls, and bronze vestibule doors decorated with an array of animals and birds. Murals in the alcoves on either side of the entrance trace the history of transportation. The bronze elevator doors are richly decorated, the vaulted banking hall is lit by chandeliers, and each desk has its own lamp. What a difference from most of the faceless skyscrapers of today! Just south of the old tower, set slightly back around a plaza at 243 Bay Street, is the bank's 57-story stainless-steel counterpart, designed by I. M. Pei in the early 1970s. ⊠ *25 King St. W.*

⑯ **Design Exchange.** A delightful example of "Streamlined Moderne" design, a later and more austere version of Art Deco, this building is clad in polished pink granite and smooth buff limestone, with wonderful stainless steel doors. Between 1937 and 1983, the DX (as it's now known) was the home of the Toronto Stock Exchange. Don't miss the witty stone frieze carved above the doors—a banker in top hat marching behind a laborer and sneaking his hand into the worker's pocket. (Only in Canada, where socialism has always been a strong force, would you find such a political statement on the side of a stock exchange.) In 1994 the building reopened as a nonprofit center devoted to promoting Canadian design. The old trading floor is now the site of rotating exhibits—check the local papers for what's on—and the ground floor has a café with good espresso. ⊠ *234 Bay St.,* ☎ *416/216–2160.* 🖃 *$5.* ⊙ *Tues.–Fri. 10–6, weekends noon–5.*

⑬ **Dominion Bank.** Erected in 1913–14 and designed by one of the architects (Frank Darling) responsible for the voluptuous Bank of Montréal branch at Yonge and Front streets, Dominion Bank is a classic Chicago-style skyscraper. You can climb the marble-and-bronze stairway to the opulent banking hall on the second floor and enjoy all the gleaming marble as well as the ornate plaster ceiling, featuring the coats of arms of what were then the nine Canadian provinces (Newfoundland did not join the Confederation until 1949). ⊠ *1 King St. W, corner of Yonge St.*

❽ **First Canadian Place.** Built in the early 1970s and also known as the Bank of Montréal tower, this building has 72 stories deliberately faced with white marble to contrast with the black of the ☞ **Toronto-Dominion Centre** to the south and with the nearby silver of I. M. Pei's

Bank of Commerce tower. This is one of the more attractive office/retail developments in the city. It is also interesting as an early and successful real estate project by the Reichman brothers, who later came to fiscal grief when their Canary Docks project in London failed to capture the imagination—and rental contracts—of that city's financial community. First Canadian Place is best known, however, as the home of the ☞ **Toronto Stock Exchange.** ⊠ *50 King St. W.*

⑭ Royal Bank. The 1913 building that predated the structure of the same name on Bay and Front streets (☞ *below*) can't quite match it for glitter, but it's no slouch in the decorative department. Note the distinctive cornice, the overhanging roof, the sculpted ox skulls above the ground-floor windows, and the classically detailed leaves at the top of the Corinthian columns. Greek culture lives! Today the once wide-awake banking floor has been taken over a company that sells mattresses. ⊠ *2 King St. E, at Yonge St.*

⑰ Royal Bank Building and Plaza. Designed by the gifted Torontonian Boris Zerafa, who was also involved in the creation of the Richmond-Adelaide Centre and the ScotiaBank Tower, this 1976 building is a classic of its kind. In this case, all that glitters *is* gold: The exterior is coated with 2,500 ounces of the precious ore in order to keep the heat in and the cold out (or vice versa, depending on the season). It's "a palette of color and texture as well as mass," in Zerafa's own words. The surface creates gorgeous reflections of sky, clouds, and other buildings; it's the jewel in the crown of the Toronto skyline. Be sure to go into the 120-ft-high banking hall and admire the lovely hanging sculpture by Jesús Raphaél Soto. The building, dramatic in almost any light, is especially stunning in a full-force sunset. ⊠ *Northwest corner of Bay and Front Sts.*

⑮ Toronto-Dominion Centre. Mies van der Rohe, a master of modern architecture, designed this five-building masterwork, even though he died in 1969 before it was fully realized. As with his acclaimed Seagram Building in New York, Mies stripped these buildings to their skin and bones of bronze-color glass and black metal I-beams. The TD Centre's tallest tower reaches 56 stories. The only decoration consists of geometric repetition, and the only extravagance is the use of rich materials, such as marble counters and leather-covered furniture. The setting is far from austere, however. In summer, the plazas and grass are full of office workers eating lunch and listening to one of many free outdoor concerts. Inside the low-rise square banking pavilion at King and Bay streets is a virtually intact Mies interior. Here you can visit the **Gallery of Inuit Art,** one of the few galleries in North America devoted to Inuit art. The Toronto-Dominion Bank's incredible collection equals that of the Smithsonian Institution. The gallery focuses attention on Canada's huge and unexplored northern frontier. ⊠ *Center: 55 King St. W; Gallery: 79 Wellington St.,* ☎ *416/982–8473.* ▣ *Free.* ☺ *Weekdays 8–6, weekends 10–4.*

NEED A BREAK?	In summer, grab a hot dog from one of the vendors at the TD Centre and enjoy people-watching. In inclement weather, venture down from here into the Underground City to pick up a sandwich.

Toronto Stock Exchange. Here beats the pulse of the Canadian economy, and to help Mr. and Ms. Public better understand how it all works, the Toronto Stock Exchange (TSE) has recently opened Stock Market Place, a dynamic state-of-the-art visitor and education center. The history and mystery of stocks and bonds, money markets, and diversified funds are explained through a variety of entertaining and educational interactive displays. A retail boutique sells related books and games. ⊠ *Main floor, 2 First Canadian Pl., 100 King St. W (between Bay and York Sts.),* ☎ *416/947–4670.* 🎟 *Free.* ☉ *Weekdays 9–4:30, Sat. 10–5.*

⑲ Underground City. This subterranean universe, which lays claim to being the largest pedestrian walkway in the world, emerged in the mid-1960s partly to replace the retail services in small buildings that were demolished to make way for the latest round of skyscrapers and partly to protect office workers from the harsh winter weather. As each major building went up, the developers agreed to build and to connect their underground shopping areas with each other and with the subway system. You can walk from beneath Union Station to the Royal York Hotel, the Toronto-Dominion Centre, First Canadian Place, the Sheraton Centre, The Bay, the Eaton Centre, "new" City Hall, and the Atrium on Dundas Street West without ever seeing the light of day. Altogether, there are nearly 11 km (7 mi) of sparklingly clean, well-lit, wheelchair-accessible tunnels, lined wall-to-wall with eateries, shops, banks, even dental offices and theaters. The 29 tunnels tie together six hotels, nearly 50 office towers, five subway stations, more than 1,000 stores and restaurants, SkyDome, the CN Tower, the Cineplex theater (16 screens), and the intercity bus and rail stations. You'll encounter everything from art exhibitions to buskers (the best are the winners of citywide auditions, licensed to perform throughout the subway system) and walkways, fountains, and trees. There are underground passageways in other parts of the city—one beneath Bloor Street, between Yonge and Bay streets, and another beneath College Street, between Yonge and Bay streets—but this is the city's most extended subterranean network. PATH maps to guide you through this labyrinth are available in many downtown news and convenience stores.

⑱ Union Station. The popular historian Pierre Berton wrote that the planning of Union Station recalled "the love lavished on medieval churches." Indeed, this train depot that anchors the financial district both visually and historically can be regarded as a cathedral built to serve the god of steam. Designed in 1907 and opened officially in 1927 by the Prince of Wales, it has a 40-ft-high ceiling of Italian tile and 22 pillars weighing 70 tons apiece. The vast main hall, with its lengthy concourse and the light flooding in from arched windows at each end, was designed to evoke the majesty of the country that spread out by rail and imagination from this spot. To this end, too, the names of the towns and cities across Canada that were served by the country's two railway lines, Grand Trunk (which was to become part of today's Canadian National) and Canadian Pacific, are inscribed on a frieze that runs along the inside of the hall. Train travel declined and the building came very near to being demolished in the 1970s, but public opposition eventually proved strong enough to save it, and Union Station is now a vital commuter hub. ⊠ *65–75 Front St. W, between Bay and York Sts.*

THE WATERFRONT

Before the drastic reduction of trucking reduced the Great Lakes trade, Toronto's waterfront was an important center for shipping and warehousing. For a long time after it fell into commercial disuse, the area was sadly neglected. The Gardiner Expressway, Lake Shore Boulevard, and a network of rusty rail yards stood as hideous barriers to the natural beauty of Lake Ontario; the area overflowed with grain silos, warehouses, and malodorous towers of malt, used by local breweries.

Since the early 1980s, however, the city has begun to reclaim this area for people-friendly purposes such as residences, shops, and parks. The reclaimed lakefront is now appealing for strolls, and myriad recreational and amusement options make it ideal for those traveling with children. As part of the restoration effort, a light rapid transit (LRT) line between Union Station and the lakefront came into operation in the summer of 1990. Seven years later the line was combined with another new LRT line constructed on Spadina Avenue. Today the red-and-white streetcars on the 510 Spadina line, which operates between Union Station and the Bloor-Danforth subway, stop at numerous locations all along the waterfront and on colorful Spadina Avenue.

Numbers in the text and in the margin correspond to points of interest on the Old Toronto, the Financial District, and the Waterfront map.

A Good Tour

The waterfront area explored here is roughly 4 km (2½ mi) long; after visits to Harbourfront Centre, SkyDome, or the CN Tower, you might want to proceed by car or a taxi because the distances between sights increase and the walking gets a bit more awkward. Start your tour at the waterfront stretch between Yonge and Bay streets, south of the Westin Harbour Castle Hotel. The docks here are the embarkation point for ferries to the **Toronto Islands** ⑳, and the surrounding plaza has a festive air, with its balloon sellers and vendors of hot dogs, cotton candy, and ice cream. When you return from the islands, walk west on Queen's Quay West about ½ km (¼ mi) to **Harbourfront Centre** ㉑; along the way you'll see Toronto's amateur sailors taking their boats out in the bay. From here, head north on York Street, then west on Ray Bremner Boulevard about 1¼ km (¾ mi) to the **CN Tower** ㉒ (you'll be going under highway bridges, but persevere). Next to the CN Tower is **Sky-Dome,** which you're more likely to visit when your favorite sport is being played. Not going to a game? Tours of SkyDome are available.

Walk south on Rees Street back to Queen's Quay West, then proceed west 1½ km (1 mi) west to Bathurst Street. Walk north on Bathurst about ½ km (¼ mi); under the expressway you'll see the entrance to **Fort York** ㉓ on your left. From Fort York, go south on Bathurst, then west 1 km (½ mi) on Lake Shore Boulevard to **Exhibition Place** ㉔, home to one of the world's largest annual expositions, the Canadian National Exhibition (CNE; mid-August-Labor Day) and various seasonal events, including a variety of trade and consumer shows in the new National Trade Centre. After Exhibition Place, use the pedestrian bridge to cross Lake Shore Boulevard to **Ontario Place** ㉕, a lakeside amusement park built by the province.

TIMING

All the attractions on this tour are open year-round, but the milder weather from May to October makes exploring them easier and more pleasant; it's also the best time to find the sights in full operation. The walk alone will take about one hour, at a strolling rate. If you're going to the Toronto Islands, add 45 minutes just to cross the bay and return on the same ferry. Depending on your interest in the various sights in the area, you can spend anywhere from half a day to three days here.

Sights to See

Canada's Sports Hall of Fame. This museum in ☞ Exhibition Place has three floors of exhibits on Canadian sports heroes throughout history, including touch-screen computers with autobiographies, highlights of famous careers, and sports quizzes. ⊠ *In the center of the CNE grounds, Dufferin St. and Lake Shore Blvd.,* ☎ *416/260–6789.* ⬚ *Free.* ☽ *Daily 10–4:30.*

★ ☺ ㉒   **CN Tower.** The tallest freestanding structure in the world at 1,815 ft and 5 inches high—yes, it's listed in the *Guinness Book of World Records*—

is tall with a cause: So many high buildings had been built over the past few decades that lower radio and TV transmission towers were having trouble broadcasting over them. It's worth a visit despite the steep fee, if the weather is clear. Six glass-fronted elevators zoom up the outside of the $63 million tower, which opened in summer 1976. It weighs 130,000 tons and contains enough concrete to build a curb along Highway 401 from Toronto to Kingston, some 262 km (163 mi) to the east. The ride takes less than a minute travelling at 20 ft a second, a rate of ascent similar to that of a jet plane takeoff. Each elevator has just one floor-to-ceiling glass wall, making it easier on anyone prone to vertigo.

The tower's ground level includes many entertainment options. The magic of digital animation allows you to imagine the thrill of bungee jumping, hang gliding, or tightrope walking from the top of the Tower. The **Marketplace at the Tower** has 12,500 square ft of shopping space with quality Canadiana sports and travel items and souvenirs. The **Fresh Market Cafe** offers a selection of foods to suit all tastes, and the **Maple Leaf Cinema** screens a 20-minute, IMAX-produced film, *Momentum—Images of Canada*. The **Themed Arcade** has the latest in simulated game experiences, including extreme sports like Alpine Racer, TopSkater, and Indy racing.

There are also four observation decks to choose from. The **Glass Floor Level,** some 1,122 ft above the ground, is just what the name describes, and it's like walking on a cloud. Above that is the **Look Out Level,** at 1,136 ft and ascending one level more, the excellent **360 Revolving Restaurant** (☞ Chapter 3). Continuing the climb, and at an elevation of 1,465 ft, is the **Sky Pod,** the world's highest public observation gallery; it's more than 30 stories higher than the other decks and a visit costs about $4 more. All the levels provide spectacular panoramic views of Toronto, Lake Ontario, and the Toronto Islands. On really clear days you can often see Lake Simcoe to the north and the mist rising from Niagara Falls to the south. Peak visiting hours are 11–4, particularly on weekends; you may wish to work around them. ⊠ *301 Front St. W,* ☎ *416/868–6937; 416/362–5411 restaurant.* ▨ *Observation levels $15; concourse attractions and Sky Pod additional cost.* ☉ *Summer, Sun.–Thurs. 9 AM–10 PM, Fri.–Sat. 9 AM–11 PM; fall–spring times vary by up to an hr, so call ahead.*

㉔ Exhibition Place. The Canadian National Exhibition (CNE or "the Ex") draws the most people to this part of the waterfront, but you'll find many other things happening here year-round. The Ex takes place the last two weeks of August and Labor Day weekend, attracting more than 3 million people each year. It began back in 1879 as primarily an agricultural show, and remnants of that tradition can still be found in the livestock exhibits. But in its second century, the Ex is a noisy, crowded, often entertaining collection of carnies pushing $5 balloons, tummy-turning midway rides, bands, horticultural and technological exhibits, parades, dog swims, horse shows, and (sometimes) top-notch happenings; the latter have included grandstand appearances by Bill Cosby, Kenny Rogers, and Whitney Houston. (Note: Never take a car to the Ex; the parking is insufficient and always terribly overpriced. Numerous buses and streetcars labeled "Exhibition" travel into the CNE grounds.) Also on the grounds is ☞ **Canada's Sports Hall of Fame.** ⊠ *Lake Shore Blvd. between Strachan Ave. and Dufferin St.,* ☎ *416/393–6000.*

★ ☾ ㉓ Fort York. The most historic site in Toronto is a must for anyone interested in the origins of the city. The founding of Toronto occurred in 1793 when the British built Fort York to protect the entrance to the harbor during the time of Anglo-American strife. Twenty years later the fort was the scene of the bloody Battle of York, in which the explorer and general Zebulon Pike led U.S. forces against the fort's out-numbered British, Canadian, and First Nations defenders. The Americans won this battle—their first major victory in the War of 1812—and burned down the provincial buildings during a six-day occupation. A year later, British forces retaliated when they captured Washington and torched its public buildings, including the President's Mansion. A tale people love to tell in Toronto is that a subsequent application of white-wash to cover the charred wood gave rise to the sobriquet "White House," a term confirmed on presidential letterhead by Teddy Roosevelt years later. Today Fort York's defensive walls surround Canada's largest collection of original War of 1812 buildings. Exhibits include restored barracks, kitchens, and powder magazines, plus a changing variety of museum displays. ⊠ *100 Garrison Rd., between Bathurst St. and Strachan Ave., north of Fleet St.,* ☎ *416/392–6907.* ⊡ *$5.* ☉ *Hrs vary; call for details.*

★ ☙ ㉑ **Harbourfront Centre.** Stretching from just west of York Street to Spadina Avenue, this culture-and-recreation center is a match for San Francisco's Pier 39 and Baltimore's Inner Harbor and is one of the highlights of a visit to Toronto. A project of the federal government, the original Harbourfront opened in 1974, rejuvenating more than a mile of city waterfront that had deteriorated badly over the years. Today, Harbourfront Centre, a streamlined version of the original concept, draws over 3 million visitors to the 10-acre site each year.

The **Queen's Quay Terminal** (quay is pronounced key) is a must-see: The former Terminal Warehouse building, where a variety of products shipped to Toronto were stored before being delivered to shops all over the city, was transformed in 1983 into a magnificent, eight-story structure with delightful specialty shops, eateries, and the handsome 450-seat Premiere Dance Theatre (☞ Chapters 5 and 7). ⊠ *204 Queen's Quay W.*

Contemporary art exhibits of painting and sculpture, architecture and video, photography and design are mounted at the **Power Plant,** which can be spotted by its tall red smokestack. It was built in 1927 as a power station for the Terminal Warehouse's ice-making plant. ⊠ *231 Queen's Quay W,* ☎ *416/973–4934.* ⊡ *$4, free Wed.* ☉ *Tues. and Thurs.–Sun. noon–6, Wed. noon–8.*

York Quay Centre offers concerts, live theater, readings, even skilled artisans at work in open craft studios. A shallow pond at the south end is used for canoe lessons in warmer months and as the largest artificial ice-skating rink in North America in more wintry times. At the nearby Nautical Centre, many private firms offer lessons in sailing and canoeing, with vessels for rent. ⊠ *235 Queens Quay W.*

An ambitious new museum (summer 1998) dedicated to all things nautical, **The Pier** provides an interactive experience with a wide range of thematic exhibits and changing programs and activities. Highlights include the Discovery Gallery, where you can guide a ship through a set of canal locks or explore a shipwreck; the Boat Shop, a special area in which artisans, using mostly forgotten skills and techniques, construct traditional watercraft; and the Livery, where you can rent these same traditional craft and explore the harbor. ⊠ *245 Queen's Quay W,* ☎ *416/338–7437.* ⊡ *$8.50.* ☉ *July–Aug., daily 10–8; May–June and Sept.–Oct., daily 10–6; Nov.–Apr., Wed.–Sun. 11-5.*

On the north side of Queen's Quay, at No. 390, you'll come to the **Harbourfront Antiques Market,** the largest antiques exchange in the city (☞ Antiques and Interiors *in* Chapter 7).

Among the seasonal events in Harbourfront Centre are an Ice Canoe Race in late January; two weekends of Winterfest in February; a jazz festival in June; Canada Day celebrations and a Parade of Lights in July; the Authors' Festival and Harvest Festival in October; and the Swedish Christmas Fair in November. Check the local newspapers or the **Harbourfront Centre Hotline** (☎ 416/973–3000) to see what's happening while you're in town. ✉ *410 Queen's Quay W (Harbourfront administrative offices)*, ☎ *416/973–4600.*

<table>
<tr><td>NEED A
BREAK?</td><td>There are plenty of places inside Queen's Quay for a quick sandwich, freshly squeezed juice, or ice cream concoction. Or check out one of the food trucks outside, selling hot, crispy french fries.</td></tr>
</table>

Music Garden. An idea developed by renowned cellist Yo-Yo Ma and garden designer Julie Moir Messervy, this park is a new addition to Toronto's reborn waterfront. Financed through private funding, the project was planned for Boston, but when that venue fell through, Toronto was the pair's next choice. The concept for the park is based on J. S. Bach's *Cello Suite No. 1* (which consists of six movements—Prelude, Allemande, Courante, Sarabande, Minuet, and Gigue), as interpreted by Yo-Yo Ma. Each movement is reflected in the park's elaborate design, using undulating riverscape, a forest grove of wandering trails, a swirling path through a wildflower meadow, a conifer grove, a formal flower parterre, and giant grass steps. The Music Garden is the latest addition to the proposed 40-acre Harbourfront Park system. ✉ *South side of Queen's Quay W, west of Spadina Ave.*

☞ ㉕ **Ontario Place.** Highlights of this waterfront complex, built on three man-made islands created out of landfill, include the **Cinesphere,** an enclosed dome with a six-story movie screen that has shows year-round; the **Haida,** a World War II and Korean War destroyer turned floating museum; the 16,000-seat outdoor **Molson Amphitheatre,** offering nightly performances by singers or rock groups; and the **Atlantis Complex,** a 32,000-square-ft entertainment and dining facility. In addition, the justly popular **Children's Village** has water games, towering tube slides, and a moon walk. It's one of the most creative playgrounds in the world, great for children 3–14. Children's theater, puppet shows, clowns, and magicians are included in the admission price to the park. In late June through early July, there are fireworks displays from six countries at 10 PM, three to four times a week; reserved seating for the event costs $5–$15. The bumper boats, pedal boats, Wilderness Adventure Ride, SeaTrek deep sea submarine simulator ride, Rush River Raft Ride, waterslides, miniature golf, and Cinesphere cost extra. ✉ *South of Lake Shore Blvd., across from Exhibition Place,* ☎ *416/314–9900 recording.* ▣ *Gate admission $9.95; Play-All-Day Pass $19.95; parking rates vary.* ☉ *Late May–Labor Day, daily 10 AM–1 AM. H.M.C.S. Haida:* ☎ *416/314–9755.* ▣ *$2.* ☉ *3rd weekend May–Labor Day, daily 10:30 AM–7 PM.*

☞ **SkyDome.** One of Toronto's newest and most famous landmarks, the home of baseball's Blue Jays was the world's first stadium with a fully retractable roof. Toronto has lost no opportunity to honor its World Series–winning team—the official address of SkyDome is 1 Blue Jays Way. One way to see the huge 52,000-seat stadium is to buy tickets for a Blue Jays game or one of the many other events that take place here. These may include cricket matches, Wrestlemania, monster truck races, family ice shows, rock concerts, or even the opera *Aïda.* You can also take a one-hour guided walking tour (including a 15-minute film). The tours are not available, however, when daytime events are scheduled. ✉ *Tour entrance: Front and John Sts., between Gates 1 and 2,* *northeast corner of SkyDome, ☎ 416/341–2770 for tours; 416/341–3663 for events and shows; 416/341–1000 for Blue Jays games. ⬚ Tour $9.50. ⊙ Tours daily; call ahead for specific times.*

★ ✋ ⑳ **Toronto Islands.** Though sometimes referred to in the singular, there are actually eight thin, tree-lined islands plus more than a dozen smaller islets that sit in Lake Ontario just off the city's downtown, providing a welcome touch of greenery. They've been attracting visitors since 1833, and why not? The more than 550 acres of parkland are irresistible, especially during the summer months when the downtown core seems to be melting as rapidly as the ice cream cones sold everywhere on the islands. (In fact, it's a good idea to bring a sweater: There's often a wind here and it's usually a few degrees cooler than it is in the city.) You'll have spectacular views of Toronto's skyline, especially as the setting sun turns the Royal Bank Tower and other skyscrapers to gold, silver, and bronze.

Sandy beaches fringe the islands, the best ones being those on the southeast tip of Ward's, the southernmost edge of Centre, and the west side of Hanlan's. (Note: Lake Ontario's water has sometimes been declared unfit for swimming in past decades, so check reports before you pack your suit.) There are free changing rooms near each, but no facilities for checking your clothes. Swimming in the lagoons and channels is prohibited. The winter can be bitter cold on the islands, but snowshoeing and cross-country skiing with downtown Toronto over your shoulder will be appealing to many. In the summer, Centre Island has rowboat and canoe rentals. Pack a cooler with picnic fixings or something you can grill on one of the park's barbecue pits.

All transportation on these interconnected islands comes to you compliments of your feet: No cars (except for emergency and work vehicles) are permitted anywhere. The boardwalk from Centre to Ward's Island is 2½ km (1½ mi) long. In summer, consider renting a bike for an hour or so—walk south from the Centre Island ferry docks to Avenue of the Islands—and working your way across the islands.

If you're not traveling with children you might want to avoid Centre Island: It gets so crowded that no bicycles are allowed on its ferry during summer weekends. Those looking to escape the city should take one of the equally frequent ferries to Ward's or Hanlan's, both of which are quiet, delightful places to picnic, sunbathe, and read under a tree.

If you've got the kids in tow, Centre Island is the one to check out first. Signs ask visitors to "Please Walk on the Grass," and a few hundred yards from the ferry docks lies **Centreville** (☎ 416/234–2345 in winter; 416/203–1113 in summer), an amusement park modeled after a turn-of-the-century children's village. On the diminutive Main Street you'll find shops, a town hall, a small railroad station, and more than a dozen rides, including a restored 1890s merry-go-round with at least four dozen hand-carved animals. There's no entrance fee to the modest, 14-acre amusement park, although there's a small charge (95¢) for the rides (day passes are $18). It's open Victoria Day (late May)–Labor Day, weekdays 10:30–6, weekends 10:30–8; Labor Day–October, weekends 10:30–6, weather permitting.

Perhaps most enjoyable for children is the free **Far Enough Farm,** which is near enough to walk to from Centreville. It has all kinds of animals to pet and feed, ranging from piglets to geese and cows. It's open daylight to dusk.

On Ward's Island you'll find the 1808 **Gibraltar Lighthouse,** the oldest monument in the city that is still standing on its original site. Next to it is a pond stocked with rainbow trout, and a concession for buying bait and renting rods.

In summer, the island ferries run between the docks at the bottom of Bay Street and the Ward's Island dock between 6:30 AM and 12:45 AM; for Centre and Hanlan's islands, they begin at 8 AM. They run roughly at half-hour intervals most of the working day and at quarter-hour intervals during peak times such as summer evenings and weekends. In the winter, the ferries run only to Ward's Island on a much more limited schedule. ⊠ *Ferries at foot of Bay St. and Queen's Quay,* ☎ *416/392–8195 for island information; 416/392–8193 or 416/392–8186 for ferry information.* 🎫 *Ferry $4.*

ALONG DUNDAS AND QUEEN STREETS

This midtown area is full of variety in architecture, purpose, and tone. It includes the town square, two city halls, Eaton Centre, a major art museum, and two ethnic areas that reflect the vitality of Toronto's continuous waves of immigrants.

Numbers in the text and in the margin correspond to points of interest on the North Central Core map.

A Good Walk

Start at the corner of **Spadina Avenue** ① and Nassau Street. Walk two blocks west on Nassau to Bellevue Avenue, turn left, and go south to Denison Square and the Kiever synagogue, a lovely leftover from the early- and mid-20th century immigration of Russian and Polish Jews to this area. Just to the southeast, at the corner of Denison Square and Augusta Avenue, **Bellevue Square** is a pretty little park with shade trees. Take Augusta Avenue one short block north to Baldwin Street, walk two short blocks east to Kensington Avenue and the overflowing stalls of **Kensington Market** ②. Continue south one block on Kensington to Dundas, turn left (east) back to Spadina, and head north two short blocks to St. Andrew's Street where, just west of Spadina, you'll see the An-shei Minsk synagogue, another testament to the Jewish influx into the area, but this one with an active congregation. Return to and cross Spadina; on the east side you'll see the Chinese Home for the Aged, which signals the approach to Toronto's original **Chinatown** ③, one block south on Spadina at Dundas.

After exploring this lively area, head east on Dundas for about four blocks to the **Art Gallery of Ontario** ④, a large beige building; be sure to visit its annex, the Grange, Toronto's oldest brick building and an earlier home to the gallery's collection. If you want to see more art, across the street is the **Ontario College of Art and Design Gallery.** Head three blocks south from the Grange on McCaul Street to Queen Street, then go three short blocks east to busy University Avenue. At the northwest corner you'll find **Campbell House** ⑤, a restored chief justice's residence.

Cross University, go north one block to Armoury Street, turn right and almost immediately take a left onto Centre Avenue to visit the **Museum for Textiles** ⑥. Now head south on Centre and east on Armory Street, where you'll approach the City Hall complex from behind. Continue along the concrete path, passing on your left a small park with a waterfall, until you reach Bay Street and the **Bell Canada Building** ⑦, with its displays of Alexander Graham Bell's early work. Walk south on Bay: At the northwest corner of Bay and Queen you'll see the expanse of **Nathan Phillips Square,** the public plaza in front of **New City Hall** ⑧. After visiting the modern building and the **Old City Hall** ⑨ diagonally across the square, turn left, walk a short block to Yonge Street, and approach the **Eaton Centre** ⑩, a gigantic shopping, office, and hotel complex. Exiting the huge mall at Yonge and Dundas, take Yonge three blocks east to Bond Street and then go south a short distance on Bond to the **Mackenzie House** ⑪.

TIMING

Although it's always nicest to stroll around in the warm weather, wintertime brings skating, Christmas caroling, and other festive activities to Nathan Phillips Square. Chinatown is at its busiest (and most fun) on Sunday. The walk itself is just under 3 km (2 mi) and should take about an hour at a strolling pace. The Campbell and Mackenzie houses merit at least half an hour each, the Art Gallery and the Grange an hour or more. And, of course, Chinatown can gobble up an entire afternoon.

Sights to See

★ ❹ **Art Gallery of Ontario.** From extremely modest beginnings in 1900, the AGO (as it's known) is now in the big leagues in terms of exhibitions and support. A 1992 renovation won international acclaim and put it among North America's top 10 art museums. The **Henry Moore Sculpture Centre** has the largest public collection of Moore's sculpture in the world. The **Canadian Wing** includes major works by such northern lights as Emily Carr, Cornelius Krieghoff, David Milne, and Homer Watson. The AGO also has a growing collection of works by Rembrandt, Hals, Van Dyck, Hogarth, Reynolds, Chardin, Renoir, de Kooning, Rothko, Oldenburg, Picasso, Rodin, Degas, Matisse, and many others. Visitors of any age can drop by the **Anne Tannenbaum Gallery School** on Sunday and explore painting, printmaking, and sculpting in Toronto's most spectacular studio space. The museum arranges numerous other workshops and special activities. All ages also enjoy climbing in and around Henry Moore's large *Two Forms* sculpture, which sits just outside the AGO, at the southwest corner of McCaul Street. Admission to AGO also gains you entrance to **The Grange,** an adjoining Georgian-style house built in 1817–18 and donated to the city in 1911. The columned front and delicately balanced wings only hint at the delightful details of the interior. There are tours, presenters in period costume, brick-oven cooking demonstrations, and special Christmas decorations. ✉ *317 Dundas St. W,* ☎ *416/979–6648.* ☎ *$5 suggested donation.* ☉ *Wed.–Fri. noon–9, weekends 10–5:30; also open holiday Mon. Call for Grange hrs.*

NEED A BREAK?

You can dine in the shadow of two Rodin sculptures at the AGO's **Gallery Grill.** Sunday brunch is particularly popular here.

☉ **Bellevue Square.** This little park with shady trees, benches, and a wading pool and playground is a good place to rest after a visit to ☞ **Kensington Market.** ✉ *Denison Sq. and Augusta Pl.*

❼ **Bell Canada Building.** Just north of the Old City Hall is a modest display of early telephones that go back to the time of Alexander Graham Bell, who dreamt up the darned thing in a town just west of Toronto. You may enjoy seeing the 1879 phone book, which listed 30 residences in Toronto, as well as the offices of 18 doctors and a single dentist. ✉ *483 Bay St.,* ☎ *416/599–6990.* ☎ *Free.* ☉ *Weekdays 9–5.*

❺ **Campbell House.** The stately Georgian mansion of Sir William Campbell, the sixth chief justice of Upper Canada, was built in 1822 in another part of town; it was moved to this site in 1972 and tastefully restored with elegant early 19th-century furniture. In one of Toronto's most charming house museums, costumed guides detail the social life of the upper class. Note the model of the town of York as it was in the

1820s, and the original kitchen. ⊠ *160 Queen St. W,* ☎ *416/597–0227.* ⊠ *$3.50.* ☉ *Oct.–mid-May, weekdays 9:30–4:30; mid-May–Oct., weekdays 9:30–4:30, weekends noon–4:30.*

NEED A BREAK?	Queen Street West is lined with cafés and restaurants. Consider the **Queen Mother Café** (⊠ 206 Queen St. W, ☎ 416/598-4719), a neighborhood favorite for wholesome meals and fabulous desserts at reasonable prices.

★ ❸ **Chinatown.** Diverse, exciting, and lively, this is the largest Chinatown in eastern Canada and one of the largest in North America. You'll pass shops selling reasonably priced silk blouses and antique porcelain, silk kimonos for less than half the price elsewhere, lovely sake sets, and women's silk suits. On Sunday, up and down Spadina Avenue and along Dundas Street, Chinese music blasts from storefronts, cash registers ring, abacuses clack, and bakeries, markets, herbalists, and restaurants do their best business of the week.

Spadina and Dundas streets were for years the anchor of Toronto's Chinatown. When a new city hall was built in the 1960s, many of the residents were uprooted from the area behind the old building, and Chinatown began to spread west. Today Chinatown—which now has to be described as the main or original one, as three other areas with large Chinese populations have sprung up elsewhere in metropolitan Toronto—covers much of the area of Spadina Avenue from Queen Street to College Street, running along Dundas Street nearly as far east as Bay Street. The population is more than 100,000, which is especially impressive when you consider that just over a century ago there was only a single Chinese resident, Sam Ching, who ran a hand laundry on Adelaide Street. A huge wave of immigration that began some two decades ago still continues today. Most of the newcomers come from Hong Kong, adding money, skills, and intelligence to an already burgeoning community. You can start a walk through this lively, interesting area on Elizabeth Street, just north of City Hall, and walk north to Dundas Street, then either east toward Bay Street or west to Spadina Avenue.

❿ **Eaton Centre.** Even if you rank shopping with the flu, you may be charmed, possibly dazzled, by this impressive environment, Toronto's top tourist attraction. The 3-million-square-ft building extends along the west side of Yonge Street all the way from Queen Street up to Dundas Street (with subway stops at each end). This is not to say the handsome collection of over 300 stores and services was not controversial when it was built in the late 1970s; some Torontonians attacked it as "a sterile and artificial environment." Others, like Jane Jacobs, author of *Death and Life of Great American Cities*, wrote that "people like the environment of the Galleria. Its popularity has lessons for Yonge Street."

The mall holds lessons for most cities of the world, as well. From its graceful glass roof, arching 127 ft above the lowest of the mall levels, to Michael Snow's exquisite flock of fiberglass Canada geese floating poetically in the open space of the Galleria, to the glass-enclosed elevators, porthole windows, and nearly two dozen long and graceful escalators, there are plenty of good reasons to visit Eaton Centre.

Such a wide selection of shops and eateries can be confusing, however, so here's a simple rule: Galleria Level 1 contains two food courts; popularly priced fashions; photo, electronics, and record stores; and much "convenience" merchandise. Level 2 is directed to the middle-income shopper, while Level 3, suitably, has the highest elevation, fashion, and prices. Eaton's, one of Canada's classic department-store chains, has a nine-floor branch here. At the southern end of Level 3 is a skywalk

32

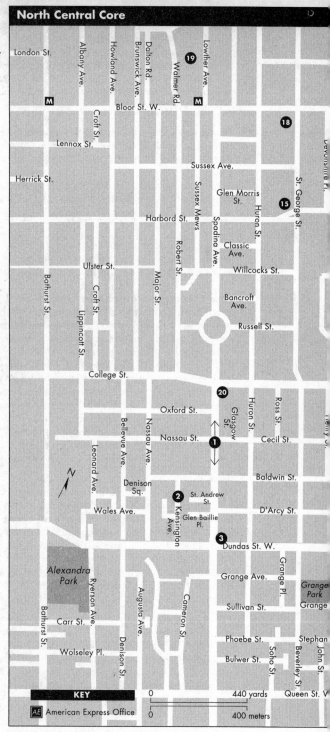

North Central Core

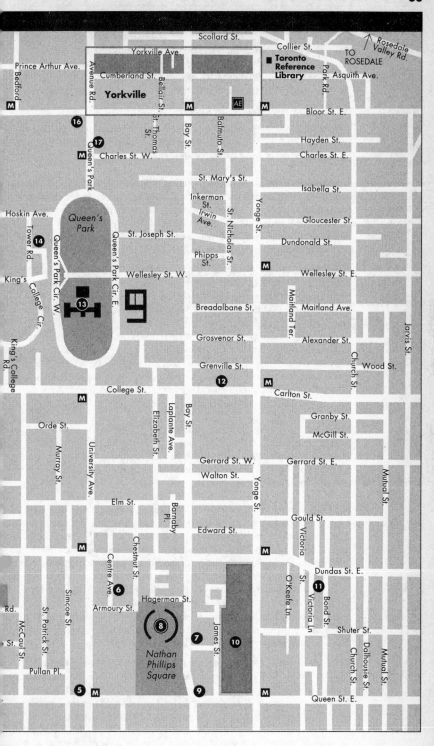

that connects the Centre to the seven-floor The Bay (formerly Simpsons) department store, across Queen Street.

A 17-theater cinema complex is west of the Dundas Street entrance. (Tuesday is half-price day for movie tickets, and it's a cheap break from shopping.) Safe, well-lighted parking garages with spaces for some 1,800 cars are sprinkled around Eaton Centre. ⊠ *220 Yonge St.,* ☎ *416/598–2322.* ⊙ *Weekdays 10–9, Sat. 9:30–6, Sun. noon–5.*

NEED A
BREAK?   If the Eaton Centre's dozens of restaurants and fast-food joints don't appeal to you, **Lick's** (⊠ Yonge St. at Dundas Sq., ☎ 416/362-5425), just across from the complex, serves tasty home-style burgers.

❷ Kensington Market. All your senses will be titillated by this steamy, smelly, raucous, European-style marketplace. Come and explore, especially during warmer weather, when the goods pour out into the narrow streets: Russian rye breads, barrels of dill pickles, fresh fish on ice, mountains of cheese, bushels of ripe fruit, and crates of chickens and rabbits that will have your children simultaneously amused and horrified.

Kensington Market sprang up just after the turn of the century, when Russian, Polish, and Jewish inhabitants set up stalls in front of their houses. Since then, the market—named after the area's major street—has become a United Nations of stores. Unlike the members of the UN, however, these vendors get along well with one another. Jewish and Eastern European shops sit side by side with Portuguese, Caribbean, and East Indian ones, as well as with a sprinkling of Vietnamese, Japanese, and Chinese establishments. Saturday is the best day to go, preferably by public transit, as parking is difficult. ⊠ *Bordered by College St. on the north, Spadina Ave. on the east, Dundas St. on the south, and Augusta Ave. on the west.* ⊙ *Daily 6–6; hrs vary; many stores closed Sun.*

NEED A
BREAK?   You'll find lots of hole-in-the-wall eateries around Kensington markets, and plenty of places selling finger foods. **Cafe La Gaffe** (⊠ 24 Baldwin St., ☎ 416/596-2397) is filled with people discussing theater, art, and politics over coffee and home-size portions of chicken brochettes, grilled fish, and fresh veggies.

⓫ Mackenzie House. One of a deceptively modest row of houses not far from the Eaton Centre, this was once home to journalist William Lyon Mackenzie, who was born in Scotland at the end of the 1700s and emigrated to Canada in 1820. Designated as a National Historic Site, the house is now operated as a museum and library. Mackenzie started up a newspaper that so enraged the powers that be (a clique known as "the Family Compact") that they dumped all his type into Lake Ontario. An undeterred Mackenzie stayed on to be elected the first mayor of Toronto in 1834 and is said to even have designed the coat of arms of his new city; his grandson, William Lyon Mackenzie King, became the longest-serving prime minister in Canadian history.

Mackenzie served only one year as mayor. Upset with the government "big shots" in 1837, he gathered about 700 supporters and marched down Yonge Street to try to overthrow the government. His minions were roundly defeated, and Willie fled to the United States with a price on his head. When the Canadian government granted him amnesty many years later, he was promptly elected to the legislative assembly and began to publish another newspaper. By this time, though, Mackenzie was so down on his luck that some friends bought his family this house. Mackenzie enjoyed the place for but a few sickly and depressing years, and died in 1861. Among the period furnishings preserved here is the fiery Scot's printing press. ⊠ *82 Bond St.,* ☎ *416/392–6915.* ☜ *$3.50.* ☺ *Jan.–Mar., weekends noon–5; Apr.–Dec., weekdays 9:30–4, weekends and holidays noon–5.*

❻ Museum for Textiles. Ten galleries include cross-cultural displays—men's costumes from Northern Nigeria, for example—as well as the latest in contemporary design. Rugs, cloth, and tapestries from around the world are exhibited. ⊠ *55 Centre Ave.,* ☎ *416/599–5515.* ☜ *$5.* ☺ *Tues., Thurs., Fri. 11–5; Wed. 11–8; weekends noon–5.*

Nathan Phillips Square. In front of the New City Hall, the 9-acre square (named after the mayor who initiated the City Hall project) has become a gathering place for the community, whether for royal visits, protest rallies, picnic lunches, or concerts. The reflecting pool is a delight in the summer, and even more so in winter, when office workers come down and skate during lunch. The park also holds a Peace Garden for quiet meditation and Henry Moore's striking bronze sculpture, *The Archer.* ⊠ *In front of 100 Queen St. W.*

❽ New City Hall. Dubbed "a urinal for the Jolly Green Giant" by some critics, Toronto's latest city hall was the outgrowth of a 1958 international competition to which some 520 architects from 42 countries submitted designs. The winning presentation by Finnish architect Viljo Revell was controversial: two towers of differing height, and curved, yet. But there is a logic to it all: An aerial view of the City Hall shows a circular council chamber sitting like an eye between the two tower "eyelids" containing offices. A remarkable mural within the main entrance, *Metropolis,* was constructed by sculptor David Partridge from 100,000 common nails. Revell died before his masterwork was opened to the public in 1965, but within months, the City Hall became a symbol of a thriving city, with a silhouette as recognizable in its own way as the Eiffel Tower. The positive influence that the development of this building has had on Toronto's civic life is detailed in Robert Fulford's 1995 book, *Accidental City.*

In front of the building is ☞ **Nathan Phillips Square,** a gathering place. Annual events at the New City Hall include the Spring Flower Show in late March; the Toronto Outdoor Art Exhibition early each July, and the yearly Cavalcade of Lights from late November through Christmas, when more than 100,000 sparkling lights are illuminated across both city halls (☞ Old City Hall, *below*). Whether the building becomes City Hall for the new megacity (the 1998 merging of Toronto and five surrounding communities) is the subject of much political debate; upgrading the building will cost millions. The underground garage holds 2,400 cars. ⊠ *100 Queen St. W,* ☎ *416/392–9111, TDD 416/392–7354.* ☺ *Weekdays 8:30–4:30.*

❾ Old City Hall. Standing in marked contrast to the ☞ **New City Hall** structure across Bay Street, this earlier city hall was created in 1899 by E. J. Lennox, who later designed Casa Loma (☞ Forest Hill, *below*). The fabulous gargoyles above the front steps were apparently the architect's witty way of mocking certain turn-of-the-century politicians; he also carved his name under the eaves on all four faces of the building. Considered one of North America's most impressive municipal halls in its heyday—note the huge stained-glass window as you enter—it's still going strong as the home of the provincial courts, the county offices, and the marriage bureau. The handsome old structure stands in delightful contrast to its daring and unique sibling. ⊠ *60 Queen St. W,* ☎ *416/327–5675.* ☺ *Weekdays 8:30–4:45.*

Ontario College of Art and Design Gallery. Across the street from the Art Gallery of Ontario (AGO), the college's third-floor gallery shows works by students, faculty, and alumni. It is one of Canada's major art institutions and an important exhibition space for emerging artists and designers. ✉ *291 Dundas St. W (enter on McCaul St.),* ☎ *416/ 977–6000, ext. 262.* ⊠ *Free.* ⊙ *Wed.–Sat. noon–6.*

❶ Spadina Avenue. Spadina, running from the lakeshore north to College Street, has never been fashionable: For decades it has contained a collection of inexpensive stores, factories that sell wholesale if you have connections, ethnic food and fruit stores, and eateries, including some often first-class, if modest-looking, Chinese restaurants sprinkled throughout the area. Each new wave of immigrants—Jewish, Chinese, Portuguese, East and West Indian, South American—has added its own flavor to the mix, but Spadina-Kensington's basic bill of fare is still bargains galore. Here you'll find gourmet cheeses, fresh (not fresh-frozen) ocean fish, fine European kitchenware at half the prices of stores in the Yorkville area, yards of remnants piled high in bins, designer clothes minus the labels, and the occasional rock-and-roll night spot and interesting greasy spoon. A new streetcar line bustles down the wide avenue to Front Street.

Toronto's widest street has been pronounced "Spa-*dye*-nah" for a century and a half, and we are too polite to point out that it really should be called "Spa-*dee*-na." The reason it is 132 ft wide, double the width of almost every other old street in town, goes back to 1802, when a 27-year-old Irish physician named William Warren Baldwin came to muddy York. He soon married a rich young woman, built a pleasant home where Casa Loma and Spadina House (☞ Forest Hill, *below*) now sit, and decided to cut a giant swath through the forest from Bloor Street down to Queen Street so they could look down—literally and socially—on Lake Ontario. Alas, their view disappeared in 1874, when a thankless granddaughter sold the land at the crescent just above College Street for the site of Knox College, which moved to the University of Toronto campus several decades later. Now covered with vines, the Victorian college building still sits in the crescent, a number of the chestnut trees planted by Dr. Baldwin remaining on the west side. Little else remains of Dr. Baldwin's Spadina, except for a handful of Victorian mansions.

NEED A
BREAK?   **Ace Bakery** (✉ 548 King St. W, ☎ 416/506–1517), 1½ blocks west of Spadina, has the best bread and sandwiches in Toronto. You can get prosciutto, mozzarella, and pesto on a panetti bun here, or Asiago cheese with grilled tomato on fresh focaccia bread.

AROUND QUEEN'S PARK

This midtown area, bounded by College Street on the south, Yonge Street on the east, Bloor Street on the north, and Spadina Avenue on the west, offers a political, cultural, and intellectual feast. Its heart is the large oval Queen's Park, south of which is the seat of the Ontario Provincial Legislature, and to the east and west the University of Toronto's main campus, which straddles the park and occupies about 160 acres. It's almost a city unto itself, with a staff and student population of more than 50,000.

The institution dates back to 1827, when King George IV signed a charter for a "King's College in the Town of York, Capital of Upper Canada." The Church of England had control then, but by 1850 the college was proclaimed nondenominational, renamed the University of Toronto, and put under the control of the province. Then, in a spirit of Christian competition, the Anglicans started Trinity College, the Methodists began Victoria, and the Roman Catholics begat St. Michael's;

by the time the Presbyterians founded Knox College, the whole thing was almost out of hand. Now the nine schools and faculties are united, and they welcome anyone who can meet the admission standards and afford the tuition, which, thanks to government funding, is reasonable. The architecture is interesting, if as uneven as one might expect from a place that's been built in bits and pieces over 150 years.

St. George Street, the major north–south hub of the campus, has suffered from the last four decades of erratic development. The buildings range from the aesthetically successful Innis and Woodsworth colleges to the graceless Sidney Smith Hall. The University has revived the streetscape by adding bike lanes, planting more trees, and adding a café and outdoor plaza in front of Sidney Smith Hall. Another project in the works would include an outdoor amphitheater, skating rink, reflecting pool, and public market. The Visitors Centre at 25 King's College Circle (☎ 416/978–4426) has information and maps; you can ask about summer walking tours.

Numbers in the text and in the margin correspond to points of interest on the North Central Core map.

A Good Walk

Start out at the northeast corner of University Avenue and College Street (Queen's Park TTC station), where you'll find yourself looking into the green expanse of **Queen's Park.** If you're traveling with kids, you might want to detour two long blocks right (east) on College Street until you come to Bay Street and the fascinating **Toronto Police Museum and Discovery Centre** ⑫. Return to University Avenue and go north toward the pink **Ontario Legislative Building** ⑬, on the site originally granted to King's College, the University of Toronto's precursor. University Avenue splits into Queen's Park Crescent. Follow Queen's Park Crescent East; when you reach Wellesley Street West, you'll find a traffic light and a safe way to cross the stream of four-lane traffic.

After visiting the parliament buildings, return to Wellesley Street West and go left (west) under an overpass onto the University of Toronto; the large green area before you is Front Campus, surrounded by King's College Circle. The circle includes some of the oldest buildings on the campus, such as the domed Convocation Hall, and some of the newest, such as the poured-concrete Medical Sciences building. Take Tower Road north from King's College Circle; almost immediately to your left, you'll see the large Romanesque Revival–style University College, the first nonsectarian college. Here the Public Affairs and Alumni Development Building provides visitor information, maps, and guided tours. It's a short block north on Tower Road to **Hart House** ⑭, a Gothic style student center.

Turn right from Hart House and walk less than a block north along another green area called the Back Campus until you reach Hoskin Avenue, where you'll cross north at the traffic light and take a left. When, after a long block, you get to Devonshire Place, you'll see Massey College, whose handsome buildings and enclosed courtyard were designed by Canadian architect Ron Thom. Past masters have included the late Robertson Davies, one of Canada's finest novelists. Continue west on Hoskin for another block until you reach the corner of St. George Street, where you'll glimpse a linked trio of poured concrete buildings. The one closest is the library school; the middle one is the Robarts Library, nicknamed "Fort Book" by students, both because of its restrictive loan policies and its slit windows, suitable for shooting arrows or pouring boiling oil on attacking hordes; and the southernmost building houses the **Thomas Fisher Rare Books Library** ⑮.

If you don't want to visit the rare books library, turn right (east) at the traffic light where Tower Road meets Hoskin Avenue; in about a block, Hoskin curves and becomes Queen's Park Crescent. Walk north on the crescent; when the street straightens out again, you'll see on your left the distinctive dome of the McLaughlin Planetarium (sadly closed indefinitely for lack of funding). Just past it is the TTC's Museum stop and, beyond that, the large stone **Royal Ontario Museum** ⑯, one of Canada's finest museums. Across the street from the ROM's main entrance is the **George R. Gardiner Museum of Ceramic Art** ⑰. At this point you are on the edge of **Yorkville,** an elegant shopping district, but don't be distracted (unless you can't resist, of course). On the north end of ROM is Bloor Street; take it west one long block to St. George Street to visit the **Bata Shoe Museum** ⑱. Catercorner from the museum is the York Club, one of the landmarks of the posh neighborhood known as **The Annex** ⑲.

TIMING

This Queen's Park walk is good any time of year because many of the attractions bring you indoors. Excluding a stroll around The Annex, the walk alone should take about half an hour at a strolling pace. The walk and a visit to the legislature and one or two of the museums or libraries would make a nice half-day (or more) program; allot at least two hours for the Royal Ontario and Gardiner museums. This area abuts the Yorkville shopping district and the Rosedale (☞ *below*) residential area and could be combined nicely with visits to either or both.

Sights to See

⑲ **The Annex.** Born in 1887, when the burgeoning town of Toronto added the area between Bathurst Street and Avenue Road north from Bloor Street to the Canadian Pacific railroad tracks at what is now Dupont Street, the countrified Annex soon became an enclave for the well-to-do; today it attracts an intellectual set. Timothy Eaton of department store fame built a handsome structure at 182 Lowther Avenue (since demolished) and the Gooderham family (of liquor fame) erected a lovely red castle at the corner of St. George Street and Bloor Street, now the home of the exclusive York Club.

As Queen Victoria gave way to King Edward, the old rich gave way to the new rich and ethnic groups came and went, until the arrival of the ultimate neighborhood wrecker—the developer. Alas, much of St. George Street has been lost to high-rises, and as you near the Spadina subway entrance along Lowther Avenue and Walmer Street, you'll see that many Edwardian mansions have fallen to very ugly 1960s-era apartment buildings.

Still, the Annex, with its hundreds of attractive old homes, can be cited as a prime example of Toronto's success in preserving lovely, safe streets within blocks of the downtown area. Even today, many examples of late 19th-century architecture can be enjoyed on Admiral Road, Lowther Avenue, and Bloor Street, west of University Avenue. Round turrets, pyramid-shape roofs, and conical (some even comical) spires are among the pleasures shared by some 20,000 Torontonians who live in this vibrant community, including professors, students, writers, lawyers, and other professional and artsy types. Bloor Street between Spadina and Palmerston keeps them fed and entertained with its bohemian collection of used record stores, crafts shops run by eccentrics, restaurants from elegant Italian to hearty Polish and aromatic Indian. Keep your eyes open, too; you may run into one of Canada's more well-known literary types, including Michael Ondatjee, Jane Jacobs, or Daniel Richler (Mordechai's son).

(18) Bata Shoe Museum. Created by Sonja Bata, of the Bata Shoe Company, this collection contains 10,000 varieties of foot coverings and, through the changing fashions, highlights the craft and sociology of making shoes. Some items date back more than 4,000 years; pressurized sky-diving boots, iron-spiked shoes used for crushing chestnuts, and smugglers' clogs are among the items on display. Elton John's boots have proved wildly popular, but Napoléon's socks give them a run for the money. ⊠ *327 Bloor St. W,* ☎ *416/979–7799.* ⊡ *$6; free 1st Tues. of month.* ☉ *Tues.–Wed. and Fri.–Sat. 10–5, Thurs. 10–8, Sun. noon–5.*

Children's Own Museum. This new museum, known as the COM, opened its doors in late 1998 in the former McLaughlin Planetarium building, one door south of the ☞ **Royal Ontario Museum**. It was specifically designed for younger children and incorporates a construction site, workshop, attic, reading nook, and theater, as well as a main street—all just the right size for small children. ⊠ *100 Queen's Park,* ☎ *416/966–9073.* ⊡ *$3.75.* ☉ *Tues. 10–8, Wed.–Sat. 10–5, Sun. noon–5.*

(17) George R. Gardiner Museum of Ceramic Art. This collection of rare European ceramics features 17th-century English Delftware and 18th-century yellow European porcelain; its pre-Columbian collection dates back to Olmec and Maya times. Most popular is the second-floor display of Italian commedia dell'arte figures, especially Harlequin. Don't miss the museum's gift shop, which stocks many unusual items. ⊠ *111 Queen's Park,* ☎ *416/586–8080.* ⊡ *$5; free Tues.* ☉ *Mon. and Wed.–Sat. 10–5, Tues. 10–8, Sun. 11–5.*

(14) Hart House. A neo-Gothic-style student center built 1911–19, Hart House represents the single largest gift to the university. Vincent Massey, a student here at the turn of the century, regretted the absence of a meeting place and gym for students and convinced his father to build one. It was named for Vincent's grandfather, Hart, the founder of Massey-Ferguson, once the world's leading supplier of farm equipment. Originally restricted to male students, Hart House has been open to women since 1972. The attached **Soldier's Tower,** with its 51-bell carrillon, was erected in 1923 as a memorial to university members who fell in World War I. Names of alumni killed in later wars have been added since then. ⊠ *Hart House Circle,* ☎ *416/978–2452.*

NEED A BREAK?

Hart House's **Gallery Grill** (⊠ Great Hall, ☎ 416/978–2445) was always worth peeking into for its impressive stained-glass windows, but since the chef of a noted restaurant/jazz bistro took over in 1996, the food is good, too. Stop in for a bowl of roasted tomato and vegetable soup, East Coast salmon sandwich, or steak salad and a glass of wine.

☾ Lillian H. Smith Branch of the Toronto Public Library. Honoring the memory of the city's first children's librarian, this branch maintains nearly 60,000 items in three children's collections, ranging from the 14th century to the present. In addition, the Merril Collection of Science Fiction, Speculation and Fantasy includes about 50,000 items on everything from parapsychology to UFOs. The Electronic Resource Centre offers on-line access to the public (even non-Canadians). ⊠ *239 College St.,* ☎ *416/393–7746.* ⊡ *Free.* ☉ *Library Mon.–Thurs. 10–8:30, Fri. 10–6, Sat. 9–5; children's and Merril collections Sun.–Fri. 10–6, Sat. 9–5; Electronic Resource Centre Mon.–Thurs. 2–8:30, Fri. noon–6, Sat. 9–5.*

OFF THE BEATEN PATH

LITTLE ITALY – Once a quiet strip of College Street with just a few unfrequented clothing shops and the odd obstinate pizzeria, Little Italy (College Street, west of Bathurst Street between Euclid Avenue and Shaw Street) has suddenly become the hippest place in Toronto. New restaurants open weekly, bars and coffeehouses are packed into the night, and every corner holds fashionable cafés and people dining outdoors. The Royal Cinema at 606 College Street is the new flagship theater for Toronto's International Film Festival. This is the southern edge of the city's Italian community, and not much remains of this heritage—most people have moved north, toward St. Clair Avenue—but the flavor lingers in the menus, food markets, pool halls, and some holdovers from a less glamorous time.

⑬ Ontario Legislative Building. Home of the provincial parliament, this mammoth study in geometric form, with rectangular towers, triangular roofs, and circular glass, was opened in 1893; you can get a taste of Ontario's history and government here. Like the New City Hall, it was the product of an international contest among architects, in this case won by a young Briton who was residing in Buffalo, New York. The Romanesque Revival–style building, made out of pink Ontario sandstone, has a wealth of exterior detail; inside the huge, lovely halls echo half a millennium of English architecture. The long hallways are hung with hundreds of oils by Canadian artists, most of which capture scenes of the province's natural beauty. Should you choose to take one of the frequent (and free) tours, you will see the chamber where the 130 MMPs (Members of Provincial Parliament) meet on a regular basis. There are two heritage rooms—one each for the parliamentary histories of Britain and Ontario—filled with old newspapers, periodicals, and pictures. The lobby holds a fine collection of minerals and rocks of the province. The many statues that dot the lawn in front of the building, facing College Street, include one of Queen Victoria and one of Canada's first prime minister, Sir John A. Macdonald. These lawns are also the site of Canada Day celebrations and the occasional political protest. These buildings are often referred to simply as Queen's Park, after the park surrounding them, or as the parliament buildings. ⊠ *1 Queen's Park,* ☎ *416/325–7500.* 🎟 *Free.* ☉ *Guided tour mid-May–Labor Day, daily on the hr 9–4, weekends every ½ hr 9–11:30 and 1:30–4; frequent tours rest of the yr; also at 6:45* PM *when evening sessions are held.*

Queen's Park. Many visitors consider this to be the soul of Toronto. Surrounding the large oval-shape patch of land are medical facilities to the south, the University of Toronto to the west and east, and the Royal Ontario Museum to the north. To most locals, Queen's Park is chiefly synonymous with politics, as the ☞ Ontario Legislative Building sits in the middle of this charming urban oasis. ⊠ *Queen's Park Circle, between College St. and Bloor St. W.*

OFF THE BEATEN PATH **ROSEDALE –** This posh residential neighborhood northeast of Queen's Park repays an hour's walk. Rosedale has the charm of curving roads (it's one of the few neighborhoods to have escaped the city's grid pattern), many small parks and large trees, and a jumble of oversize late 19th-century and early 20th-century houses in Edwardian, Victorian, Georgian, and Tudor styles. In the 1920s, Sheriff William Jarvis and his wife, Mary, settled here on a 200-acre estate in what was then the country. She named her home Rosedale for the wildflowers that bloomed in profusion. Most of the roses are gone now, as are the magnificent trees for which Elm Avenue was named. Morley Callaghan, the Toronto novelist and longtime neighborhood resident (who also boxed with Ernest Hemingway and quarreled with F. Scott Fitzgerald in Paris), called this "a fine and private place." While some of the fine old houses have been carved up into small apartments, the neighborhood is still the home of old and new wealth and many who wield power and responsibility. The neighborhood is bounded by Yonge Street on the west, the Don Valley Parkway on the east, St. Clair Avenue to the north, and the Rosedale Ravine, just above Bloor Street East, to the south.

★ ☕ ⑯ **Royal Ontario Museum.** Ongoing renovations have restored the ROM to its status as—in the words of the Canada Council—"Canada's single greatest cultural asset." Since its inception in 1912, Canada's largest museum has continued to collect—always with brilliance—reaching more than 6 million items altogether. What makes the ROM unique is that science, art, and archaeology exhibits are all appealingly presented under one roof. A good place to begin a visit is the restored **Samuel Hall– Currelly Gallery,** with its magnificent glass and mosaic ceiling. The gallery displays some outstanding artificats and serves as an orientation center.

The **Sigmund Samuel Canadiana Collection,** a worthy assemblage of 18th- and 19th-century Canadian furnishings, glassware, silver, and period rooms, is part of the Canadian Heritage gallery. A particular strength of the ROM is the **T. T. Tsui Galleries of Chinese Art,** with stunning sculptures, paintings, and many other artifacts. The **Roman Gallery** has the most extensive collection of Roman artifacts in Canada. The brilliant **Ancient Egypt Gallery** is connected with the newer **Nubia Gallery;** both exhibit artifacts that illuminate the ancient cultures. The **European Musical Instruments Gallery** has a revolutionary audio system and more than 1,200 instruments dating back to the late 16th century.

Sciences aren't given short shrift, either. The **Evolution Gallery** has an ongoing audiovisual program on Darwin's theories of evolution. The **Discovery Centre** allows children six years and older to handle objects from the ROM's collections and to study them, using microscopes, ultraviolet light, and magnifying glasses. A **Bat Cave** contains 4,000 freeze-dried and artificial bats in a lifelike presentation; there's a guided walk through a dimly lit replica of an 8-ft-high limestone tunnel in Jamaica, filled with sounds of dripping water and bat squeaks. Children and adults alike can appreciate the extensive **Dinosaur Collection.**

The new ☞ **Children's Own Museum** is in the former McLaughlin Planetarium building, one door south of the ROM, but it is not part of the museum. ✉ *100 Queen's Park,* ☎ *416/586–8000.* 💲 *$10; by donation Tues. after 4:30.* ☉ *Mon. and Wed.–Sat. 10–6, Tues. 10–8, Sun. 11–6; Discovery Centre hrs vary, so call ahead.*

⑮ **Thomas Fisher Rare Books Library.** Early writing artifacts such as a Babylonian cuneiform tablet, a 2,000-year-old Egyptian papyrus, and books dating to the beginning of European printing in the 15th century are shown here in rotating exhibits, which change four or five times annually. Subjects of these shows might include Shakespeare, Galileo, Italian opera, or contemporary typesetting. ✉ *120 St. George St.,* ☎ *416/ 978–5285.* 💲 *Free.* ☉ *Weekdays 9–4:45.*

NEED A
BREAK?   One block north of the library, on St. George Street and Sussex Avenue, **the cafe of Innis College** (✉ 2 Sussex Ave., ☎ 416/598–0575) purveys good sandwiches and strong espresso; in summer, there's a patio with barbecue and a salad bar.

☕ ⑫ **Toronto Police Museum and Discovery Centre.** Highlights are a replica of a 19th-century police station, the array of firearms, and exhibits of infamous crimes. Interactive displays include everything from information on drugs, computers that help track down missing children, and "Did You Know?" quizzes. You can also study your own fingerprints. Kids like the 1914 paddywagon, crash car videos, and, especially, the brand-new Harley Davidson they can jump on; they also enjoy climbing in and out of a car sliced in half and hearing a dispatcher squawk at them. ⊠ *40 College St.,* ☎ *416/808–7020.* 🎟 *Free.* ⊘ *Daily 9–9.*

Toronto Reference Library. Designed by one of Canada's most admired architects, Raymond Moriyama, who also created the Ontario Science Centre, this library is arranged around a large atrium, affording a wonderful sense of open space. Among the highlights is a fabric sculpture, *Lyra,* designed by artist Aiko Suzuki; it overhangs the pool and waterfall in the foyer. Glass-enclosed elevators glide swiftly and silently up and down one side of the atrium, allowing you to admire the banners that hang from the ceiling, announcing the collections on each floor. Fully one third of the more than 4 million items—spread across 45 km (28 mi) of shelves—are open to the public. Audio carrels are available for listening to your choice among the nearly 30,000 music and spoken-word recordings. Open on Saturday from 2 to 4 and by appointment, the **Arthur Conan Doyle Room** will be of special interest to Baker Street regulars. It houses the world's finest public collection of Holmesiana, including records, films, photos, books, manuscripts, letters, and even cartoon books starring Sherlock Hemlock of *Sesame Street.* ⊠ *789 Yonge St.,* ☎ *416/393–7131.* ⊘ *Mon.–Thurs. 10–8, Fri.–Sat. 10–5.*

Yorkville. One of the most dynamic and expensive areas of the city is known to some as Toronto's Rodeo Drive; other people call it Toronto's Madison Avenue. One thing is certain: These blocks are packed with restaurants, galleries, specialty shops, and high-price stores specializing in designer clothes, furs, and jewels (☞ Chapter 7). ⊠ *Bordered by Avenue Rd., Yonge and Bloor Sts., and Yorkville Ave.*

CABBAGETOWN

The area that the late Cabbagetown-born-and-bred novelist and short story writer Hugh Garner described in his 1950 novel *Cabbagetown* as "the world's largest Anglo-Saxon slum" has turned into one of downtown's most popular neighborhoods. Mockingly named by outsiders for the cabbages that grew on tiny lawns and were cooked in nearly every house, the moniker is used with a combination of inverse pride and almost wistful irony today. Beginning in the 1970s, rehabbers turned houses that sold in the $25,000 range into ones that now fetch $500,000 and more—part of the insistent gentrification of Toronto's downtown. Although there are few tourist attractions per se here, it's fun to stroll around and enjoy its architectural diversity. The borders extend roughly from Parliament Street on the west (about 1½ km/1 mi due east of Yonge Street) to the Don River on the east, and from Bloor Street on the north to Queen Street East on the south.

Numbers in the text and in the margin correspond to points of interest on the Metropolitan Toronto map.

A Good Walk

Start at the southeast corner of Carlton and Parliament Streets (the latter so named because the first government buildings were built near its foot in the closing years of the 18th century). Walk south, through the busiest part of the **Parliament Street** commercial area. Most of the buildings on the west side date from the 1890s, though the storefronts are more recent.

Turn left at **Spruce Street,** the first block you come to. Of note are No. 35 and No. 41, two buildings that were once part of Trinity College Medical School. Continuing east to the northwest corner of Spruce and Sumach streets, you'll see Spruce Court, one of the city's earliest low-income housing projects and now a residential cooperative. Around the corner to the right, on **Sumach Street,** check out No. 289, once the Ontario Women's Medical College. Now turn around and walk north on Sumach Street. After crossing Spruce Street, look to your right at the attractive terrace of workers' cottages at 119–133 Spruce Street.

Continue north on Sumach Street back to **Carlton Street,** where you'll see some of the area's largest homes. (Note the redbrick surface of the street to the east.) Among the most outstanding are No. 288, No. 286, and No. 295. Continue west on Carlton Street to **Metcalfe Street,** which, thanks to all its trees, fences, and unbroken rows of terraces, is one of the most beautiful streets in Toronto. Look down on the sidewalk on the east side nearest Carlton Street to see a utility-hole cover from the Victorian era, bearing the date 1889. Proceed north to look at No. 37, a mix of Victorian and beaux-arts styles. At the northeast corner of Metcalfe and Winchester streets is the handsome St. Enoch's Presbyterian Church.

Turn left now, which will take you west along **Winchester Street** back to Parliament. At the southeast corner of Winchester and Parliament you'll see the most prominent building in the area, the Hotel Winchester, erected in 1881. South of the Hotel Winchester, on Parliament Street, stand Nos. 502–508, an imposing row of large Victorian houses. At the northwest corner of Parliament and Wellesley streets loom the overwhelming apartment towers of St. James Town, built in the 1960s and reviled ever since because they wiped out many attractive older homes. On the east side of Parliament Street, just north of Wellesley Street, is the beautiful **St. James Cemetery** ①.

From the cemetery, turn right (east) along **Wellesley Street.** Be sure to take note of No. 314. Farther east, turn north up the lane marked **Wellesley Cottages.** Back on Wellesley Street, walk north up the lane just east of number 402 to see the 1893–94 Owl House, named for the bird on a small terra-cotta plaque under one of its windows. Wellesley Street comes to an end at **Wellesley Park.** Framing the park are parts of the Don Valley, the **Necropolis Cemetery** ②, and a row of houses to the south. Proceed south through Wellesley Park, and turn right along Amelia Street to Sumach Street. Head south again, past Winchester Street, and make a left (east) into Riverdale Park, which once hosted the city's main zoo and is now home to **Riverdale Farm** ③, a living-history farm museum.

TIMING

This Cabbagetown walk covers 2–3 mi and should take an hour or two at a leisurely pace. Since the main reason to explore the neighborhood is its architecture, a clear day in any season is the best time to visit.

Sights to See

Carlton Street. Some of Cabbagetown's largest homes, dating from the late 19th century, are on this street. **No. 288** is a Second Empire–style house built in 1882 of solid brick with white stone trim. **No. 286,** next door, was built in 1883 and has the familiar steep gable and bargeboard trim. Check out the wrought-iron cresting over the round bow window. **No. 295,** an earlier house of Victorian Gothic design, was originally the home of an executive of Toronto's first telephone company—keep in mind that the wondrous machine was envisioned by Alexander Graham Bell in Brantford, Ontario, just an hour west of Toronto—and had one of the first telephones in the city.

Metcalfe Street. The street's rows of trees, fences, and terraces make it one of Toronto's most beautiful. Superimposed on the side of the simple but picturesque Victorian **No. 37** are 1891 and 1912 additions in beaux-arts classical forms. The Romanesque **St. Enoch's Presbyte-**

rian Church, at the northeast corner of Metcalfe and Winchester streets, was erected in 1891.

❷ Necropolis Cemetery. This "city of the dead" is home to many of Toronto's pioneers. Among the most famous (and notorious) are Toronto's first mayor, William Lyon Mackenzie, who led a revolt against the city in 1837; Samuel Lount and Peter Matthews, two of Mackenzie's followers, who were hanged for their part in that rebellion; and George Brown, founder of the **Globe** newspaper and one of the fathers of Canada's Confederation. The beautiful chapel, gate, and gatehouse of the nonsectarian burial ground, erected in 1872, constitute one of the most picturesque groupings of small Victorian buildings in Toronto. The Necropolis is also known for its great variety of trees, flowering shrubs, and rare and exotic plants. ⊠ *Corner Winchester and Sumach Sts.,* ☎ *416/923–7911.* ⊙ *Daily 8–8.*

Parliament Street. This busy commercial and residential Cabbagetown street is particularly noteworthy for its houses dating from the late 19th century. **Nos. 502–508,** erected in 1879, are among the largest and most elaborately decorated Second Empire structures still standing in Toronto. While you're on the street, St. James Town and ☞ **St. James Cemetery** are also worth seeing.

❸ Riverdale Farm. Not only is this museum one of Toronto's most delightful attractions and a special treat for children, but it's also free. The most interesting structure is the original Pennsylvania German–style barn, built in 1858 and moved to the farm in 1975 from suburban Markham, many miles north of the city. Inside are various implements such as a light sleigh from the turn of the century and an exact replica of the type of Conestoga wagon used by German-speaking immigrants to this country early in the last century. Demonstrations of turn-of-the-century crafts such as quilting and spinning are offered daily. Bring along bathing suits for the very young children: The lovely park adjacent to the farm has a wading pool. ⊠ *201 Winchester St.,* ☎ *416/392–6794.* ☞ *Free.* ⊙ *Daily 9–4, crafts demonstrations 10–3.*

❶ St. James Cemetery. Laid out in the 1840s, the burial ground contains the graves of many of Toronto's prominent citizens from the days when the place was still called the town of York, as well as some of the more interesting burial monuments in Toronto. While you are there, observe the small yellow-brick Gothic **Chapel of St. James-the-Less,** built in 1858 and considered one of the most beautiful church buildings in the country. ⊠ *Northeast corner of Parliament and Wellesley Sts.*

Spruce Court. Now a residential cooperative, Spruce Court was originally constructed between 1913 and 1926 for the Toronto Housing Company as one of the city's earliest and most attractive low-income housing projects. The individual units not only provided modern conveniences and street access but also opened to a grassy courtyard. ⊠ *Northwest corner of Spruce and Surmach Sts.*

Spruce Street. In the heart of the city's Cabbagetown neighborhood, this street is of architectural and historical note. The little brick cottage set far back from the street at **No. 35** was built in 1860–61 and once was home to the dean of Trinity College Medical School. The fence also dates from the last century. **No. 41** was built in 1871 and served until 1903 as a medical school; it has now been recycled as part of a residential development. Its history is outlined on the Toronto Historical Board plaque on its front lawn. Down the street is ☞ **Spruce Court.** Numbers **119–133** on Spruce Street are characteristic of Toronto's residential architecture between 1875 and 1890. These workers' cottages were erected in 1887 in Second Empire style, typified by high mansard roofs punctuated by dormers with marvelous details such as carved wooden brackets and metal decorative devices.

Sumach Street. Of particular historical importance on this Cabbagetown street is **No. 289.** The Ontario Women's Medical College, built in 1889 and a forerunner of Women's College Hospital (Canada's less-than-enlightened attitudes toward women barred them from male-only medical schools and city hospitals), was formerly housed here. The attractiveness of this brick-and-stone structure demonstrates the success with which Victorian architects and builders managed to integrate institutions into mostly residential streetscapes.

Wellesley Cottages. Much of Toronto's inexpensive housing of the 19th century was built in the same simplified Gothic style, faced with wood lath and stucco, as this row of 1886–87 workers' houses. ⊠ *Off Wellesley St.*

Wellesley Park. From 1848 to 1888, the park was the site of the area's major industry: the P. R. Lamb Glue and Blacking Factory; today it's a small, pleasant neighborhood park and playground, surrounded by the Don Valley, the ☞ **Necropolis Cemetery,** and a row of houses to the south. ⊠ *End of Wellesley St.*

Wellesley Street. A park, a cemetery, and a variety of architectural styles can be found on this Cabbagetown street (☞ **Wellesley Cottages, Wellesley Park,** and ☞ **Necropolis Cemetery**). **No. 314,** built in 1889–90, has stonework around the windows and carved stone faces above the door and in the keystones.

Winchester Street. Walk along this Cabbagetown street and admire the repeated sunburst patterns of carved wood in many of the gables and the large amount of stained glass, much of it original, some of it recently installed by lovers of Victoriana. The **Hotel Winchester,** a venerable but sadly decaying building at the southeast corner of Winchester and Parliament, is one of the neighborhood's most prominent. It opened in 1888 as the Lake View Hotel and was so named because from its roof one could see all the way south to the blue waters of Lake Ontario.

FOREST HILL AND BEYOND

A golden square of about 948 acres, Forest Hill is bounded by Bathurst Street on the west, Avenue Road on the east, Eglinton Avenue on the north, and St. Clair Avenue West on the south. Its major draws for visitors, besides handsome streets and houses, are the Casa Loma and Spadina house museums. The area is home to approximately 25,000 well-heeled people, although it numbered but some 2,100 souls in 1923 when it chose to become a village on its own. Its first reeve (local official) passed a bylaw requiring that a tree be planted in front of every house; you can see the shady results of his campaign today. At that time, there were no paved streets. Eglinton Avenue was a wagon trail, and Old Forest Hill Road was part of an old Indian path that meandered from the Humber River to Lake Ontario.

Forest Hill remained its own little village, with its own police and fire departments and school system, until it was incorporated into Toronto in 1967. A sense of this community can be obtained by recalling a 1982 controversy: Would the former village of Forest Hill continue to have backyard garbage pickup, or would the villagers have to drag their rubbish out front like everyone else? The City Council finally voted to con-

The Beaches, **28**
Beth Tzedec Museum, **8**
Black Creek Pioneer Village, **19**
Casa Loma, **7**
The Danforth, **27**
David Dunlap Observatory, **21**
Edward's Gardens, **23**
Gibson House, **20**
High Park, **11**
Highland Creek Ravine, **30**
James Gardens, **13**
Kortright Centre, **16**
McMichael Canadian Art Collection, **18**
Montgomery's Inn, **12**
Necropolis Cemetery, **2**
Ontario Science Centre, **25**
Paramount Canada's Wonderland, **17**
Riverdale Farm, **3**
Scarborough Bluffs, **29**
Scarlett Mills Park, **14**
Sherwood Park, **24**
Sir Casimir Gzowski Park, **10**
Spadina, **6**
St. James Cemetery, **1**
Sunnyside Park, **9**
Todmorden Mills Historic Site, **26**
Tommy Thompson Park, **31**
Toronto Zoo, **22**
Upper Canada College, **4**
Wild Water Kingdom, **15**
Winston Churchill Park, **5**

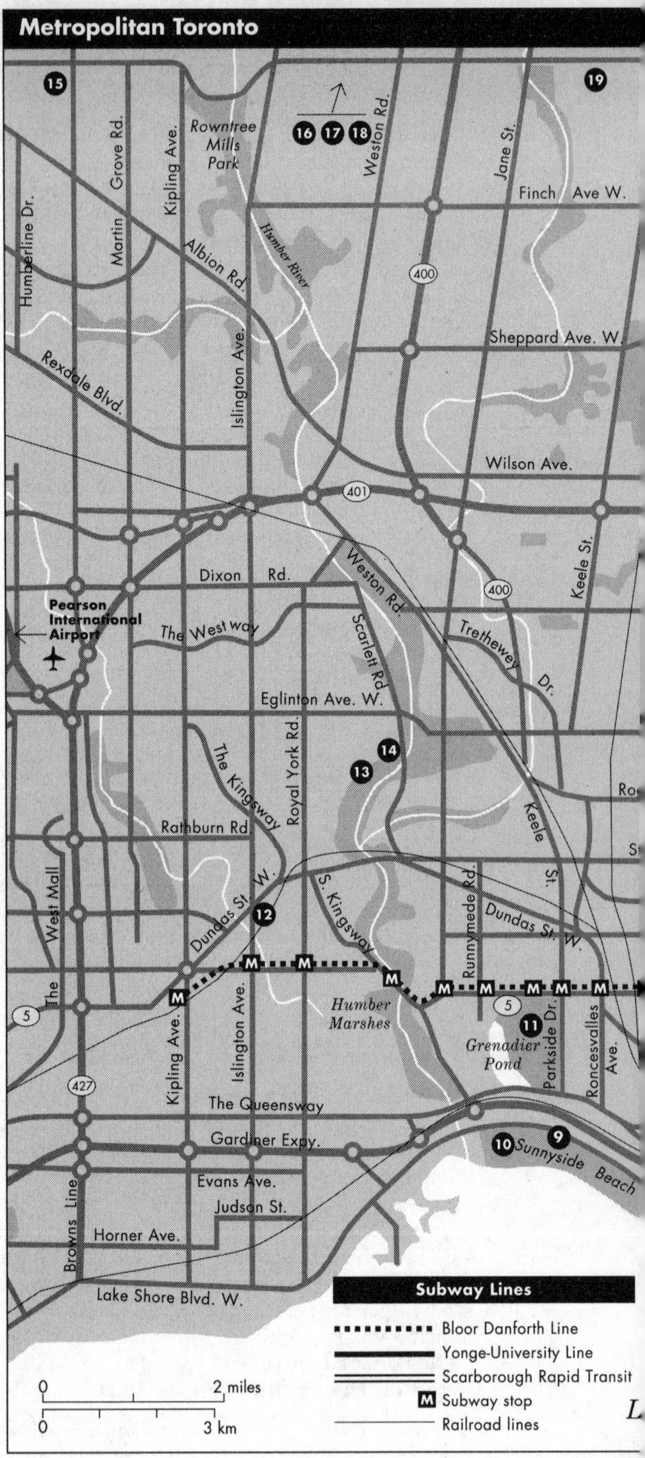
Metropolitan Toronto
15
19
16 17 18
Rowntree Mills Park
Martin Grove Rd.
Kipling Ave.
Weston Rd.
Jane St.
Finch Ave W.
Humberline Dr.
Albion Rd.
Humber River
400
Sheppard Ave. W.
Islington Ave.
Rexdale Blvd.
Wilson Ave.
401
Keele St.
Dixon Rd.
Weston Rd.
400
Pearson International Airport
The Westway
Scarlett Rd.
Trethewey Dr.
Eglinton Ave. W.
14
13
The Kingsway
Royal York Rd.
Rathburn Rd.
Keele St.
West Mall
Dundas St. W.
12
S. Kingsway
Runnymede Rd.
Dundas St. W.
The
5
Kipling Ave.
Islington Ave.
Humber Marshes
5
11
Grenadier Pond
Parkside Dr.
Roncesvalles Ave.
427
The Queensway
Gardiner Expy.
10 Sunnyside Beach
9
Browns Line
Evans Ave.
Judson St.
Horner Ave.
Lake Shore Blvd. W.
Subway Lines
Bloor Danforth Line
Yonge-University Line
Scarborough Rapid Transit
M Subway stop
Railroad lines
0 2 miles
0 3 km

TO ④④④

G. Ross
Lord
Park

Dufferin St.

Bathurst St.

Yonge St.

㉑

Finch Ave. W.

Finch
East
Park

Finch Ave. E.

E.

Downsview
Airport

Earl Bales
Park

⑳ ⑪

Bayview Ave.

Sheppard Ave. E.

Don Mills Rd.

Don Valley Pkwy.

㉒

401

Allen Expwy.

Dufferin St.

Lawrence Ave. W.

Avenue Rd.

York Mills Rd.

Leslie St.

Lawrence Ave. E.

Don Mills Rd.

Don Valley Pkwy.

Wigmore
Park

Victoria Park Ave.

Clinton Ave. W.

Oakwood Ave.

⑧

FOREST
HILL

④

Spading Rd.

Mount Pleasant Rd.

㉔

Eglinton Ave. E.

Sunnybrook
Park

㉓

Don Valley

Laird Dr.

㉕

Taylor Creek
Park

Dawes Rd.

St. Clair Ave. W.

⑤

⑦

⑥

Davenport Rd.

Dupont St.

Bathurst St.

TORONTO

Bayview Ext.

㉖

O'Connor Dr.

Broadview Ave.

Pape Ave.

Greenwood Ave.

Coxwell Ave.

Lansdowne Ave.

Dufferin St.

oor St. W.

Danforth Ave.

Woodbine Ave.

Gerrard St. E.

College St.

㉒ ①

Kingston Rd.

Dundas St. W.

③

Gerrard St. E.

Leslie St. E.

㉚

Queen St. W.

Dundas

Queen St. E.

㉙

King St. W.

Eastern
Ave.

㉘

Exhibition
Place

CABBAGE
TOWN

Lake Shore Blvd. E.

Ashbridges
Bay Park

Ontario
Place

Harbourfront
Centre

Toronto City
Centre
Airport

Inner Harbour

ke Ontario

Toronto Islands

㉛

tinue the special service, on the principle that "invisible garbage" was one of the unwritten terms of Forest Hill's amalgamation with Toronto.

Numbers in the text and in the margin correspond to points of interest on the Metropolitan Toronto map.

A Good Walk
The following suggested walk takes you through the heart of Forest Hill and a bit farther south.

Start at Forest Hill Road, just west of Avenue Road and St. Clair Avenue (take the St. Clair streetcar or Avenue Road bus). You are now entering the thick of Forest Hill, with its handsome English manors and splendid Georgian homes. At the northeast corner of Forest Hill and Lonsdale roads is **Upper Canada College** ④, a prominent private boys school. Several blocks to the west of UCC is **Bishop Strachan** (pronounced strawn) **School,** a similar facility for girls. Admire the homes along Old Forest Hill Road, then head up and down the streets that run north–south: Dunvegan, Warren, and Russell Hill. South of St. Clair Avenue, Russell Hill Road becomes a showpiece of impressive mansions.

If you take Spadina Road south from St. Clair Avenue, you'll pass **Winston Churchill Park** ⑤ on your left. Continue farther south on Spadina to reach **Spadina** ⑥, a magnificently restored Victorian home. Across the street is **Casa Loma** ⑦, a European-style fairy-tale castle.

TIMING
Allow about an hour just to stroll along the area's residential streets. If you want to spend time in Winston Churchill Park, Spadina, or Casa Loma, give yourself at least another hour at each place. You can do this walk in any season. Spring and fall provide the pleasure of extensive gardens and stands of trees blossoming, blooming, and fading. But in winter you'll have a better view of the buildings' architectural details.

Sights to See
Bishop Strachan School. A neighborhood counterpart to ☞ **Upper Canada College,** the girls get their shot at success at this much admired, much attended, and very expensive school. ⊠ *200 Lawnsdale Rd.*

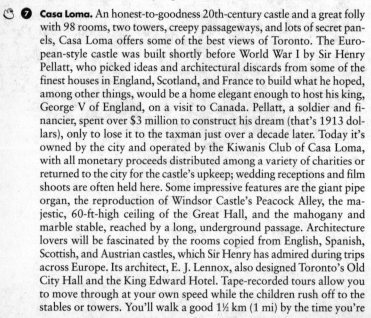

⑦ **Casa Loma.** An honest-to-goodness 20th-century castle and a great folly with 98 rooms, two towers, creepy passageways, and lots of secret panels, Casa Loma offers some of the best views of Toronto. The European-style castle was built shortly before World War I by Sir Henry Pellatt, who picked ideas and architectural discards from some of the finest houses in England, Scotland, and France to build what he hoped, among other things, would be a home elegant enough to host his king, George V of England, on a visit to Canada. Pellatt, a soldier and financier, spent over $3 million to construct his dream (that's 1913 dollars), only to lose it to the taxman just over a decade later. Today it's owned by the city and operated by the Kiwanis Club of Casa Loma, with all monetary proceeds distributed among a variety of charities or returned to the city for the castle's upkeep; wedding receptions and film shoots are often held here. Some impressive features are the giant pipe organ, the reproduction of Windsor Castle's Peacock Alley, the majestic, 60-ft-high ceiling of the Great Hall, and the mahogany and marble stable, reached by a long, underground passage. Architecture lovers will be fascinated by the rooms copied from English, Spanish, Scottish, and Austrian castles, which Sir Henry has admired during trips across Europe. Its architect, E. J. Lennox, also designed Toronto's Old City Hall and the King Edward Hotel. Tape-recorded tours allow you to move through at your own speed while the children rush off to the stables or towers. You'll walk a good 1½ km (1 mi) by the time you're done, so wear sensible shoes. ⊠ *1 Austin Terr.,* ☎ *416/923–1171.* 🖰 *$9.* ⊙ *Daily 9:30–4.*

6 **Spadina.** Pronounced "spa-*dee*-na," as the avenue should be but never is, this 1866 house is filled with arts and artifacts of the James Austin family, prominent in the natural gas, railroad, and banking businesses. Members of the family lived here from Victorian times until 1982, when it was turned over to public ownership. The 50-room house has been restored with period wallpaper, upholstery, and furniture, and crystal chandeliers burn softly with natural gas. Docents tend the magnificent gardens and the small orchard; they make jam in summer and bread in winter and, additionally, give guided tours. ⊠ *285 Spadina Rd.,* ☎ *416/392–6910.* 🖰 *$5.* ⊙ *Jan.–Mar., weekends noon–5; Apr.–Dec., weekdays 9:30–4, weekends and holidays noon–5.*

4 **Upper Canada College.** One of the country's most prestigious boys' private schools, UCC has educated both the reverent (the Eatons as well as numerous bankers, mayors, and prime ministers) and the ir-reverent (humorist Stephen Leacock and the late author Robertson Davies). The school is for grades 1 to 13—yes, Canada's schools have one more year than those in the States. ⊠ *200 Lonsdale Rd.*

☞ 5 **Winston Churchill Park.** In summer, a sweet playground and tennis courts attract Torontonians; folk-dancing is held on some nights. In winter, a serious hill offers the most terrifying—and hence the best—tobog-gan run in the city. Year-round, it's a favorite of joggers. ⊠ *Southeast corner of St. Clair Ave. W and Spadina Rd..*

SOUTHWEST TORONTO

Ethnic enclaves, parks, and museums make Southwest Toronto an in-teresting area to visit. High Park is the main green space, but James Gar-dens and Scarlet Mills Park are two smaller parks also worth a stroll. Area museums include the Beth Tzedec Museum and the restored Mont-gomery's Inn. You can easily reach all of these sights by mass transit.

TIMING

It will probably take you anywhere from an hour to most of a day to visit each of the sights in this area. Plan to explore each sight inde-pendently or to combine a couple of sights in a trip. You might visit the Polish community and High Park during the same morning or af-ternoon, for example. Or consider renting a bike in Sir Casimir Gzowski Park on the lake and riding it up the Humber Valley Parkland (☞ North-west Toronto, *below*). The 19-km (12-mi) trip could take you most of the day, depending on how fast you ride. It's possible to spend from one to two hours in the historic Montgomery's Inn, then walk or take the subway one stop to the lovely James Gardens. Another hour or two could be spent wandering around the West Indian community. The Beth Tzedec Museum, which isn't really close to any other sights in the area, deserves one–two hours of its own.

Numbers in the margin correspond to points of interest on the Metropoli-tan Toronto map.

Sights to See

8 **Beth Tzedec Museum.** Set in a Conservative synagogue of the same name, the museum houses one of the largest collections of Jewish artifacts in Canada. In addition to displays of ritual objects relating to Jewish cel-ebrations and life cycle, the museum mounts original exhibitions that provide a geographic, cultural, and historic view of Jewish life. High-lights of the collection include a treasury of illuminated marriage con-tracts and a unique circumcision chair from Berlin, dated 1766. Tours can be arranged. ✉ *1700 Bathurst St., 2 blocks south of Eglinton Ave,* ☎ *416/781–3514, ext. 32.* 🎫 *Free.* ☼ *Mon., Wed., Thurs. 11–1, 2–5; Sun. 11–2, and by appointment.*

★ ⓫ **High Park.** One of North America's loveliest parks, High Park (at one time the privately owned "farm" of John George Howard out in the countryside) is especially worth visiting in summer, when the many special events include free productions of Shakespeare. The small **Grenadier Pond** in the southwest corner is named after the British soldiers who, it is said, crashed through the soft ice while rushing to defend the town against invading American forces in 1813. Today the pond is home today to thousands of migrating birds. You can fish in its well-stocked waters, either from the shore or from a rented rowboat. There are Sunday afternoon concerts in summer and supervised skating in winter.

The **High Park Zoo** is more modest than the Toronto Zoo in the northeast quadrant of the city, but it's a lot closer, and it's free. Even young children won't tire walking among the deer, Barbary sheep, peacocks, rabbits, and buffalo.

Colborne Lodge, at the south end of the park, was built more than 150 years ago by John Howard on a hill overlooking Lake Ontario. This Regency-style "cottage" contains the original fireplace, bake oven, and kitchen, as well as many of Howard's own drawings and paintings. From High Park subway station, enter the park and follow signs for the lodge. It's open weekdays 9:30–4 and weekends noon–5 from April to December; weekends noon–5 from January to March; and holidays noon–5. The cost is $3.50. For more information call 416/392–6916.

Other highlights of the park are a large swimming pool, tennis courts, fitness trails, and hillside gardens with roses and sculpted hedges. To get here, take the TTC to the High Park station and walk south, or the College Street streetcar to the eastern end of the park and walk west. There's limited parking along Bloor Street, just north of the park, and along the side streets on the eastern side. ✉ *6 km (4 mi) due west of Bloor and Yonge Sts.*

⓭ **James Gardens.** These lovely formal gardens are reachable from Edenbridge Drive, east of Royal York Road. Just to the north is ☞ **Scarlet Mills Park.** ☼ *Daily until sunset.*

⓬ **Montgomery's Inn.** This restored inn, built in the early 1830s by an Irish immigrant, is a good example of the Loyalist architecture—an early American style similar to Georgian—of the time. Costumed staff go about the museum quilting, rug hooking, and cooking traditional foods. There are many tours and a daily afternoon tea. To get here, take the subway to Islington station and then take the Islington bus. ✉ *4709 Dundas St. W,* ☎ *416/394–8113.* 🎫 *$3.* ☼ *Tues.–Fri. 9–4:30, weekends 1–5.*

Polish Community. Roncesvalles Avenue, a long north–south street just east of High Park (☞ *above*), is the commercial heart and soul of Toronto's Polish community, filled with butcher shop after butcher shop, each selling homemade sausages just like grandmother should have made, if she had the skill and time. (Consider buying a few to grill in High Park.) On the west side of High Park is Runnymede Road. Here, and along Bloor Street West, you move both west and east across Europe: Both German and Ukrainian shops come into view, selling fine food and clothing.

⓮ **Scarlett Mills Park.** An appealing wildflower reserve can be found at this park just north of ☞ **James Gardens.** ✉ *Look for signs for the park on Edenbridge Dr.* ☼ *Daily to sunset.*

☙ ⑩ **Sir Casimir Gzowski Park.** From this park you have marvelous views of the Toronto Islands, Ontario Place, and the downtown skyline, both from a paved lakeshore-hugging trail—ideal for jogging, biking, and rollerblading—as well as from a new boardwalk made of Trex, a product derived from recycled plastic garbage bags. The park is accessible by the 501 Queen and 504 King streetcars and is right next to ☞ **Sunnyside Park.**

☙ ⑨ **Sunnyside Park.** Once the site of a large, rollicking amusement park, Sunnyside is now a favorite place for a swim in the heated water of the "tank" or a quick snack in the small restaurant inside the handsome restored 1922 Sunnyside Bathing Pavilion. One of the few remnants of the old amusement park is the Palair Royale dance hall, which still reverberates with the sounds of the big bands most weekends. The park is easily accessible by streetcar from the King, Queen, Roncesvalees, Queensway intersection. Nearby is ☞ **Sir Casimir Gzowski Park.**

West Indian Community. The city's West Indian community is concentrated along Eglinton Avenue, just east of Dufferin Street; along Bloor Street West near Christie Street; and along Bathurst Street, north of Bloor Street. It's fun to explore and great if you like *roti*—spicy Jamaican meat patties.

NORTHWEST TORONTO

This primarily residential area is great for a family visit; it encompasses a huge theme park, a conservation center, a pioneer village, a significant art collection, and a large park stretching along the Humber River.

The northwest is also home to the ever-widening and always vibrant Italian community, which is concentrated in areas that extend from College and Bathurst streets west to Dufferin Street and beyond, and north all the way to the city limits of Steeles Avenue. Its heart is St. Clair Avenue West, running from Bathurst Street to Dufferin Street. On many evenings, especially Sunday, the street is filled with thousands of men and women promenading between *gelaterias,* eyeing each other, and generally enjoying their neighbors.

A car is a necessity for visiting the Kortright Centre and Paramount Canada's Wonderland and is helpful for getting to other sights as well.

TIMING
Each of the sights in this area deserves a separate excursion. You could probably spend half a day at the Black Greek Pioneer Village, especially if you are interested in mid-19th-century Ontario history, or at the Michael Canadian Art Collection in Kleinburg. The Gibson House is another good spot for history buffs—count on an hour or two here, plus the half-hour trip from downtown. Set aside half a day or more for the many activities at the Kortright Centre. Kids, young and old, can last a whole day at Paramount Canada's Wonderland and a half day at Wild Water Kingdom. The Italian community is a good place to spend an afternoon and evening wandering around, drinking espressos at one of the many cafés and eating at one of the excellent restaurants. Of course, many of these excursions require good weather as most of the sights are outdoors.

Numbers in the margin correspond to points of interest on the Metropolitan Toronto map.

Sights to See

☙ ⑲ **Black Creek Pioneer Village.** Less than a half hour's drive from downtown Toronto is a rural, mid-19th-century living-history museum village that makes you feel as if you've gone through a time warp. Black Creek Pioneer Village is a collection of more than three dozen period buildings that have been moved to their current site: a town hall, weaver's shop, printing shop, blacksmith's shop, and a school, complete with dunce cap. The mill dates from the 1840s and has a 4-ton wood waterwheel that still grinds up to a hundred barrels of flour a day (bags are available for purchase).

You can watch men and women in period costumes go about the daily routine of mid-19th-century Ontario life—cutting tin, shearing sheep, tending gardens (weather permitting), fixing and even making horseshoes, baking bread, weaving, printing a newspaper, stringing apple slices, and dipping candles. They explain what they're doing and how they do it, and answer all questions about pioneer farm life.

Free wagon rides, a decent restaurant, and many farm animals all contribute to a satisfying outing. And in the winter, there's also skating, tobogganing, and sleigh rides. Special events include Spring and Fall fairs and celebrations of Canada Day, Thanksgiving, and Christmas (from the middle of November). ⊠ *1000 Murray Ross Pkwy., corner of Jane St. and Steeles Ave.,* ☎ *416/736–1733.* ⊒ *$9, parking $4.* ☉ *May–Dec., daily 10–4.*

⑳ **Gibson House.** It's the Little House in the Suburbs, a 10-room residence built in 1851 by one of the supporters of William Lyon Mackenzie's 1837 rebellion. True, David Gibson's original home was burned to the ground by anti-Mackenzie men while the surveyor was off in a decade-long exile in the United States (during which time he assisted in constructing the Erie Canal), but when he returned to Toronto, he built this. Men and women in 19th-century costumes demonstrate the cooking and crafts of the pioneers. ⊠ *5172 Yonge St., about 1½ km (1 mi) north of Sheppard Ave. and Hwy. 401,* ☎ *416/395–7432.* ⊒ *$2.50.* ☉ *Tues.–Fri. 9:30–5, weekends noon–5; also open Mon. holidays.*

Humber Valley Parkland. This park stretches along the Humber River ravine, from north of the city limits (Steeles Avenue) down to where the Humber flows quietly into Lake Ontario, not far from High Park (☞ Southwest Toronto, *above*). It's well worth a hiking/jogging/biking tour.

⑯ **Kortright Centre.** This delightful conservation center, only 15 minutes north of the city and just a groundhog's shadow away from ☞ **Paramount Canada's Wonderland,** holds three aquariums and more than 16 km (10 mi) of hiking trails through forest, meadow, river, and marshland. During the winter, some of the trails are reserved for cross-country skiing (bring your own skis or snowshoes and dress warmly). In the magnificent woods, there have been spottings of foxes, coyotes, rabbits, deer, wild turkeys, pheasants, chickadees, finches, and blue jays. Seasonal events include a winter carnival, spring maple syrup festival, and Christmas craft fair. ⊠ *9550 Pine Valley Dr., Woodbridge (drive north along Hwy. 400, exit west at Major Mackenzie Dr., continue 1.9 mi to Pine Valley Dr., then turn left),* ☎ *905/832–2289.* ⊒ *$5.* ☉ *Daily 10–4.*

★ ⑱ **McMichael Canadian Art Collection.** Set on 100 acres of lovely woodland in Kleinburg, 30 km (19 mi) northwest of downtown Toronto, the McMichael is the only major gallery in the country with the mandate to collect Canadian art exclusively. The museum holds impressive works by Tom Thomson, Emily Carr, and the Group of Seven landscape painters (as well as their contemporaries) from the turn of the century. These artists were inspired by the wilderness and sought to capture it in bold, original styles. First Nations art and prints, drawings, and sculpture by Inuit artists are well represented. Strategically placed windows help you appreciate the scenery as you view art that took its inspiration from the vast outdoors; inside, wood walls and fireplace set a country mood. ✉ *10365 Islington Ave., west of Hwy. 400 and north of Major Mackenzie Dr., Kleinburg,* ☎ *905/893–1121.* ✑ *$7.* ☉ *May–Oct., daily 10–5; Nov.–Apr., Tues.–Sat. 10–4, Sun. 10–5.*

☝ ⑰ **Paramount Canada's Wonderland.** Yogi Bear, Fred Flintstone, and Scooby Doo are part of this theme park (it was Canada's first) filled with games, rides, restaurants, and shops. Entertainment ranges from pop and rock musical performances to sea lion shows. The season runs from May to Labor Day (plus a few weekends either side of the main season). The park is close to Toronto—barely 30 minutes from downtown by car or special GO Transit bus.

Attractions include Kidzville, home of the Rugrats; "A License to Thrill," with secret agent James Bond in the Paramount F/X Theatre; and the Top Gun looping inverted jet coaster. Splash Works, a 20-acre water park, has an outdoor wave pool called Whitewater Bay; the Black Hole, a fully enclosed water thrill slide; and a children's interactive water play area. Other draws are strolling Star Trek characters, Paramount Studio Store and memorabilia, cliff divers, minigolf, and batting cages. The high-quality **Kingswood Music Theatre** (☎ 905/832–8131) has excellent pop and rock acts through the summer. There are 7,000 reserved seats under a covered pavilion and 8,800 additional seats on the sloping lawn.

The park can run up to $38 per adult if you take all the rides (except "pay as you play" rides); call for information about the day and season passes that are available and check newspapers, chain stores, and hotels for special discount tickets. ✉ *9580 Jane St.,* ☎ *905/832–7000 information; 416/870–8000 tickets.* ✑ *$22 for grounds admission without rides.* ☉ *May–Labor Day, daily from 10 AM; Labor Day–2nd Mon. in Oct, weekends from 10 AM; closing time varies.*

☝ ⑮ **Wild Water Kingdom.** The largest park of its kind in Canada, Wild Water Kingdom has huge water slides, river rapids, giant outdoor hot tubs, a fantastic wave pool, and a delightful area for younger children to splash around in. Right next to it is a sports complex, Emerald Green, which has miniature golf, batting cages, and more. ✉ *Finch Ave. W and Hwy. 427,* ☎ *905/794–0565.* ✑ *$17.* ☉ *Water park June–Labor Day, daily 10–8; minigolf Apr.–Oct., daily 10–8.*

NORTHEAST TORONTO

Consisting mostly of upper-middle-class residences, this suburban area is popular for its parks and ravines, as well as for the Toronto Zoo and the David Dunlap Observatory. Most of the sights in this part of town can be reached by public transit, but not as easily as those in some parts of the city; you'll have to build in a lot of time if you don't have a car.

TIMING

Plan on spending between a couple of hours and a half day at each of the sights in Northeast Toronto. The grounds of Edward's Gardens are a pleasant place to pass an hour wandering through the well-designed landscape and watching newlyweds have their photos taken. If you have a bike, take a nice half-day ride from Edward's Gardens south to the lake. Sherwood Park deserves a half hour to an hour; from here you can also walk or bike to the lake. Another good spot for biking, jogging, and even cross-country skiing is the Highland Creek Ravine. The sprawling Toronto Zoo is a good place to spend a morning or afternoon, especially if you have kids. Save a couple of hours on Saturday night from mid-April to late September for stargazing at the David Dunlap Observatory.

Numbers in the margin correspond to points of interest on the Metropolitan Toronto map.

Sights to See

㉑ David Dunlap Observatory. Constructed in 1935, this research facility is both a photo gallery of things astronomical, featuring sunspots, nebulae, and galaxies, and the largest observatory in Canada—only 24 km (15 mi) north of downtown. Visitors eight years and older are admitted for educational lectures on Wednesday mornings year-round and for stargazing on Saturday nights from mid-April to late September. You can also climb a ladder and peek through the 25-ton telescope to see the planet, star, or moon that is "playing" that night. It can get chilly under the unheated dome, even in midsummer, so dress warmly for your close encounter. From downtown Toronto it takes about an hour by car or mass transit to get here. ⌧ *123 Hillsview Dr.,* ☏ *905/ 884–2112.* ⌧ *Wed. lecture free; evening viewing sessions $2.50; no children under 8 admitted.* ⊙ *Lecture/tour Wed. 10–11:30 AM; stargazing mid-Apr.–late Sept., Sat. nights from ½ hr after sunset.*

★ ☝ **㉓ Edward's Gardens.** The beautiful 35-acre Edward's Gardens (once the private enclave of industrialist Rupert Edwards) flow into one of the city's most visited ravines. Paths wind along colorful floral displays and exquisite rock gardens. Refreshments and picnic facilities are available, but no pets are allowed. A new "teaching garden" helps children learn the pleasures to be found in a garden. For a great ravine walk, start out at the entrance of Edward's Gardens (southwest corner of Leslie Street and Lawrence Avenue East) and head south through **Wilket Creek Park** and the winding Don River valley. Pass beneath the Don Valley Parkway and continue along Massey Creek. After hours of walking (or biking, or jogging) through almost uninterrupted parkland, you'll end up at the southern tip of **Taylor Creek Park** on Victoria Park Avenue, just north of the Danforth. From here you can catch a subway back to your hotel. ⌧ *Entrance at southwest corner of Leslie St. and Lawrence Ave. E.*

㉚ Highland Creek Ravine. The ravines at Highland Creek are considered the most beautiful in Toronto. They are ideal for cross-country skiing, biking, and jogging. Both **Colonel Danforth Park** and **Morningside Park** follow Highland Creek. The **Colonel Danforth Trail** begins south of Kingston Road, on the east side of Highland Creek bridge, and Morningside Park is accessible off Morningside Avenue, between Kingston Road and Ellesmere Avenue. ⌧ *Parks can be entered from the grounds of Scarborough College, 1265 Military Trail.*

㉔ Sherwood Park. This park is one of the best-kept secrets in Toronto: It has one of the finest children's playgrounds in the city, a lovely wading pool, and a hill that seems to go on forever. A ravine begins at the bottom of the hill; you can follow it across Blythwood Road, all the way to Yonge Street and Lawrence Avenue. There, subways and buses await you—as do the beautiful rose gardens in **Alexander Muir Park.** Or walk or bike southeast to **Sunnybrook Park,** then head south along the ravine to the lake (13 km, or 8 mi). ⌧ *Near Lawrence Ave. E. and Mount Pleasant Rd.*

★ ☝ **㉒ Toronto Zoo.** With its varied terrain, from river valley to dense forest, the Rouge Valley was an inspired choice of site for this 710-acre zoo, in which mammals, birds, reptiles, and fish are grouped according to their natural habitats. In the enclosed, climate-controlled pavilions you'll also find botanical exhibits, such as the Africa pavilion's giant baobab tree. The Events Guide distributed at the Main Entrance will help you plan your day. The "Around the World Tour" takes approximately three hours and includes the **Africa, Americas, Australasia,** and **Indo-Malayan pavilions.** The Zoomobile (seasonal operation) glides silently through the outdoor exhibit area without disturbing the animals. A daily program of special events provides opportunities to chat with animal keepers and watch animal and bird demonstrations. Coming with kids? You'll want to visit the **Children's Web** (seasonal attraction) to see displays including "Backyard Bugs," "Backyard Pond," and "Butterfly Garden." This area also has a playground and pony rides. Camel rides are also offered in the zoo's **Marco Polo area** (June–September, daily; October–May, weekends and holidays only). The **African Savanna** is the country's finest walking safari, a dynamic reproduction of "big-game" country that brings rare and beautiful animals and distinctive geological features to the city's doorstep. You can also dine in the Savanna's Safari Lodge and camp overnight in the Bush Camp (reservations required). ⊠ *Meadowvale Rd. north of Hwy. 401, 30-min drive from downtown, or take Bus 86A from Kennedy subway station,* ☎ *416/392–5900.* 🎟 *$12; parking $5 (free Nov.–Feb.)* ☉ *Summer 9–7:30; winter 9:30–4:30.*

SOUTHEAST TORONTO

Longtime residents mix with recent immigrants in urbanized Southeast Toronto, which is well served by public transit from downtown. Ethnic neighborhoods include The Danforth (also known as Greektown) as well as an Indian community, concentrated along Gerard Street East near Greenwood Avenue. Also worth a visit in the vicinity of The Danforth is the Todmorden Mills Historic Site, where you can see a number of the city's oldest buildings. A boardwalk, in The Beaches, and a series of parks flank Lake Ontario in this part of town. The impressive Ontario Science Centre, at the area's northern boundary, could also be combined with a visit to some of the sights in Northeast Toronto.

TIMING

To see the sights in Southeast Toronto you'll need to set aside anywhere from one hour to at least half a day for each, depending on your interests. An afternoon or evening could easily be spent in The Danforth, which has lots of shops, restaurants, cafés, bars, and an active streetlife. You might not need as much time in the Indian community, which is a place to go for a specific reason—to buy hard-to-find foods or to eat out, for example. The Todmorden Mills Historic Site is a good spot for a picnic lunch, followed by an hour viewing some of the old, restored buildings. If you're interested in birds, head for Tommy Thompson Park on Lake Ontario for an hour or two of bird-watching. You could easily connect a visit to the park with an afternoon trip to The Beaches; from The Beaches, take the paved Martin Goodman Trail to the park or drive out to Scarborough Bluffs for a more dramatic view of the lake. Two hours is just enough to scratch the surface at the Ontario Science Centre; you may want to go for an entire day.

Numbers in the margin correspond to points of interest on the Metropolitan Toronto map.

Sights to See

28 **The Beaches.** Known either as The Beach or The Beaches, the charming section east of downtown has attracted tens of thousands of people drawn to the chance to live in a small town that has easy access to Toronto via public transport and even easier access to Lake Ontario. The area is bounded by Kingston Road to the north, the Greenwood

Raceway to the west, Victoria Park Avenue to the east, and the lake to the south. It's easy to spend an afternoon strolling the delightful, safe, and (in summer) often crowded boardwalk, graced by huge, shady trees. Other options are taking a dip in the free Olympic-size Somerville Pool at Woodbine Avenue or window shopping on Queen Street East (☞ Chapter 7).

A soldier from London, Joseph Williams, first settled the area in 1853, having arrived in Toronto with the 2nd Battalion Rifle Brigade five years earlier. His 25-acre grant was named Kew Farms, after London's Kew Gardens, and it was there that he raised vegetables, selling them at the St. Lawrence Market on Saturday mornings. When Williams chose to turn his property into a park in 1879, he naturally called it Kew Gardens. The youngest son of the *paterfamilias,* named Kew Williams, built a handsome house of stone with a circular staircase and a tower. Today it serves as home to the park's keeper.

This part of town was soon flooded by hundreds of hot and sticky Torontonians attracted by the advertisements for "innocent amusements" and the prohibition of "spirituous liquors." The cottages that once stood on the lakeshore vanished with the waves in 1932, at which time Kew Gardens, Scarborough Beach Park, and Balmy Beach became one large park called Kew Beach Park. But on a leisurely walk along the thoroughfares that run north from the lake to Queen Street, you'll still find hundreds of New England–style clapboard-and-shingle houses, often standing next door to formal stucco mansions in the Edwardian tradition.

㉗ The Danforth. This area along Danforth Avenue is a dynamic ethnic mix, although it is primarily a Greek community. Once English-settled (although it was named after Asa Danforth, an American contractor who cut a road in the area back in 1799), the neighborhood is now Italian, Greek, East Indian, Latin American, and, increasingly, Chinese. But a large percentage of the 120,000 Greek Canadians in metropolitan Toronto live here, and the area is still referred to as Greektown. Late-night taverns, all-night fruit markets, and some of the best ethnic restaurants in Toronto abound. Since 1982, 50 English/Greek street signs have been installed.

★ ☺ ㉕ **Ontario Science Centre.** It has been called a museum of the 21st century, but it's much more than that. Where else can you stand at the edge of a black hole, work hand-in-clamp with a robot, or land on the moon? Even the building itself is extraordinary. Three linked pavilions float gracefully down the side of a ravine and overflow with exhibits that make space, technology, and communications fascinating. A dozen theaters show films that bring the natural world to life. Live demonstrations—lasers, glassblowing, papermaking, electricity, and more—take place regularly throughout the day; check the schedule when you arrive at the museum. The Human Body, the Information Highway, and the Sport Show are major newer exhibits, and the domed Omnimax theater (separate charge) shows films on subjects from deep space to deep science. You need at least two hours to scratch the surface; you may want to spend an entire day. Children will love this place, probably more than any other in Toronto, but most adults will be intrigued, too. The museum has a cafeteria, a restaurant, and a gift store with a cornucopia of books and scientific doodads. ⊠ *770 Don Mills Rd.; Yonge St. subway from downtown to Eglinton station and Eglinton East bus to Don Mills Rd. stop,* ☎ *416/429–4100; 416/696–3127 recording.* ▣ *$10; parking $5.* ☉ *Daily 10–5; extended evening hrs in summer.*

㉙ Scarborough Bluffs. This is the most scenic of the bluff parks along Lake Ontario in the southeastern part of Toronto. It affords wonderful vistas, as does **Cathedral Bluffs** at its western edge. ✉ *From downtown take Kingston Rd. east, past Midland, and right on Brimley Rd.*

㉖ Todmorden Mills Historic Site. Bring a picnic to this open parkland, where a number of the city's oldest buildings have been restored on their original sites. Among the structures built by the English settlers are two pioneer houses, a brewery (1821), a paper mill (1825), and the old Don Train Station (1891), designed to serve two once-great railroads, the Canadian National and Canadian Pacific. ✉ *67 Pottery Rd., just off the Bayview Ave. Extension,* ☎ *416/396–2819.* ▦ *$2.25.* ☉ *May–Sept., Tues.–Fri. 10–4:30, weekends and holidays noon–5; Oct.–Dec., weekdays 10–4.*

㉛ Tommy Thompson Park. Known until 1985 as the Leslie Street Spit, the park comprises a peninsula that juts 5 km (3 mi) into Lake Ontario. It was created from the sand dredged for a new port of entry and the landfill of a hundred skyscrapers. It has quickly become one of the best areas in the city for cycling, jogging, walking, sailing, photography, and, especially, bird-watching: The strange, man-made peninsula is home (or stopover) to the largest colony of ring-billed seagulls in the world and for dozens of species of terns, ducks, geese, and snowy egrets. To get here, go east along Queen Street to Leslie Street, then south to the lake. No private vehicles are permitted, but on weekends, mid-May to early October, two vans operate free of charge from the main gate. ✉ *Leslie St.,* ☎ *416/392–8186.* ☉ *Mid-May–early Oct., weekends and holidays 9–6.*

3 Dining

Canada may be a commonwealth country, but don't think British when it comes to Toronto's eateries: Starchy pub food has become a thing of the past. New Canadian cooking means fresh local ingredients put together in delightfully creative ways. And Toronto's melting-pot character means an abundance of ethnic restaurants—especially Italian and Asian—to choose from.

THE TORONTO RESTAURANT SCENE is in a state of perpetual motion. The economy, reluctant no longer, surges forward. Meeting the demands of a savvy dining public, new restaurants are opening at a vigorous rate, making the search for that elusive, perfect restaurant a simpler task.

By Sara Waxman

Even formal haute cuisine establishments, which had all but faded into Toronto's gastronomic history, are experiencing a renaissance, joining the ever-swelling ranks of bistros, cantinas, tavernas, trattorias, tapas bars, noodle bars, wine bars, and smart cafés. Red meat is making a comeback, and along with steak houses have come cigar and martini lounges. Meanwhile, the cuisines of the world have appeared on Toronto's doorstep. Recipes need no passports to cross borders. Little Italy, a half dozen individual Chinatowns, urban and suburban, Little India, and, of course, the cooking of Southeast Asia—a tidal wave of Korean, Vietnamese, Laotian, Thai, and Malaysian restaurants—are taking our taste buds by storm with their assertive, clean flavors: chili, ginger, lemongrass, coconut, lime, and tamarind.

Toronto's brilliant young chefs recognize that when most customers start requesting "sauce on the side," the public's collective taste is changing; those with a vision are looking over their shoulders toward California and Asia for a more creative marriage of fresh market ingredients.

Smoking is prohibited in most Toronto restaurants. If this is important to you, call to check on the status of the law.

Servers expect 15% tip on the pre-tax bill. An easy formula is GST (7%) plus PST (8%) equals tip (15%). There's no need to tip on the total after-tax bill.

Unless noted below, dress in Toronto is casual but neat. In the more elegant and/or expensive restaurants, men are likely to feel more comfortable wearing a jacket.

CATEGORY	COST*
$$$$	over $40
$$$	$30–$40
$$	$20–$30
$	under $20

*per person, in Canadian dollars, for a three-course meal, excluding drinks, service, and 15% sales tax (7% GST plus 8% PST)

American/Casual

$$$ ✕ **Cities.** While some kitchens just play, this tiny café creates symphonies in a space with brown paper–covered tables and hand-painted walls hung with the works of local artists. There's never an empty seat in the place. What gives? Appetizers like whole tomatoes with balls of *bocconcini* (fresh mozzarella) on leafy lettuce and fresh sautéed mangoes with goat cheese are the draws. The menu always has a vegetarian entrée, besides an ever-changing variety of main courses: free-range chicken breast, lamb chops, witty pairings of grilled fruits and vegetables. ✉ *859 Queen St. W, ☎ 416/504–3762. Reservations essential. AE, DC, MC, V. No lunch Sat.–Mon.*

$–$$ ✕ **Marché.** This Old World market square in a downtown office tower ★ is really a self-service restaurant. Herbs grow in pots; fresh fruits and vegetables are piled high; an enormous snowbank holds bright-eyed fish and fresh seafood; fresh pasta spews from pasta makers, ready to be cooked to order. A rotisserie roasts lacquer-crisp game birds and

60

Metropolitan Toronto Dining

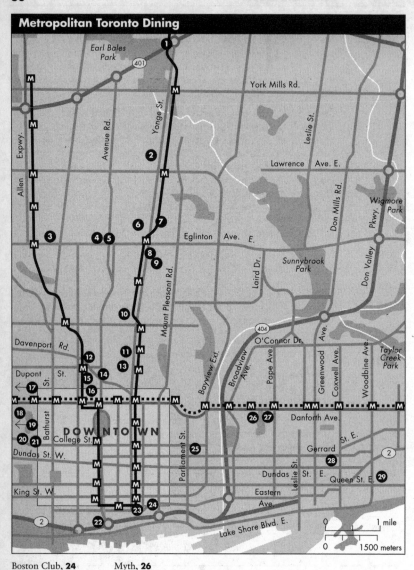

Boston Club, **24**
Centro, **6**
Chiado, **21**
Cuisine of India, **1**
Edo, **5**
Future Bakery &
Café, **17**
Giovanna, **20**
Grano, **9**
Herbs, **2**
House of Chan, **3**
Il Fornello, **10, 29**
Joso's, **14**
Le Paradis, **12**
Lolita's Lust, **27**
Madras Express
Cafe, **28**
Mandarin, **8**
Mistura, **15**

Myth, **26**
North 44, **7**
Pastis, **11**
Provence, **25**
Shopsy's, **23**
Sotto Sotto, **16**
Southern Accent, **18**
Thai Magic, **13**
360 Revolving
Restaurant, **22**
Trattoria
Giancarlo, **19**
Vanipha Lanna, **4**

European sausages. Bread and croissants are baked before your eyes, and pizza is prepared to order. Pick up a shopping "credit card" and a tray and stroll through the marketplace, choosing as much or as little as you want. This high-concept, low-price dining adventure is open Wednesday–Saturday 7:30 AM–2 AM and Sunday–Tuesday 7:30 AM–1 AM; there are smaller versions all over town. ⊠ *BCE Place, 42 Yonge St., Yonge and Wellington Sts.,* ☎ *416/366–8986. Reservations not accepted. AE, DC, MC, V.*

$–$$ ✕ **Masquerade Caffè Bar.** An eclectic array of primary-color furnishings, stoves, and Murano glass mosaics fills this Fellini-esque environment. The daily-changing Italian menu lists a variety of risottos, divine ravioli, and a choice of *panini*—Italian sandwiches on homemade breads with scrumptious meat, cheese, and veggie fillings. Zabaglione, whipped to a thick, frothy cream and poured over fresh berries, is a knockout dessert. ⊠ *BCE Place, Front and Yonge Sts.,* ☎ *416/363–8971. Reservations not accepted. AE, DC, MC, V. Closed Sun.*

$–$$ ✕ **7 West Cafe.** Three creative young women have converted a narrow row house into a 24-hour haven for the hip and hungry. It's surprising how many people hunger for pasta primavera, vegetarian chili, or a bagel melt at 3 AM. Everything comes with a green salad, and every item is homemade. Soups like Moroccan lentil, carrot, and potato-leek are delicious. Pasta salad is fresh and yummy, and dinner-size sandwiches (grilled honey and herb chicken breast, for example) are huge. The chic antipasto/wine bar on the main floor is very trendy. ⊠ *7 Charles St. W,* ☎ *416/928–9041. MC, V.*

Barbecue

$–$$ ✕ **Red Devil.** Where there's smoke, there's barbecue. Almost everything on the vast menu of this generous, good family restaurant has a hint of the smoky great outdoors—wood-roasted Portobello mushroom salad; roasted garlic Caesar salad textured with crunchy bacon. Cutlery is wrapped in colored dish towels that, unrolled, make nice absorbent napkins, a necessity when digging into a mess of Bad-to-the-Bone ribs: barbecued, mustard-glazed, jalapeño pepper–crusted, and smoked prime rib bones. Other choices are smokin' chicken, steak, and shrimp. The waiters know their p's and bbq's. ⊠ *14 Duncan St.,* ☎ *416/598–5209. AE, DC, MC, V.*

Cafés

$ ✕ **Future Bakery & Café.** A European-style bakery has blossomed into a small chain of cafeterias supplied by their own dairy. Old European recipes have remained: beef borscht, buckwheat cabbage rolls, and potato cheese *varenycky* slathered with thick sour cream. This place is beloved by students for its generous portions, by homesick Europeans hungry for goulash and knishes, by the cheesecake-and-coffee crowd, by health-conscious foodies looking for fruit salad with homemade yogurt and honey, and by people-watchers looking for people worth watching from 7 AM to 2 AM. ⊠ *483 Bloor St. W,* ☎ *416/922–5875;* ⊠ *2199 Bloor St. W,* ☎ *416/769–5020;* ⊠ *739 Queen St. W,* ☎ *416/504–8700;* ⊠ *St. Lawrence Market, 95 Front St. E,* ☎ *416/366–7259. Reservations not accepted. MC, V.*

Cajun/Creole

$$–$$$$ ✕ **Southern Accent.** This funky Cajun-style restaurant fits hand in glove with its neighbors on a street born for browsing, chockablock with antiques shops, bookstores, and galleries. You can perch at the bar, order a martini and hush puppies, and look around. Whimsical

62

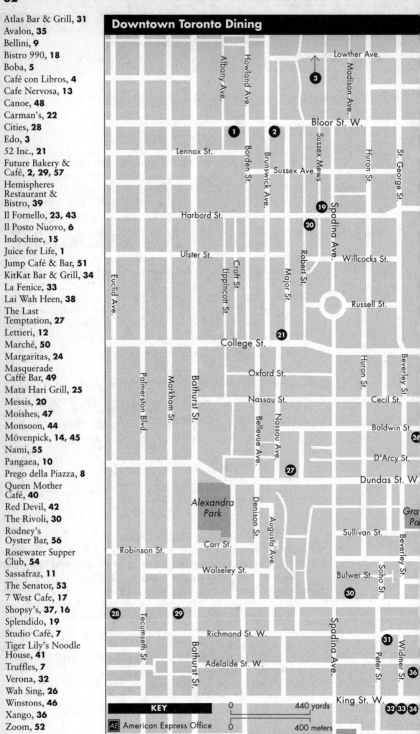

Downtown Toronto Dining

KEY

AE American Express Office

0   440 yards
0   400 meters

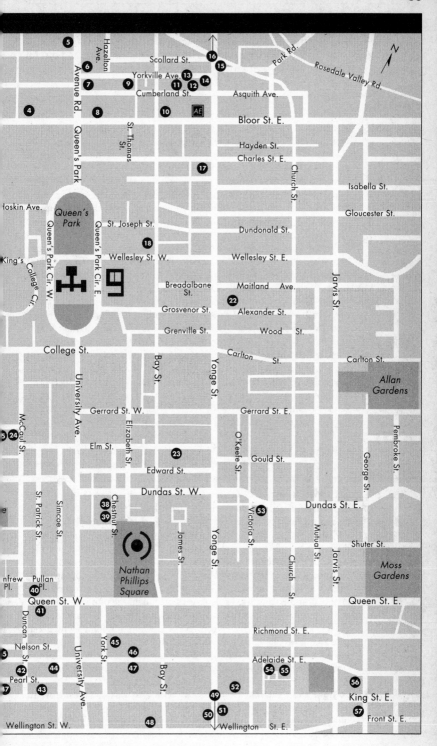

knickknacks adorn every inch of the place. One flight up, the dining room offers a changing, market-fresh menu. Fortunately, bayou chicken, southern fried with dark and spicy sauce; cracker catfish (a fillet coated with spiced crackers) served with swamp lime tartar sauce; and shrimp étouffee with carmelized vegetables are constants. ⊠ *595 Markham St.,* ☎ *416/536–3211. AE, DC, MC, V. No lunch.*

Canadian

$$$$ ✕ **Canoe.** A delicious homage to regional foods is sifted through the world's finest cuisines. There's a breathtaking view of the Toronto Islands and Lake Ontario from the huge windows on the 54th floor of the Toronto Dominion Bank Tower. Some inspirational dishes here are lobster baked in potato skin, glazed with aged cheddar, and Québec foie gras with roasted potatoes, grilled duck livers, late-harvest Riesling dressing, and quince jam. Canadiana courses through the menu with entrées like herb-stuffed breast of Ontario pheasant on spaetzle with roasted apples. The adventurous meat eater might enjoy roast hind of Yukon caribou with wild-mushroom celeriac and corn-bread cobbler. Vegetarian and spa dishes are also available. ⊠ *Toronto-Dominion Center, 66 Wellington St. W, 54th floor,* ☎ *416/364–0054. Reservations essential. AE, DC, MC, V. Closed weekends.*

$$$$ ✕ **360 Revolving Restaurant.** A glassed-in bridge and a glass elevator carry you to the top of the tallest freestanding structure in the world. In the distance are New York State and the twinkling lights of Niagara Falls. The curved leather booths and windowside tables circle the core, which holds the kitchen and the award-winning Wine Cellar in the Sky. The menu is unabashedly Canadian. The kitchen blackens quails and sautées them with preserved kumquats for an intense orange glaze. Scallops in the shell are steamed in a roasted garlic and white wine bath. Rack of lamb is crusted with fresh herbs, garlic, and peppers and paired with wild rice. You can even try locally farmed ostrich steaks. ⊠ *CN Tower, 301 Front St. W,* ☎ *416/362–5411. Reservations essential. AE, DC, MC, V.*

Chinese

$$$–$$$$ ✕ **Lai Wah Heen.** For Cantonese culinary fireworks, phone and pre-order ★ Lustrous Peacock. When it arrives, an explosion of white vapor reveals an arrangement of melon, barbecued duck, chicken, honeyed walnuts, and more exotic ingredients. The mahogany-color lacquer-crisp Peking duck is wheeled in on a trolley, where it is sliced and diced and presented with panache. Some excellent choices from the 100-dish inventory are wok-fried shredded beef and vegetables in a crisp potato nest; fillet of sole done two ways—steamed with asparagus and fenced in by crisply crumbed and fried sole fingers. At lunch, the dim sum is divine: translucent dumplings and pouches bursting with juicy fillings of shark's fin sprinkled with bright red lobster roe; shrimp dumplings with green tops that look like baby bok choy; and more. The service is French, in an elegant room with a sculptured ceiling, etched-glass turntables, and silver serving dishes. ⊠ *Metropolitan Hotel, 118 Chestnut St., 2nd floor,* ☎ *416/977–9899. Reservations essential. AE, DC, MC, V.*

$–$$ ✕ **Tiger Lily's Noodle House.** Many come to this clean and bright hand-painted café for real egg rolls and shrimp- and spinach-dumpling-like pot stickers in a light lemony sauce. But most people come for the noodles, cooked in many ways and combinations: Hawaiian duck long-rice soup, redolent with coconut lemongrass, plump with chicken and seafood, is one option. Soups include noodles, wontons, meat or vegetable broth, and garnishes of barbecued pork, Shanghai chicken, or veggies. If you want your Chinese food steeped in tradition, not grease, you'll find double happiness here. ✉ *257 Queen St. W,* ☎ *416/977–5499. AE, MC, V.*

$–$$ ✗ **Wah Sing.** Just one of a jumble of Asian restaurants clustered together on a tiny Kensington Market street, this meticulously clean and spacious restaurant has two-for-the-price-of-one lobsters (in season, which is almost always). With black bean sauce or ginger and green onion, they're scrumptious and tender. You can choose giant shrimps Szechuan-style or one of the lively queen crabs from the tank. Chicken and vegetarian dishes for landlubbers are good, too. ✉ *47 Baldwin St.,* ☎ *416/599–8822. AE, MC, V.*

$ ✗ **Mandarin.** Diners may be weak in the knees at the sight of the smorgasbord of Chinese food. The options are endless: First, heap your plate with salad bar selections and large shrimp in the shell, and then attack the hot and sour soup, the wonton soup, or both. The food has no MSG, no preservatives. Eager to please, the servers explain each dish and invite you to come back for seconds of honey garlic ribs, deep-fried shrimp and chicken wings, breaded chicken, spring rolls, sweet and sour dishes, chicken curry, mixed vegetables, seafood stir-fries, and more—even sliced beef with gravy and roast potatoes. Desserts include tarts, cookies, and ice cream. ✉ *2200 Yonge St.,* ☎ *416/486–2222. AE, DC, MC, V.*

Contemporary

$$$$ ✗ **Centro.** Massive columns, a bright blue ceiling, salmon-color walls
★ lined with comfortable banquettes, and creative lighting turn this vast eatery into intimate spaces. Owners Tony Longo and award-winning chef Marc Thuet set city standards of excellence. French-Mediterranean style filters through fine regional ingredients in specialties such as terrine of Québec foie gras marinated with Inniskillin ice wine; a duo of fruitwood-smoked Bay of Fundy salmon and Asian cured gravlax is served with sherry-marinated Vidalia onions and Arctic char caviar dressing. The kitchen scores with pan-charred Chilean sea bass and grilled Delft Blue veal chop. Ask about the chef's daily *plat classique* special. Service is urbane, although the noise level is sometimes an obstacle to conversation. ✉ *2472 Yonge St.,* ☎ *416/483–2211. Reservations essential. AE, DC, MC, V. Closed Sun.*

$$$$ ✗ **North 44.** Mirrored sconces hold exotic floral arrangements; a steel compass is embedded in a gorgeous marble floor. This is the place to awaken your taste buds with appetizers of hot smoked Arctic char with mustard-seed crust and potato parfait or panfried oysters with cornmeal nut crust. Just try to choose from owner-chef Marc McEwen's creative alchemy, found in his seven-page menu. Exciting main courses are center-cut veal chop with toasted rosemary peppercorn crust, or oven-roasted striped sea bass with black bean sauce and shrimp dumplings. Pasta and pizzas are other options, and 50 wines sold by the glass complement every dish. North 44 is noisy but fun. ✉ *2537 Yonge St.,* ☎ *416/487–4897. AE, DC, MC, V. Closed Sun. No lunch.*

$$$$ ✗ **Truffles.** Through the impressive wrought-iron gates of Truffles,
★ pale wood walls glow in the reflected soft light of handcrafted candelabra. This restaurant has won the hearts of discerning gastronomes with dishes like date and goat cheese wrapped in *brique* (pastry) leaves, spaghettini with Périgord black truffles, a splendid sautéed lobster flambéed with vodka, and triumphant poached and braised veal tournedos. Leave room for esoteric desserts including mocha soufflé and baked bosc pear with ivory Bavarian cream. Patrick Lin is the new chef at one of the finest restaurants in Canada. ✉ *Four Seasons Hotel, 21 Avenue Rd.,* ☎ *416/928–7331. Reservations essential. AE, DC, MC, V. Closed Sun. No lunch.*

$$$-$$$$ ✕ **Avalon.** A narrow marble staircase opens to Avalon's pretty, understated dining room, where loaves of bread on an ancient butcher block table share space with a lush bouquet. You can start with three large plump sardines, the fresh, oceanic, saltwater scent still hovering, grilled over a wood fire till the exact moment when flesh lifts easily from bone. They are accompanied by a unique salad of string-cut celery root, nubbins of green olives, and subtly citric preserved lemon. The triumph of the mixed grill is Ontario lamb loin chop, tenderloin, and kidneys. Wood-roasted half chicken, fresh minced basil leaves stuffed under the crisp, golden skin, is simplicity itself. ⊠ *270 Adelaide St. W,* ☎ *416/979–9918. Reservations essential. AE, DC, MC, V. Closed Sun.–Mon. No lunch Tues., Sat.*

$$$-$$$$ ✕ **Boba.** Owners Bob Bermann and Barbara Gordon (Boba) are a sophisticated culinary couple who cook in a charming brick house personalized with robust and gorgeous color. The dishes they've dreamed up are original and delicious: Rice paper–wrapped chicken breast on Thai black rice and big-eye tuna grilled rare with coconut noodles, mango and avocado salsa, and black bean sauce are favorites, or try the traditional grilled bone-in rib steak with Yukon Gold frites. Vegetable dinners are spontaneously created. The couple's flamboyant presentations bring to mind gourmet chefs at play; Boba also has one of the city's prettiest patios for summer dining. ⊠ *90 Avenue Rd.,* ☎ *416/961–2622. AE, MC, V. No lunch weekdays.*

$$$-$$$$ ✕ **Hemispheres Restaurant & Bistro.** An ordinary hotel facade has been transformed from duckling to beautiful swan by this dazzling restaurant. You can watch the chefs strut their stuff through the window wall of the vast kitchen. Award-winning chef Neal Noble puts an exciting East/West spin on the finest local ingredients: duck breast with preserved plums, miso orange jus, and three-potato terrine. Noble sautées foie gras and black truffle and encases it in crisply deep-fried balls of Japanese bread crumbs. Reconnecting with the Canadian theme, he roasts tenderloin of Manitoba bison and sets it on wildberry risotto. A changing, fresh market menu is consistently witty and surprising. ⊠ *Metropolitan Hotel, 110 Chestnut St.,* ☎ *416/599–8000. Reservations essential. AE, DC, MC, V.*

$$$-$$$$ ✕ **Jump Café & Bar.** Look up through the atrium and you'll see that you're surrounded by towering skyscrapers. A glass wall abuts the interior courtyard, which, from May to September, becomes a vast flower- and fountain-filled patio with a menu of appetizers such as grilled calamari with anchovies, capers, and olives. Chef Herbert Barnsteiner roasts honeyed rack of lamb with a pumpkinseed crust and presents veal liver with buttermilk mashed potatoes. From 5 to 7, a smartly dressed, downtown office crowd packs the bar. ⊠ *Court Level, Commerce Court East, Yonge and Wellington Sts.,* ☎ *416/363–3400. Reservations essential. AE, DC, MC, V. Closed Sun. No lunch Sat.*

$$$-$$$$ ✕ **Pangaea.** Partners Peter Geary and chef Martin Kouprie use unprocessed, seasonal ingredients and the bounty of produce the world has to offer. Soups are celestial, cream-free compositions; salads are creative constructions. Grilled jumbo quail is paired with Portobello mushrooms and honey lemon vinaigrette; grilled calamari sings and dances with vivacious flavors. Vegetarians will find bliss in this caring kitchen. And, on the other side of the food chain, rack of lamb gets dolled up with sunflower crust, sweet-potato mash, and apple chips. Afternoon tea with all the sweet and savory goodies is a joy for Bloor Street shoppers. The tranquil room has an aura of restrained sophistication. ⊠ *1221 Bay St.,* ☎ *416/920–2323. AE, DC, MC, V.*

$$$-$$$$ ✕ **Rosewater Supper Club.** A historic landmark building with 22-ft-high ceilings, hardwood and marble floors, and thronelike blue velvet banquettes for two is a place to go when you're in the party mood.

In case you want to be welcomed there.

We're here to see that you're always welcomed at establishments everywhere. That's why millions of people carry the American Express® Card – for peace of mind, confidence, and security, around the world or just around the corner.

do more

Cards

In case you're running low.

We're here to help with more than 118,000 Express Cash locations around the world. In order to enroll, just call American Express before you start your vacation.

do more

Express Cash

And just in case.

We're here with American Express® Travelers Cheques and Cheques *for Two.*® They're the safest way to carry money on your vacation and the surest way to get a refund, practically anywhere, anytime.

Another way we help you...

do more ®

Travelers Cheques

The scintillating appetizers and beautifully presented entrées include saffron risotto with leeks, lobster and caviar, and Asian-spiced chicken supreme with sweet chili sauce. Not ready to commit to dinner? A lounge with a baby grand and a slinky torch singer can hold your attention. Or you can play a game of billiards, nibble from a tapas menu, and relax in luxe comfort in the downstairs lounge. ⊠ *19 Toronto St.,* ☎ *416/214–5888. AE, DC, MC, V. Closed Sun. No lunch Sat.*

$$–$$$$ ✕ **Studio Café.** At this well-lit, comfortable café—a combination hotel coffee shop, restaurant, and contemporary glass-and-art gallery—you can have a full Japanese or Canadian breakfast; order nutritionally balanced meals; and indulge in trend-setting dishes such as smoked salmon and sea scallops with angel-hair pasta, and porcini mushroom risotto. The Atlantic cod fish-and-chips and roast leg of lamb with sweet garlic and toasted couscous prove there's something for everyone. Still, the sandwiches, such as hand-carved turkey breast or open-faced lobster salad on grilled brioche, are what draw the gourmets. ⊠ *Four Seasons Hotel, 21 Avenue Rd. (just north of Bloor St.),* ☎ *416/964–0411. AE, DC, MC, V.*

Delicatessen

$–$$ ✕ **Shopsy's.** In 1945, when the three Shopsowitz brothers came into the business started by their parents in 1921, you'd pay 8¢ for a corned-beef sandwich. Today Shopsy's belongs to a food conglomerate, and such a sandwich costs $5.75. The corned beef is always freshly cooked and firm, and piled on fresh rye bread slathered with mustard; there's nothing like it. Soups are satisfying, salads are huge, and hot dogs are legendary. All locations are in the heart of the theater and business district. The deli often has a wait at peak hours. ⊠ *33 Yonge St.,* ☎ *416/365–3333;* ⊠ *1535 Yonge St.,* ☎ *416/967–5252;* ⊠ *284-A King St. W,* ☎ *416/599–5464. AE, DC, MC, V.*

Eclectic

$$$–$$$$ ✕ **Zoom.** Huge white globes traced with letters and symbols that mean something to someone hang from a 21-ft-high ceiling. Glass planets, suns, baubles, and lenses are everywhere; lovely curtains sashed in gold add softness to the hard-edged, steel tables and chairs. The kitchen, as inventive as the setting, ties salmon steaks into rounds with ribbons of leek and fills vegetable blossoms with seasoned goat cheese, creating fancy edible sculptures. Start with chili-rubbed roasted sweetbreads or pumpkin-crusted oysters, and then consider the merits of lobster and scallop paella with olive tapenade or other glitzy choices from a seasonal menu. Zoom isn't everyone's daily bread but part of everyone's fantasy. ⊠ *18 King St. E,* ☎ *416/861–9872. AE, DC, MC, V. Closed Sun. No lunch Sat.*

$$–$$$ ✕ **Messis.** The lights on the romantic patio wink an enticing invitation, in stark contrast to the spare, hard-edged dining room. Penne arrives al dente; its tomato pesto sauce has bite, and its crown of veal medallion and roasted pine nuts is delicious. The textures and flavors of spaghettini with bay scallops, smoked trout, sweet peppers, and snappy snow peas in lemony cream sauce unfurl smoothly. Grilled Atlantic salmon, rich and satisfying as a steak, is elevated on a crop of produce—roasted new potatoes, red and yellow grilled peppers, a chunk of sweet corn, the earthy flavors of chard and spinach. Menus adapt to the seasons. ⊠ *97 Harbord St.,* ☎ *416/920–2186. AE, DC, MC, V. No lunch.*

$$ ✕ **Atlas Bar & Grill.** This restaurant–bar–jazz club–raw bar combines California cool and New York glitz. The main floor bar, with its high grazing tables and savory tapas menu, opens in summer to a vast streetside patio. You can watch it all from a balcony table in the din-

ing room. There is an intensity of flavor to the lobster vegetable spring rolls with mango chutney. Hong Kong barbecue beef burger with watercress and noodle salad fulfills a craving—as does sassy and brassy Tennessee mountain barbecue half-chicken with grilled corn. The fab-u-lous head for the Satellite Lounge on the top floor for cigars and dancing. ✉ *129 Peter St.,* ☎ *416/977–7544. Reservations essential. AE, MC, V. Closed Mon. No lunch weekends.*

$–$$ ✕ **Café con Libros.** In this second-floor hideaway across from the Royal Ontario Museum, heavy oak bookshelves line the walls floor-to-ceiling, spilling over with books on every subject imaginable. The kitchen delivers a divine dish of warm scallop salad tossed with tomatoes, chilies, and herbs. Gnocchi, tossed with sun-dried tomato and pine-nut pesto, is just one of several vegan dishes on the menu. New Zealand lamb is partnered with goat cheese cannelloni, and medallions of beef are finished in a red wine and wild mushroom sauce. You can gaze into your lover's eyes over a fondue (after 10:30 PM) or be surprised by an original copy of *The Table Talk of Samuel Marchbanks* on the shelf behind his head. Wednesday through Saturday, live music adds a Latin element. A $5 donation will buy you any book and help support the Children's Wish Foundation. ✉ *208 Bloor St. W,* ☎ *416/923–6520. AE, MC, V. Closed Sun.*

$–$$ ✕ **Myth.** Both menu and theme in this Greektown restaurant walk a tightrope between garishness and genuine glamour, taking a nontraditional route to the Mediterranean with a detour through California. Perch at the bar and munch on a cold meze platter—a vast assortment of dips with pita, or nibble on a pizza. If table service is more your style, consider an uncomplicated pasta or an adventurous Moroccan chicken with a cumin and coriander infusion. Rack 'em and stack 'em at five pool tables; graze, sip, and mingle. ✉ *417 Danforth Ave.,* ☎ *416/461–8383. AE, DC, MC, V.*

French

$$$$ ✕ **Winstons.** The ceilings are gold leaf, the walls turquoise, the banquettes
★ velvet, in a room that's a vision of luxury. The menu is a gastronomic tour of French haute cuisine. The chef roasts rack of wild boar and loin of fallow deer, and wraps turbot from the English Channel around lobster mousse. Truffles from France and caviar from the Caspian Sea are his garnishes. A dazzler is roast guinea fowl arranged over sautéed spinach, the breast carved on the bone and slightly fanned, the leg meat boned, rolled round fresh herbs, and sliced into pinwheels of brilliant flavor. Two sauces ring the bird, and a shower of wild mushrooms adds earthy elements. Winstons is eloquent yet unpretentious. ✉ *104 Adelaide St. W,* ☎ *416/360–8888. AE, MC, V. Closed Sun. No lunch Sat.*

$$$–$$$$ ✕ **Pastis.** Diners may well feel they're in the south of France as they sit
★ within lush raspberry and violet walls, munching on fresh radishes and slices of baguette and butter, spooning up traditional fish soup with rouille, croutons, and grated cheese. Simply roasted grain-fed chicken is glazed with an intense natural jus and garlic cloves. Cut into four neat sections, it perches on a crisp potato pancake and gives a totally satisfying variety of taste and texture. The adventurous palate will rhapsodize over sweetbreads sautéed with shallots, white wine, and veal jus, paired with a ragout of vegetables. This place could run on the Gallic charm of owners Georges Gurnon and Claude Bouillet alone. ✉ *1158 Yonge St.,* ☎ *416/928–2212. AE, DC, MC, V. Closed Sun.–Mon. No lunch.*

$$–$$$ ✕ **Bistro 990.** A superior kitchen combined with bistro informality is
★ the successful recipe here. Start with traditional pâté maison, slices of smooth chicken liver pâté crusted with coarsely crushed peppercorns and partnered with crunchy green gherkins and plenty of homemade

crutons. Corn-crusted sea bass with artichoke ragout and risotto cake is a treat, and roasted half-chicken with herbed garlic jus crackles with crispness and Provençal flavor. The purist kitchen uses artesian spring water for all stocks and homemade breads. Faux stone walls stenciled with Cocteau-esque designs, sturdily upholstered chairs, and a tiled floor create a sophisticated but comfortable ambience. ⊠ *990 Bay St.,* ☎ *416/921–9990. Reservations essential. AE, DC, MC, V. Closed Sun. No lunch Sat.*

$$–$$$ ✕ **Herbs.** Paintings of lush gardens adorn the walls, while brown
★ butcher paper covers floral-clothed tables. For starters, there's great bread. The plain menu doesn't do justice to what's on the plate. Among the superb appetizers, try the silken liver pâté, seasoned with port and cognac—it comes in a teacup, ringed with fresh figs and garlicky crutons—or gravlax and smoked Arctic char, twirled on a plate with asparagus vinaigrette. Specialties may include roasted pork tenderloin with a glaze of fresh fig and mint, and breast of free-range pheasant roasted with fruits and berries. The *tarte tatin* (caramelized apple cake) will transport you to Paris. The young chef cooks like a dream, but don't expect to eat and run. ⊠ *3187 Yonge St.,* ☎ *416/322–0487. Reservations essential. AE, MC, V. Closed Sun. No lunch Sat.*

$$–$$$ ✕ **Provence.** Whitewashed walls hung with provocative artwork make
★ this pretty villa seem like a little corner of the south of France. In summer the front garden is an especially beautiful place to dine. Fois gras from Québec is prepared in a terrine and served simply, with a small salad of oak-leaf lettuce. Duck confit, preserved in its own fat and then crisped in the oven and presented with seasonal vegetables, is outstanding. Authentic French patisserie like chocolate hazelnut torte or a tarte Tatin of luscious brown caramelized apples on a good pastry crust makes a fine ending. ⊠ *12 Amelia St.,* ☎ *416/924–9901. AE, MC, V.*

$–$$ ✕ **Le Paradis.** It's an authentic French bistro on a budget. Well-traveled university types, writers, actors, and producers from this downtown neighborhood come for the ambience and gently priced wine list. To the staff, all diners are created equal and all get the same casual service. Steak and fries, crisp herb-roasted chicken, and exotic *tajine de volaille* (a Moroccan stew of chicken, prunes, olives, and a shopping list of seasonings) get the creative juices flowing. Pay heed to the daily fixed-price menu. ⊠ *166 Bedford Rd.,* ☎ *416/921–0995. AE, MC, V.*

Indian

$$ ✕ **Cuisine of India.** Civic progress has placed this casual, unassuming restaurant a few blocks away from the magnificent Ford Centre for the Performing Arts. Puffy, crusty, buttery-center *naan* (white-flour flat bread) comes from the depths of the tandoor over. A whole leg of lamb for two, halved chicken breasts, and giant shrimp can all be ordered oven-baked, too. The vegetable dishes are diverse in their seasonings and come with fragrant basmati rice. ⊠ *5222 Yonge St.,* ☎ *416/229–0377. Reservations essential. AE, DC, MC, V.*

Italian

$$$–$$$$ ✕ **Prego della Piazza.** This chic Italian eatery is filled with the who's who of the city's highly visible film and TV industry. The glitterati nibble on carpaccio della casa and arugula with strawberries and indulge in butterfly trout with capers and burnt butter or crisp roast baby chicken with *peperonata* (a mix of onions, garlic, tomatoes, and sweet peppers cooked in olive oil). Daily fresh fish is a treat. Next door at Enoteca della Piazza, a design award–winning wine bar, the hip and cheerful sip wine and nibble on pizza and antipasti. A third separate room is called Black and Blue, a tribute to fine steaks and wines. Upstairs, the lounge is a luxe cigar smoke-easy. Come summer, the outdoor patio is in full bloom in this busy see-and-be-seen spot. ⊠ *150 Bloor St. W,* ☎ *416/920–9900. Reservations essential. AE, DC, MC, V. Closed Sun.*

$$$–$$$$ ✕ **Splendido.** Torontonians love the sophisticated ambience here and
★ respect chef-owner Arpi Magyar's sparkling contemporary menu. Ricotta and potato are coaxed into plump gnocchi and served splashed with lemon butter, Parmesan, cracked pepper, and sage. Veal is the chef's masterpiece: Oven-baked rack set on garlic mashed potatoes comes with fresh horseradish, pesto sauce, sautéed kale, and sun-dried tomato mayonnaise. Casual good taste meets the eye at every turn. The bar is popular for nightcaps. ⊠ *88 Harbord St.,* ☎ *416/929–7788. Reservations essential. AE, DC, MC, V.*

$$–$$$$ ✕ **Bellini.** From the street, it's a few steps down to this comfortable, flower-filled, romantic spot. The beef carpaccio and the warm, herb-crusted goat cheese and grilled eggplant are excellent. Try the veal osso buco with garlic mushroom risotto, or the special Bellini chicken with roasted artichokes, wild mushrooms, and baked polenta. Pasta dishes are the kitchen's pride. Service pampers, and a friendly host greets you at the door. ⊠ *101 Yorkville Ave. W,* ☎ *416/929–9111. AE, DC, MC, V. No lunch.*

$$–$$$$ ✕ **La Fenice.** Luigi Orgera has been serving classic, unself-conscious northern Italian cuisine to the power-lunching business elite for decades, before Italian food was trendy. Whole grilled Arctic char is sensational, presented sizzling on the platter, skin crispy and slicked with extra virgin olive oil. It's then whisked away to be deboned and returned—a luxurious dish for a fish lover. A double-cut, extra thick veal chop is grilled with sage and braised pearl onions. La Fenice offers pure Italian flavor and professional, nonintrusive service. ⊠ *319 King St. W,* ☎ *416/585–2377. AE, DC, MC, V. Closed Sun. No lunch Sat.*

$$–$$$$ ✕ **Mistura.** This place has the buzz that's made it one of the hottest
★ new, modern Italian restaurants in town. Two hip hospitality professionals have come up with an innovative, unclichéd menu in a space that combines comfort with casual luxury. Start with a mix and match of four out of six bruschetta: some choices are grilled radicchio, Gorgonzola, and roasted onion as well as mushroom, eggplant, and roasted garlic. Crispy roast chicken with garlic mashed potatoes and rosemary sauce delights. Grilled turkey breast paillard is a carefully thought-out triumph for calorie counters. Vegetarians will find true happiness here, too. ⊠ *265 Davenport Rd.,* ☎ *416/515–0009. AE, DC, MC, V. Closed Sun. No lunch.*

$$–$$$$ ✕ **Sotto Sotto.** A coal cellar in a turn-of-the-century home was dug out,
★ its stone walls and floor polished, and a restaurant created in what has become a dining oasis for locals and international jet-setters alike. The menu gives a tantalizing tug to the taste buds. Of the 14 pasta dishes, appetizer or main-course size, *orecchiette* (tiny, disk-shape pasta) with a toss of prosciutto, mushrooms, black olives, and fresh tomatoes is a symphony of textures. Gnocchi are made daily. Cornish hen is marinated, pressed, and grilled to juicy brownness; swordfish and fresh fish of the day are beautifully done on the grill. Lots of nooks and corners and flickering candles cast uneven shadows in these charming, cavelike rooms. ⊠ *116-A Avenue Rd.,* ☎ *416/962–0011. AE, DC, MC, V. No lunch.*

$$–$$$ ✕ **Grano.** What started as a bakery and take-out antipasto bar has grown
★ into a cheerful collage of the Martella family's Italy. Come for animated talk, good food, and great bread in lively rooms with faux ancient plaster walls, wooden tables, and bright chairs. Choose, if you can, from 40 delectable vegetarian dishes and numerous meat and fish antipasti. Lucia's homemade gnocchi and ravioli are divine, as is the white chocolate and raspberry pie. ⊠ *2035 Yonge St.,* ☎ *416/440—1986. Reservations essential. AE, DC, MC, V. Closed Sun.*

$$–$$$ ✕ **KitKat Bar & Grill.** This eclectic and eccentric southern Italian eatery is built around a massive tree. A theater-district locale means pre- and post-theater hours are really busy. Choose from window tables in the front, perch at the long bar, enjoy the privacy of an old-fashioned wooden booth, or sit at a picnic table in the rear. Portions are enormous. An antipasto platter for two is a meal; pastas, seafood, roast chicken, and grilled steak are all delectable. Owner Al Carbone welcomes everyone like long-lost family. ⊠ *297 King St. W, ☎ 416/977–4461. AE, DC, MC, V. Closed Sun. No lunch Sat.*

$$ ✕ **Verona.** The kitchen sends over homemade savories as soon as
★ you're seated: diced marinated vegetables in olive oil, lush olive spread, and a basket of fresh breads. You might start with opulent pan-seared sea scallops on truffled asparagus spears with champagne cream, or goat cheese wrapped in prosciutto with marinated eggplant. The kitchen blesses angel-hair pasta with tiger shrimp, scallops, and woodland mushrooms. A specialty is hazelnut-crumbed pork tenderloin. Upstairs, a comfortable lounge served by the same kitchen offers cigars, fine wines, and live music on weekends. ⊠ *335 King St. W, ☎ 416/593–7771. AE, DC, MC, V. Closed Sun. No lunch Sat.*

Japanese

$$–$$$$ ✕ **Edo.** A paint job and a face-lift have given Edo a dramatic new setting. Aficionados of Japanese food will have to stop themselves from ordering everything on the menu, and even the uninitiated will be mesmerized by the intriguing dishes carried by servers, including plates of *yaki kinoko* (grilled mushrooms or thickly sliced eggplant baked to a silken texture with mildly sweet and sour flavors). If soft-shell crab is on the menu, it's a worthy choice. The chef is an artist with sushi and sashimi, but if you can't decide, the set menus will give you a balanced and exciting Japanese meal. ⊠ *359 Eglinton Ave. W, ☎ 416/481–1370; ⊠ 439 Spadina Rd., ☎ 416/482–8973. Reservations essential. AE, DC, MC, V. No lunch at Eglinton Ave. W.*

$$–$$$$ ✕ **Nami.** In this large, attractive restaurant, diners can choose to eat at
★ the sushi bar, in tatami rooms with nontraditional wells under the tables, or at the *robatayaki* (a cooking grill surrounded by an eating counter). The chef douses soft-shell crabs with a special sauce and puts them on the grill. Scallops, shrimp, Atlantic salmon, mackerel, and ocean perch sizzle on skewers. Special dinner combos at a table or booth include soup, salad, tempura, yakitori (skewers of chicken) or a beef or salmon teriyaki dish, rice, and dessert. ⊠ *55 Adelaide St. E, ☎ 416/362–7373. Reservations essential. AE, DC, MC, V. Closed Sun. No lunch Sat.*

Latin

$$$–$$$$ ✕ **Xango.** The beautiful people know that the discreet, red capital X on a black tile is where the action is. A three-tiered rack of appetizers can include "Honduran Fire and Ice" (fresh tuna-loin seviche with coconut chilies and ginger) and fried oysters with sweet plantain, bacon, and spinach. Salvadorean chicken perched on saffron mashed potatoes and sea bass baked on a cedar plank with calamari rice have blasts of flavor. Coco Cabana, a coconut custard, and flan Borracho are dazzling desserts. Upstairs is for tango and tapas fans. ⊠ *106 John St., ☎ 416/593–4407. Reservations essential. AE, MC, V. Closed Sun. No lunch.*

Malaysian

$–$$ ✕ **Mata Hari Grill.** Dusky mauves and plums give this jewel-box interior a calm yet exotic aura, and there's a fresh scent in the room. Sticky rice mixed with shrimp and spices is wrapped in a banana leaf and grilled.

Crackling spring rolls filled with shrimp and jicama arrive with little dishes of hot sweet-and-sour sauce. Satays sizzle with the heat of freshly ground spices: sea scallops and red pepper, marinated beef, and chicken speak eloquently with mysterious Malay-Thai flavors. ✉ *39 Baldwin St.,* ☎ *416/596–2832. Reservations essential. AE, DC, MC, V. Closed Mon. No lunch weekends.*

Pan-Asian

$$–$$$$ ✕ **Monsoon.** A fragrant, eclectic consort of Pan-Asian–inspired cuisine is served in a dining-and-lounge environment with a black-brown color scheme that evokes a serene yet dynamic atmosphere. It's hard to pass up any of the raft of incredible small dishes. Tandoori salmon is wrapped in seaweed and rice paper, painted with miso and sesame, and splashed through hot oil to crisp. A covered ceramic bowl holds wok-steamed mussels in a breathtaking ginger and curry broth. Main courses excite the palate: A whole bamboo-steamed snapper is glazed with a lush sauce of coconut and kaffir lime curry; chicken breast is barbecued, laced with Thai chili, and enhanced with banana-fig curry and water spinach. The ambience here is unsnobbish sophistication. ✉ *100 Simcoe St.,* ☎ *416/ 979–7172. AE, DC, MC, V. Closed Sun. No lunch Sat.*

$–$$ ✕ **Indochine.** A century of French colonization of Vietnam had a great influence on that country's food; India and China have also left an indelible stamp. Appetizers are stunning: Two large west-coast rock oysters on the half shell poach in a bubbling hot sauce of butter, garlic, and shallots, and there's French bread to dip up savory oceanic juices. Chicken *grandmère* cooks in its own clay pot; the server lifts the lid, pours in clear and spicy sauce, mixes it through the chicken and rice, and ladles it onto the plates. Vegetarians go for noodle soups, fragrant with tamarind and lemongrass. Try Vietnamese coffee—a filtered mix of milk, sugar, and strong coffee. ✉ *4 Collier St.,* ☎ *416/922–5840. AE, DC, MC, V. No lunch weekends.*

Patio Dining

At the first sign of warm weather, and until the evenings turn cool in September, Torontonians hit the deck, the patio, the courtyard, and the rooftop terrace. White plastic tables and chairs sprout around every restaurant that has a patch of frontage to call its own.

In summer, Yorkville lives again; Cumberland Park between Avenue Road and Bellair Street bursts into bloom. Wildflowers, an herb garden, fountains, and groves of trees present a one-word invitation: picnic. The surrounding eateries oblige with pizza, deli sandwiches, salads, and gourmet lunches to go. **Sassafraz** (✉ 100 Cumberland St., ☎ 416/ 964–2222) is cool and contemporary. **Lettieri** (✉ 94 Cumberland St., ☎ 416/515–8764) is an Italian café. **Cafe Nervosa** (✉ 75 Yorkville Ave., ☎ 416/961–4642) serves up pizza, pasta, and salads. Don't miss the off-street flower filled terraces of **Il Posto Nuovo** (✉ 148 Yorkville Ave., ☎ 416/968–0469), **Prego della Piazza** (☞ Italian, *above*) and **Boba** (☞ Contemporary, *above*).

The passage to Indian cuisine (Gerrard Street between Coxwell and Victoria Park Avenues) is filled with exciting sights and sounds. Streets are crowded, and everywhere there is food and the scintillating aroma of spices. Sit at an outdoor table at **Madras Express Cafe** (✉ 1438-A Gerrard St., ☎ 416/461–7470) and eat a *masala dosa,* a folded, foot-long, crunchy rice flour pancake filled with potato and mustard seed.

Kensington Market (between Dundas and College streets, west of Spadina Avenue), home to melting pot cuisine, is an area to which immigrants have moved for generations. **The Last Temptation** (⊠ 12 Kensington Ave., ☎ 416/599–2551) is great for spicy roti or fresh fruit salad. **Margaritas** (⊠ 14 Baldwin St., ☎ 416/ 977–5525) is known for great guacamole and fajitas. You can sample Chinese/Thai food at pretty **Mata Hari Grill** (⊠ 39 Baldwin St., ☎ 416/596–2832).

When they're rolling up the sidewalks elsewhere, Greektown (Danforth Avenue between Chester and Jones avenues) is just getting lively. Bouzouki music fills the air, and dozens of Greek restaurants on both sides of the street are filled with night owls nibbling on traditional appetizer platters and warm pita bread. The sidewalk patio of **Lolita's Lust** (⊠ 513 Danforth Ave., ☎ 416/465–1751) is a good place to check out the scene. **Myth** (☞ Eclectic, *above*) has pool as well as a patio.

The Italians have practically invented the art of sipping espresso and watching the world go by. Little Italy (College Street between Euclid Avenue and Shaw Street) is packed with trattorias, wine bars, bistrettos, and traditional pool halls. **Giovanna** (⊠ 637 College Ave., ☎ 416/538–2098) serves great roast chicken with Tuscan bread salad. Tasty grilled meats are favored at **Trattoria Giancarlo** (⊠ 41 Clinton St., ☎ 416/533–9619).

Where's everyone going? The Entertainment District (King Street west of University, Duncan, John, Simcoe, and Peter) teems with suited afterwork crowds seeking an outdoor terrace and a cool drink. If you see an empty table, take it. Queen Street, between University Avenue and Bathurst Street, is filled with Gen-X dining adventure—pizza, sushi, pad thai, tortillas, pasta. **The Rivoli** (⊠ 322 Queen St. W, ☎ 416/596–1908) is a hot spot. The rear garden at the **Queen Mother Café** (⊠ 208 Queen St. W, ☎ 416/598–4719) is a cool place for East/West dishes.

Pizza

$–$$$ ✕ **Il Fornello.** Pizza aficionados especially love Il Fornello's 10-inch, thin-crust pie, baked in a wood-burning oven. Orchestrate your own medley from over 100 traditional and exotic toppings that include braised onion, *cappicola* (spicy Italian sausage), provolone, calamari, eggplant, and anchovies. Pastas, veal dishes, and salads are available, too. Wheat-free pizza crust and dairy-free cappuccino are also on the menu. Customer clamor has prompted the opening of more venues. ⊠ *55 Eglinton Ave. E,* ☎ *416/486–2130;* ⊠ *214 King St. W,* ☎ *416/977–2855;* ⊠ *1560 Yonge St.,* ☎ *416/920–8291;* ⊠ *1968 Queen St. E,* ☎ *416/691–8377;* ⊠ *1218 St. Clair Ave. W,* ☎ *416/658–8511;* ⊠ *35 Elm St.,* ☎ *416/598–1766;* ⊠ *576 Danforth Ave.,* ☎ *416/466–2931. AE, MC, V.*

Portuguese

$$$–$$$$ ✕ **Chiado.** Service is bilingual (Portuguese and English), and the fish are flown in from the Azores and Madeira. French doors lead to polished wood floors, tables set with starched white napery, and plum velvet armchairs. Most days you'll find bluefin tuna, piexe aspado, swordfish, and boca negra, along with monkfish, sardines, squid, and salmon. Traditional Portuguese dishes like *asorda* of seafood, a kind of soufflé, are served from a silver tureen. There's much for meat eaters to enjoy, too: beef tenderloin blessed with a wild-mushroom tawny port sauce, and roasted rack of lamb that sparkles with Duoro wine sauce. ⊠ *864 College St. W,* ☎ *416/538–1910. Reservations essential. AE, DC, MC, V. Closed Sun.*

Seafood

$$$–$$$$ ✕ **Boston Club.** The sophisticated ambience of the dining room evokes a realistic Beacon Hill look that is matched with an authentic New En-

gland kitchen. Pewter fixtures, candlelight, and a pianist at a polished baby grand set the tone. For pre- or post-theater noshing, the lounge is glowing and gorgeous. You can ask for the specials or start with an array of fine raw and prepared seafood for two. Follow with Vermont cheddar cheese soup (made with six-year-old cheddar) or clam chowder plump with littlenecks, razor clams, nubbins of smoky bacon, and potatoes. Main courses include a whole panfried flounder, crackercrumbed scrod, or lamb London broil. ⊠ *4 Front St. E,* ☎ *416/860–0086. AE, DC, MC, V. Closed Sun. No lunch Sat.*

$$$–$$$$　✕ **Joso's.** Joso Spralja—artist, musician, and restaurateur—has filled
★　　his two-story midtown restaurant with his sensual paintings of nudes and the sea, signed celebrity photos, and intriguing wall hangings. The kitchen prepares dishes from the Dalmatian side of the Adriatic Sea, and the international artistic community who frequent the place adore the unusual and healthy array of seafood and fish. *Risotto carajoi* is Joso's own creation of rice and sea snails simmered in an aggressively seasoned tomato sauce. Try porgy from Boston, salmon trout from northern Ontario, or baby clams from New Zealand. Grilled prawns, their charred tails pointing skyward, is a dish often carried aloft by speedwalking servers. ⊠ *202 Davenport Rd.,* ☎ *416/925–1903. Reservations essential. AE, DC, MC, V. Closed Sun. No lunch Sat.*

$$–$$$$　✕ **Rodney's Oyster Bar.** This playful, basement raw bar is a hotbed of
★　　bivalve variety frequented by dine-alones and showbiz and agency types. Among the offerings are salty Lewis Islands from Cape Breton, perfect Malpeques from Rodney Clark's own oyster beds in P.E.I., or New York Pine Islands. A zap of Rodney's own line of condiments or a splash of vodka and freshly grated horseradish are certain eye-openers. Soft-shell steamers, quahogs, and oyster slapjack chowder are among the array of oceanic delights. Shared meals and half-orders are okay with Rodney. Be sure to ask to hear the daily white-plate specials. ⊠ *209 Adelaide St. E,* ☎ *416/363–8105. Reservations essential. AE, DC, MC, V. Closed Sun.*

Steak

$$$–$$$$　✕ **Carman's.** The 40-year history of this restaurant unfolds as you walk along the photograph-lined hall inside the front door. Inside, pewter and copper utensils hang from every inch of the ceiling and fill the shelves. A leather-bound book contains the menu, a five-page wine list, a copy of Abraham Lincoln's work ethic, and great reviews. In the steak-house tradition, Carman's has plenty of pre-eats: feta-filled phyllo pastries, garlic toast, olives, dill pickles, and cottage cheese. All the right steaks—rib, T-bone, fillet, slabs of barbecued ribs—come on wooden steak boards. ⊠ *26 Alexander St.,* ☎ *416/924–8697. AE, DC, MC, V. No lunch.*

$$$–$$$$　✕ **House of Chan.** Some people actually come here for the Chinese food, but it's the U.S. prime beef and the huge lobsters filling the tank that are considered by those in the know to be the best in town. Slide into a red leather booth and order a T-bone, New York strip steak, or fillet in the size you can handle—ditto for the lobster. Go-withs are sliced fresh vegetables, crunchy batter-fried onions, and home fries. While you're waiting, have an egg roll. ⊠ *876 Eglinton Ave. W,* ☎ *416/781–5575. Reservations not accepted. AE, DC, MC, V. No lunch.*

$$$–$$$$　✕ **Moishes.** This Montréal landmark has crossed the border to take up spiffy new quarters. Courtesy reigns supreme, from complimentary valet parking after 6 PM to bar and smoking lounge service, and is carried through to the posh upstairs dining room. Steak, any way you like it, is king. The chopped liver appetizer piled high with fried onions is a must, but don't ignore the variety of fresh fish, chicken, and vegetables.

Potato Monte Carlo, stuffed and baked, or french fries come with the main courses. Wonderful coleslaw, pickles, and a bread basket are brought with the menu. ✉ *First Canadian Place, 77 Adelaide St. W,* ☎ *416/363–3509. AE, DC, MC, V.*

$$–$$$$ ✕ **The Senator.** Throngs of theatergoers get a sense of occasion here, amid sumptuous leather booths with rich leather framing and numbered Victorian private dinettes with 8-ft dividing walls windowed with stained glass. (Dinette #7 is ventilated for pipe and cigar smoking.) The kitchen goes for the classics—grilled liver and onions is wonderful, a mixed grill of swordfish and tuna satisfies, and there's a good choice of U.S. imported beef steaks. This food warms the soul. After dinner, it's one flight up to the Top O' The Senator, a late-night jazz club. ✉ *253 Victoria St.,* ☎ *416/364–7517. AE, DC, MC, V. Closed Mon. No lunch weekends.*

Swiss

$–$$$ ✕ **Mövenpick.** Swiss hospitality makes these downtown restaurants all
★ things to all people. Among the dinner specialties are *Zürcher G'Schnatzlets,* the famous Swiss dish of thinly sliced veal and mushrooms in a creamy white wine sauce served with *rösti* (panfried) potatoes; *Kasseler,* a juicy smoked, grilled pork chop served with braised savoy cabbage; and red wine herring from Iceland marinated in wine and spices. The Swiss Farmers Sunday Brunch (York Street location only) is a vast buffet of food stations. The Yorkville location offers a thrilling ice-cream/dessert menu, in addition to the traditional Swiss selections, and downstairs at La Pécherie, schools of fish are cooked with respect. ✉ *165 York St.,* ☎ *416/366–5234;* ✉ *133 Yorkville Ave.,* ☎ *416/926–9545. AE, DC, MC, V.*

Thai

$$ ✕ **Thai Magic.** Bamboo trellises, cascading vines, fish and animal carvings, and a shrine to a mermaid goddess make a magical setting for coolly saronged waiters and hot-and-spicy Thai food. "Hurricane Kettle" is a dramatic presentation of fiery seafood soup. Whole coriander lobster sparkles with flavor; chicken with cashews and whole dried chilies is for the adventurous. ✉ *1118 Yonge St.,* ☎ *416/968–7366. Reservations essential. AE, MC, V. Closed Sun. No lunch Sat.*

$–$$ ✕ **Vanipha Lanna.** People can't get enough of the clean and bright fla-
★ vors, grease-free cooking, and lovingly garnished Lao-Thai presentations at this tidy, colorful restaurant. The bamboo steamer of dumplings with minced chicken and seafood, sticky rice in a raffia cylinder, and chicken and green beans stir-fried in lime sauce are exceptional. Rice is served from a huge silver tureen. ✉ *471 Eglinton Ave. W,* ☎ *416/ 484–0895. Reservations essential. AE, MC, V. Closed Sun.*

Vegetarian

$–$$ ✕ **Juice for Life.** There's no gloom that can't be cured by Super Energy Cocktail, Einstein's Theory, or Rocket Fuel Fix, to name just a few of the energy elixirs at this funky gourmet juice bar and vegan café. Sunday's Feast for Life brunch includes hemp-seed French toast with maple syrup and sliced fruits, grilled corn and potato cakes with warm salsa, and a three-page menu of delicious hot and cold dishes made without dairy, meat, or any animal matter whatsoever. There is a long bar with stools and a whole row of cozy ancient wooden booths. ✉ *521 Bloor St. W (1½ blocks east of Bathurst),* ☎ *416/531–2635. V.*

$ ✕ **52 Inc.** Two young creative people founded this café on the belief that responsible consumption can be good business. Carefully seasoned gazpacho, Greek salad, grilled vegetables, and extraordinary soups are handcrafted from scratch. Even the espresso is brewed from organically grown beans. Most of the unusual and attractive fixtures were rescued from the demolition of a Victorian house. ✉ *394 College St.,* ☎ *416/960–0334. V. Closed Mon.*

4 Lodging

Modernity may have won out over nostalgia in most of Toronto's hotels— only a few historic lodgings survive in the city—but old-style service and luxury are by no means a thing of the past. You can choose to be pampered at any number of establishments, or you can find basic lodgings pleasantly convenient to the city's highlights. The value of the U.S. dollar in relation to Canadian currency makes many terrific hotels a real bargain.

Updated by
Terrence
Moloney

PLACES TO STAY in this cosmopolitan city range, as
might be expected, from luxurious hotels to budget motels to bed-and-breakfasts in private homes.
The city once had more charming old lodgings, but only a few, including
the King Edward (now Le Royal Meridien King Edward), the Royal
York, and the Grand Bay (formerly the Park Plaza) have survived. Most
other high-quality hotels are part of well-known American, European,
or Asian chains. The deluxe Four Seasons chain got its start here and
set the pace for service and amenities. Generally there is a good relationship between price charged and value received: Toronto has thank-
fully avoided the hotel price inflation of cities like London.

When planning your trip, take into account the fact that the city draws
many conventions and is also increasingly popular with leisure travelers, particularly outside the winter months of late November through
March. Book well in advance, and—if conventioneers bother you—
inquire if there will be any large groups in the hotel you're interested
in at the time of your projected stay.

Some hotels cut prices nearly in half over weekends (which sometimes
start on Thursday) and during special times of the year; many Toronto
hotels drop their rates a full 50% in January and February. When you
book, don't forget to ask about family deals and special packages. And
remember that every U.S. dollar buys about $1.38 Canadian dollars,
so that a C$100-room in Toronto costs about US$72.

If you plan to do a good deal of sight-seeing, you're best off staying in
the downtown area, where you will find Harbourfront Centre, the CN
Tower, Eaton Centre, the Toronto Islands, SkyDome, Chinatown, and
most of the finest shopping and restaurants. If you are staying only a
day or two with kids, and are mainly interested in visiting the zoo, the
Ontario Science Centre, and Paramount Canada's Wonderland, look
into some of the places along the airport strip or outside the downtown core. Most of these have plenty of rooms during the weekend
and frequently offer steep discounts for weekend travelers.

Toronto Visitor Information Line (☎ 416/203–2500 or 800/363–1990)
is a good resource for finding hotel rooms in the price range you want.
More than two dozen private homes scattered across the city are af-
filiated with **Toronto Bed & Breakfast** (✉ 253 College St., Box 269,
Toronto, Ontario M5T 1R5, ☎ 416/588–8800, ℻ 416/927–0838).
Most of them tend to fall into the less expensive price categories.

Bridge Street Accommodations (✉ 1000 Yonge St., Suite 301, Toronto,
Ontario M4K 2Y2, ☎ 416/923–1000, ℻ 416/924–2446) supplies business and leisure travelers with short- and long-term rentals of furnished
apartments and town houses. The company serves visitors to Toronto
and also has access to rentals across North America. With fully equipped
kitchens and maid service, these are often more comfortable and less
expensive than hotels. Apartments are near the financial, business, and
theater districts, and in finer residential neighborhoods like the Annex
and Forest Hill.

Ontario Farm and Country Accommodations (✉ R.R. 2, Alma, Ontario
N0B 1A0, ☎ 519/846–9788, ℻ 519/896–9378) can help if you think
you (and your children) might enjoy staying on a farm near Toronto.
Rates range from $35 to $100 per person per night, including breakfast, with a weekly average of only $200 per person. Some locations
have riding stables and hot tubs.

At the hotels listed in the top two price categories, you can expect wheel-chair accessibility, room service, twice-daily maid-service, minibars, hair dryers, nonsmoking rooms, business services and meeting rooms, and laundry and dry cleaning service. Unless otherwise noted, all hotels have air-conditioning and private baths.

CATEGORY	COST*
$$$$	over $250
$$$	$170–$250
$$	$90–$170
$	under $90

All prices are for a standard double room, excluding 7% GST (Goods and Services Tax), 5% room tax, and optional service charge, in Canadian dollars.

Downtown and Midtown

$$$$ ★ **Four Seasons Toronto.** It's hard to imagine a lovelier or more ex-clusive hotel than the elegant Four Seasons. The location is one of the most ideal in the city: in Yorkville, a few yards from the Royal Ontario Museum and the University of Toronto. Rooms are tastefully appointed and come with comfortable bathrobes, oversize towels, and fresh flowers. Ask for upper rooms with views facing downtown and the lake. The Studio Café is one of the best business breakfast, lunch, or dinner spots in town; the formal dining room, Truffles (☞ Chapter 3), is highly acclaimed; La Serre is a good place for cocktails; and a lovely afternoon tea service is offered in the lobby. ⊠ *21 Avenue Rd., a block north of Bloor St., M5R 2G1,* ☎ *416/964–0411,* FAX *416/964–2301. 230 rooms, 150 suites. 2 restaurants, bar, lobby lounge, in-room modem lines, indoor-outdoor pool, health club, bicycles, baby-sitting, business services. AE, DC, MC, V.*

$$$$ **Grand Bay Hotel Toronto.** Formerly the Park Plaza, the luxurious, completely renovated Grand Bay opened in summer 1998. The hotel, one of the best situated in town, is a short distance from the Royal Ontario Museum and the upscale Yorkville shopping areas, with views south over Queen's Park and to Lake Ontario. The renovations added a pool and a Golden Door spa as well as larger rooms. The Roof Restaurant, a writers' haunt, was once described by novelist Mordecai Richler as "the only civilized place in Toronto." It offers wonderful service along with sparkling nighttime views of the skyline. The experience here is *très* New York Park Avenue. ⊠ *4 Avenue Rd., at Bloor St. W, M5R 2E8,* ☎ *416/924–5471 or 800/977–4197,* FAX *416/924–4933. 348 rooms. 3 restaurants, bar, lounge, in-room modem lines, pool, health club, business services. AE, D, DC, MC, V.*

$$$$ ★ **Inter-Continental Toronto.** This handsome postmodern high-rise, part of a respected international chain, is just a half block west of the major intersection of Bloor Street, Avenue Road, and University Avenue, making it a two-minute walk to the Royal Ontario Museum and the Yorkville shopping area. Edwardian and art deco touches enhance the public areas and the spacious, well-appointed guest rooms. The lobby lounge is especially nice for tea after a hard morning of shopping. Service here is top-notch. ⊠ *220 Bloor St. W, M5S 1T8,* ☎ *416/960–5200 or 800/327–0010,* FAX *416/324–5920. 209 rooms, 12 suites. Restaurant, lobby lounge, outdoor café, in-room modem lines, indoor lap pool, massage, sauna, exercise room. AE, DC, MC, V.*

$$$$ **Sheraton Centre.** This busy conventioneer's favorite is across from the New City Hall and just a block from Eaton Centre, which is accessible through an underground passage. The below-ground level is part of Toronto's labyrinth of shop-lined corridors, the Underground City. The Long Bar, overlooking Nathan Phillips Square, has an unimpeded view of Ontario's highest court of law across the street; it's a

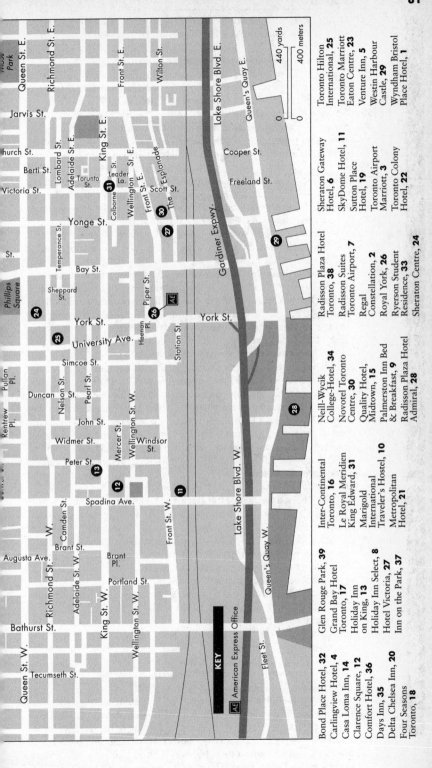

Bond Place Hotel, **32**
Carlingview Hotel, **4**
Casa Loma Inn, **14**
Clarence Square, **12**
Comfort Hotel, **36**
Days Inn, **35**
Delta Chelsea Inn, **20**
Four Seasons
Toronto, **18**

Glen Rouge Park, **39**
Grand Bay Hotel
Toronto, **17**
Holiday Inn
on King, **13**
Holiday Inn Select, **8**
Hotel Victoria, **27**
Inn on the Park, **37**

Inter-Continental
Toronto, **16**
Le Royal Meridien
King Edward, **31**
Marigold
International
Traveler's Hostel, **10**
Metropolitan
Hotel, **21**

Neill-Wycik
College-Hotel, **34**
Novotel Toronto
Centre, **30**
Quality Hotel,
Midtown, **15**
Palmerston Inn Bed
& Breakfast, **9**
Radisson Plaza Hotel
Admiral, **28**

Radisson Plaza Hotel
Toronto, **38**
Radisson Suites
Toronto Airport, **7**
Regal
Constellation, **2**
Royal York, **26**
Ryerson Student
Residence, **33**
Sheraton Centre, **24**

Sheraton Gateway
Hotel, **6**
SkyDome Hotel, **11**
Sutton Place
Hotel, **19**
Toronto Airport
Marriott, **3**
Toronto Colony
Hotel, **22**

Toronto Hilton
International, **25**
Toronto Marriott
Eaton Centre, **23**
Venture Inn, **5**
Westin Harbour
Castle, **29**
Wyndham Bristol
Place Hotel, **1**

KEY
AE American Express Office

440 yards
400 meters

favorite of lawyers, especially after winning a case. All views are marvelous; to the south are the CN Tower and SkyDome; to the north, both city halls. ⊠ *123 Queen St. W, M5H 2M9,* ☎ *416/361–1000,* ℻ *416/947–4874. 1,384 rooms. 3 restaurants, bar, coffee shop, lobby lounge, in-room modem lines, no-smoking floors, indoor-outdoor pool, hot tub, massage, sauna, exercise room, summertime children's program (ages 18 months–12 years). AE, DC, MC, V.*

$$$$ ★ **Sutton Place Hotel.** The elegant, 33-story Sutton Place draws many visiting film and stage stars because of the combination of attentive service and privacy it provides them. The spacious rooms have comfortable, traditional-style furnishings; Oriental rugs, tapestries, flowers, and plush chairs fill the public areas. The hotel is also a favorite of lobbyists, who like the proximity of the Ontario legislature and its bureaucrats. Leisure travelers appreciate the location near the Royal Ontario Museum, Yorkville, and excellent restaurants. Some rooms have full kitchens and VCRs. ⊠ *955 Bay St., M5S 2A2,* ☎ *416/924–9221 or 800/268–3790,* ℻ *416/924–3084. 230 rooms, 60 suites. Restaurant, in-room modem lines, indoor pool, beauty salon, health club, business services. AE, DC, MC, V.*

$$$$ **Westin Harbour Castle.** The Westin, just steps from Harbourfront and the Toronto Islands ferry, offers the best views of Lake Ontario of any hotel in the city. A free shuttle bus and the Harbourfront LRT (light rail transit) provide links to Union Station, the subway, and downtown business and shopping. The hotel is a favorite with conventioneers because of its enclosed bridge to the large convention center across the street. The Toronto Island ferries dock at the plaza in front of the hotel, and all waterfront attractions are within half an hour's walk or a quick cab ride. Rooms are well appointed and tastefully modern; all look out onto the lake, but you may want to ask for one of the corner rooms, which look up to the glittering banks and office towers to the north. The revolving Lighthouse restaurant, atop the 37th floor, has a spectacular view. The Grand Yatt Dynasty Chinese restaurant serves fine Hong Kong–style seafood. ⊠ *1 Harbour Sq., M5J 1A6,* ☎ *416/ 869–1600 or 800/228–3000,* ℻ *416/869–3682. 980 rooms. 2 restaurants, coffee shop, lobby lounge, pool, barbershop, beauty salon, tennis court, health club, squash, playground. AE, DC, MC, V.*

$$$–$$$$ **Delta Chelsea Inn.** Toronto's largest hotel has also become known as the city's theater hotel because it's within walking distance of the Pantages, Elgin, and Winter Garden theaters. You can also book tickets with your room. This friendly spot has long been popular with tour groups and with business travelers. It has more rooms than any other hotel in the British Commonwealth, so be prepared for a bustle of activity. Ask for the southeast and southwest rooms in the south wing, overlooking downtown and the lake. A creative, supervised day-care service for children runs from 9:30 AM to 10 PM. The Delta Chelsea is a couple of short blocks north of Eaton Centre, and the College subway station is across the street in the basement of College Park shopping center. ⊠ *33 Gerrard St., M5G 1Z4,* ☎ *416/595–1975 or 800/ 243–5732,* ℻ *416/585–4375. 1,594 rooms, 18 suites. 2 restaurants, 4 lounges, 2 pools, sauna, hot tub, exercise room, business services, children's program (ages 3–8). AE, D, DC, MC, V.*

$$$–$$$$ ★ **Le Royal Meridien King Edward.** The grande dame of downtown Toronto hotels, this beauty built in 1903 attracts a well-heeled clientele. (In the past, everyone from Rudyard Kipling to the Beatles stayed here.) The "King Eddie," a new member of a European hotel chain, still has an air of understated elegance, with its vaulted ceiling, marble pillars, and palm trees. The hotel's restaurants, Chiaro's and the Café Victoria, are favorites among Toronto power brokers. For a genteel afternoon pastime, take tea in the lobby lounge. What other hotel gives you not only bathrobes and hair dryers, but also umbrellas? ⊠ *37 King St. E, M5C 1E9,* ☎ *416/863–3131,* FAX *416/863–4102. 298 rooms. 2 restaurants, lobby lounge, beauty salon, spa, business services, meeting rooms. AE, DC, MC, V.*

\$\$\$–\$\$\$\$ 🏨 **Metropolitan Hotel.** One of Toronto's largest hotels, this handsome,
★   contemporary 26-floor property with a glass-enclosed atrium lobby could hardly be more convenient: It's just steps behind City Hall, a few short blocks from Eaton Centre, and near the theater district. The Metropolitan is also on the edge of one of the most dynamic Chinatowns outside mainland China. The guest rooms, which include eight for travelers with disabilities, are all well decorated, with finely crafted furniture and desks; some have king-size beds, and executive rooms have a work center with printer and fax. Dining options include the excellent Hemispheres, Lai Wah Heen (☞ Chapter 3), and the Mezzanine Café. ⊠ *108 Chestnut St., M5G 1R3,* ☎ *416/977–5000 or 800/668–6600,* FAX *416/977–9513. 481 rooms. 3 restaurants, 2 bars, in-room modem lines, indoor pool, sauna, hot tub, health club, playground, business services. AE, D, DC, MC, V.*

\$\$\$–\$\$\$\$ 🏨 **Royal York.** One of Canada's famous railway hotels, this grand hostelry was built by the Canadian Pacific Railway for the convenience of passengers using nearby Union Station. Although no longer the largest hotel in the British Commonwealth, a title it held for decades, the Royal York is still a monster of a place. The service is efficient but sometimes impersonal, and there's always a convention of some sort going on. Still, it's venerable, comfortable, and close to the financial district, waterfront attractions, and many theaters. An award-winning refurbishment of the hotel has returned the lobby to its classic 1929 decor, with travertine walls and columns. The health club and skylit lap pool feature rich marblework and a stunning hand-painted trompe l'oeil wall mural. You can have full afternoon tea at the Royal Tea Room or sample wine from the Acadian Room's extensive wine list. The hotel's links to Union Station and the Underground City make it very handy in cold weather. ⊠ *100 Front St. W, M5J 1E3,* ☎ *416/368–2511 or 800/663–7229,* FAX *416/368–9040. 1,408 rooms. 6 restaurants, 4 bars, in-room modem lines, indoor lap pool, health club, business services, travel services. AE, D, DC, MC, V.*

\$\$\$–\$\$\$\$ 🏨 **SkyDome Hotel.** Billing itself as the "World's Only Sports and Entertainment Hotel," the SkyDome fulfills the fantasies of Torontonians and visitors by providing them with the opportunity to watch their favorite sports team, pop star, or even a monster-truck rally from the comfort of a hotel room. A Canadian Pacific Hotel, it bears little resemblance to the chain's flagship, the nearby Royal York (☞ *above*). Seventy rooms are built into the north wall of the SkyDome stadium and look right onto the field; the price of those rooms varies with the event. Laminated jerseys, signed baseball bats, and other assorted sports paraphernalia adorn the hotel halls and lobby. Guests can also book one of the four skyboxes for meetings and parties. Still, unless you want to watch a game, the hotel may not be to your taste: it maintains a very modern look with embossed steel and bare concrete, even in the guest rooms. ⊠ *1 Blue Jays Way, M5C 1E9,* ☎ *416/341–7100 or 800/341–1161,* FAX *416/341–5090. 323 rooms, 23 suites. Restaurant, lobby lounge, indoor pool, health club, business services. AE, DC, MC, V.*

\$\$\$ 🏨 **Holiday Inn on King.** In the heart of the entertainment district, the Holiday Inn is just three blocks north of the Metro Toronto Convention Centre, SkyDome, and the CN Tower; also nearby is Queen Street and its lively club scene. Although the structure is 20 floors high, half of that is office space; the hotel occupies the 9th–20th floors. You can request views of either Lake Ontario, the downtown skyline, or SkyDome. Executive suites have whirlpool bathtubs. The swimming pool is tiny, but the exercise room is appealing. You get a lot for your money at this chain hotel, a frequent award winner. ⊠ *370 King St. W, M5V 1J9,* ☏ *416/599–4000 or 800/263–6364,* 🆋 *416/599–7394. 426 rooms. 2 restaurants, refrigerators, pool, massage, sauna, exercise room, business services, meeting rooms. AE, D, DC, MC, V.*

$$$ 🏨 **Radisson Plaza Hotel Admiral.** This intimate hotel is on the edge of Lake Ontario, overlooking Harbourfront Centre; it's only a short walk to the CN Tower, SkyDome, Harbourfront Antiques Market, and Queen's Quay Terminal shopping, and there's a light rail connection to the subway system just outside the door. Rooms are handsomely furnished, and the public areas maintain a nautical look with gleaming lacquered wood and polished brass. The Promenade Deck on the fifth level, surrounding the heated outdoor pool, allows for fabulous views of the bustling harbor and the hotel's mooring for private boats. The Commodore's Restaurant has equally stunning views. ⊠ *249 Queen's Quay W, M5J 2N5,* ☏ *416/203–3333,* 🆋 *416/203–3100. 157 rooms, 8 suites. 2 restaurants, bar, pool, health club, squash. AE, D, DC, MC, V.*

$$$ 🏨 **Radisson Plaza Hotel Toronto.** This pleasant, relatively small and modern hotel is one that Torontonians tend to forget, but it's near the busy intersection of Yonge and Bloor streets, convenient for both business and leisure travelers. Matisse Restaurant and Bar is popular for its colorful Provençal decor, good service, and mixture of Southern California, southern United States, and Far Eastern cooking. ⊠ *90 Bloor St. E, M4W 1A7,* ☏ *416/961–8000,* 🆋 *416/961–9581. 258 rooms. Restaurant, in-room modem lines, health club, business services. AE, D, DC, MC, V.*

$$$ 🏨 **Toronto Hilton International.** The Hilton's proximity to the financial district, theaters, and the CN Tower makes it a convenient base for many visitors. Hallways are bright, done in pleasant peach with flecks of black, and rooms are cheerful, in light pastel shades. The indoor-outdoor pool is modest, but the view of the city from the glass-enclosed elevators is a thrill. ⊠ *145 Richmond St. W, M5H 2L2,* ☏ *416/869–3456,* 🆋 *416/869–1478. 600 rooms. 3 restaurants, indoor-outdoor pool, sauna, hot tub, health club. AE, DC, MC, V.*

$$$ 🏨 **Toronto Marriott Eaton Centre.** This link in the Marriott chain has a terrific location: It's part of the Eaton Centre, Toronto's number-one attraction, and within easy walking distance of SkyDome, the Metro Toronto Convention Centre, and the theater and financial districts. The hotel's pretty guest rooms, all decorated in shades of dusty rose and gray, have larger bedrooms than most you will find in Toronto; irons, ironing boards, and hair dryers are standard. The indoor rooftop swimming pool provides a fabulous view of the city. At the airy Parkside Café on the main floor, you can sip your coffee while basking in the light pouring in from the enormous windows, which overlook the Church of the Holy Trinity. Character's, a sports bar with a dozen TVs, has pool tables. ⊠ *525 Bay St., M5G 2L2,* ☏ *416/597–9200 or 800/ 228–9290,* 🆋 *416/597–9211. 435 rooms, 24 suites. 2 restaurants, lobby lounge, sports bar, indoor pool, health club, billiards, business services. AE, DC, MC, V.*

$$–$$$ 🏨 **Novotel Toronto Centre.** The Novotel—part of a few-frills French chain—has comfortable modern rooms that are a good value. All rooms have a hair dryer, voice mail, and video checkout, and there are a good number of fitness facilities for the price range. This nine-floor hotel, convenient to Old Toronto and the financial districts, is just behind the Hummingbird Centre for the Performing Arts and within walking distance of the St. Lawrence market. ⊠ *45 The Esplanade, M5E 1W2,* ☏ *416/367–8900,* 🆋 *416/860–5166. 266 rooms. Restaurant, minibars, no-smoking floors, indoor pool, hot tub, sauna, exercise room, meeting rooms. AE, DC, MC, V.*

$$–$$$ ⊞ **Toronto Colony Hotel.** The Colony offers somewhat less expensive ac-
commodations than many of the large hotels in the downtown core. It
has an ideal location, close to the subway, the theater district, and Eaton
Centre. The lobby is drab but functional, while the rooms are simple but
pleasant; some have spectacular, unimpeded views of downtown Toronto.
⊠ *89 Chestnut St., M5G 1R1,* ☎ *416/977–0707,* FAX *416/585–3164.
721 rooms, 15 suites. Restaurant, sports bar, in-room modem lines,
minibars, indoor pool, outdoor pool, business services. AE, DC, MC, V.*

$$ ⊞ **Bond Place Hotel.** If you're on a limited budget but want a central
location, this hotel just two blocks from Eaton Centre is a good choice.
It has clean, spacious rooms with color TVs and phones but few other
frills. Although the Garden Café serves breakfast, lunch, and dinner,
you'll find a wider variety of food at Eaton Centre. The Bond Place is
also a few minutes' walk from the Elgin, Pantages, and Winter Gar-
den theaters. ⊠ *65 Dundas St. E, M5B 2G8,* ☎ *416/362–6061 or 800/
268–9390 in Canada and northeastern U.S.,* FAX *416/362–9372. 286
rooms. Restaurant, no-smoking floors. AE, DC, MC, V.*

$$ ⊞ **Clarence Square.** On the edge of the entertainment and financial dis-
★ tricts, this newly opened bed-and-breakfast has elegant accommoda-
tions in a beautiful Victorian town house. It also overlooks a small park.
A marble fireplace, French doors, and a 12-ft ceiling enhance the delightful main salon, and all guest rooms come with whirlpool tubs and
TV. Host and owner Susan Walker assiduously cares for the well-
being of her guests. This property is at the lower end of the price cat-
egory. ⊠ *13 Clarence Sq., M5V 1H1,* ☎ *416/598–0616,* FAX *416/
598–4200. 3 rooms. AE, DC, MC, V.*

$$ ⊞ **Comfort Hotel.** This intimate hotel is close to the University of Toronto,
several museums, and the Yorkville shopping district. You could not be
closer to the center of town and still get a quiet night's sleep. Jazz piano
aficionados will enjoy the atmospheric Louis Janetta's Place next to the
hotel. ⊠ *15 Charles St. E, M4Y 1S1,* ☎ *416/924–1222 or 800/228–5150,*
FAX *416/927–1369. 108 rooms. Restaurant, piano bar. AE, DC, MC, V.*

$$ ⊞ **Days Inn.** Tour groups and families from the United States, Japan,
and Europe are the mainstays at the economical downtown Days Inn.
It has resisted the temptation (to which many downtown Toronto hotels have succumbed) to increase rates in light of the improving economy. Located next to Maple Leaf Gardens and within walking distance
of downtown, the theater district, and Yorkville, the hotel offers the
advantage of being near top attractions without the expense of being
right in the thick of them. It's unglamorous but clean and reliable; rooms
have an unambitious yet practical modern look. ⊠ *30 Carlton St., M5B
2E9,* ☎ *416/977–6655,* FAX *416/977–0502. 536 rooms. Restaurant,
coffee shop, sports bar, indoor pool, beauty salon, sauna, meeting
rooms. AE, DC, MC, V.*

$$ ⊞ **Hotel Victoria.** Travelers on budgets will appreciate the personal ser-
★ vice and quiet atmosphere of this Victorian-era hotel on Yonge Street
hotel a block east of Union Station. Clean and cozy, it's a good choice
for those who want to be near everything downtown without paying
dearly. The Victoria is at the low end of its price category. ⊠ *56 Yonge
St., M5E 1G5,* ☎ *416/363–1666, 800/363–8228 in Canada and
N.Y.,* FAX *416/363–7327. 48 rooms. Restaurant, bar. AE, DC, MC, V.*

$$ ⊞ **Quality Hotel, Midtown.** The Choice Hotel chain has four downtown locations plus four hotels near the airport. This one is close to
the University of Toronto, the Royal Ontario Museum, and the Yorkville
shopping district. Rooms are comfortable but not luxurious. The St.
George subway stop is steps away, and underground parking is available. It's hard to beat the combination of convenience and price here.
⊠ *280 Bloor St. W, M5S 1V8,* ☎ *416/968–0010,* FAX *416/968–7765.
210 rooms. Restaurant, coffee shop. AE, D, MC, V.*

$–$$ 🏨 **Casa Loma Inn.** Hidden within the tree-lined avenues of Toronto's hip
Annex neighborhood, the Casa Loma has been welcoming the bed-and-
breakfast crowd for 13 years. The rooms of this Victorian mansion built
in 1893 are well furnished, if somewhat dated. The inn has an unassuming
air—still, quiet, tidy, and a little old-fashioned—and the owners are
kind and solicitous. Breakfast can be brought to your room; there's no
breakfast room. Despite being nestled in a quiet residential area, the inn
is close to downtown and Yorkville, and only five minutes from the subway. All rooms have televisions and microwaves; four have functioning
fireplaces. ⊠ *21 Walmer Rd., M5R 2W7,* ☎ *416/924–4540,* FAX *416/
975–5485. 23 rooms. Refrigerators, coin laundry. AE, MC, V.*

$–$$ 🏨 **Palmerston Inn Bed & Breakfast.** The new owner of the Palmerston
★ has wrought a veritable revolution in the establishment. Capitalizing
on her experience as an interior decorator, Judy Carr has breathed new
life into a Georgian mansion built in 1906. Each room has the name of
a regular guest, and floral-pattern linens and curtains enliven the antique furniture. Discreetly watching over the rooms are ubiquitous
porcelain dolls perched upon mantels and closets. A covered and heated
outdoor patio also serves as a breakfast room. Palmerston Boulevard
is one of Toronto's most pleasant downtown streets, with attractive gates
at either end and iron streetlights. You can stroll down the tree-lined
boulevard to bustling Bloor Street or to ultrahip College Street bars and
restaurants. ⊠ *322 Palmerston Blvd., M5G 2N6,* ☎ *416/920–7842,*
FAX *416/960–9529. 8 rooms. Breakfast room, lobby lounge. MC, V.*

$ 🏨 **Neill-Wycik College-Hotel.** This is an attractive option for young peo-
★ ple or families on a tight budget who don't mind sharing bathroom facilities. From early May through late August, this college residence
near Dundas and Yonge streets becomes Toronto's best hotel value. There
is one bath/shower for every five or six guests. The cedar roof deck has
a great view of the city; barbecues are available. ⊠ *96 Gerrard St. E,
M5B 1G7,* ☎ *416/977–2320 or 800/268–4358,* FAX *416/977–2809.
325 rooms. Cafeteria, kitchenettes, sauna, coin laundry. MC, V.*

$ 🏨 **Ryerson Student Residence.** Short-term lodging is available in the
heart of downtown at Ryerson from early May to late August every
year. True, the rooms are all singles, sharing bathrooms, but there are
kitchenettes, laundry facilities, and TV lounges on every floor; each
room has a phone. No children under 12 (or pets of any age) are allowed, but for prices ranging from about $30 per night and $150 weekly
for students (about $50/$250 for nonstudents), it's hard to do better
anywhere else. ⊠ *160 Mutual St., M5B 2M2,* ☎ *416/979–5296. 450
rooms. Coin laundry. MC, V.*

Northeast

$$–$$$ 🏨 **Inn on the Park.** Just off Don Valley Parkway and about 20 min-
★ utes from downtown Toronto, this is the only resort in the city. A low-
rise unit was built in 1963 as part of the Four Seasons chain, and two
larger towers were added in the 1970s. The property became two separate hotels in 1996, the Inn on the Park (in a 23-story building) and
a Holiday Inn (with 300 rooms); the two share facilities, but reservations are separate. The hotel is across the street from the Ontario Science Centre and from 600 acres of parkland that include extensive
jogging and cross-country ski trails. From May through September children can take advantage of a supervised program with swimming, arts
and crafts, and other activities. ⊠ *1100 Eglinton Ave. E, M3C 1H8,*
☎ *416/444–2561,* FAX *416/446–3308. 270 rooms. 2 restaurants,
lounge, indoor pool, outdoor pool, health club, bicycles, children's programs (ages 5–12), business services. AE, DC, MC, V.*

Southwest

$ ▦ **Marigold International Traveler's Hostel.** A charming little private hostel near High Park in western Toronto is associated with the Backpacker's and Rucksacker's networks. It's a bit off the beaten path but well connected to downtown by the Dundas streetcar. It's also close to Roncesvalles, one of Toronto's underrated neighborhoods—a mixed community of Poles, Somalis, and yuppies in which you can munch on pierogis while waiting for the falafel shops to open after devout Muslims have completed their prayers. Some rooms are available for couples, but most contain bunk beds and are usually rented as single-sex dormitory rooms or shared by families; the per-person rate is $22.35. In summer you can lounge on sundecks in the front and back. There are coin lockers and a TV lounge, and free coffee, tea, and doughnuts are set out in the morning. The hostel opens at 2 PM and has no curfew. ⊠ *2011 Dundas St. W, M6R 1W7, ☎ 416/536–8824 (only after 7 PM),* FAX *416/588–2678. 11 rooms with 2–8 beds. Coin laundry. No credit cards.*

The Airport Strip

Lester B. Pearson International Airport is 32 km (18 mi) northwest of downtown, so staying near the airport is an option to consider. Keep in mind, however, that in rush hour the drive can take more than an hour. If you don't have a car, taxis and buses provide service into town.

$$$ ▦ **Radisson Suites Toronto Airport.** All-suite hotels such as the Radisson provide an excellent alternative for families or anyone staying for more than a weekend. The affable staff will be happy to include a microwave in your suite, which comes with useful extras like umbrellas, two televisions, and a couch that's also a fold-out bed. All rooms are decorated in a light green, as is the lobby, which is among the tiniest on the Dixon Road hotel strip. The restaurant cooks up basic fare, and plenty of inexpensive restaurants are nearby. ⊠ *640 Dixon Rd., M9W 1J1, ☎ 416/242–7400,* FAX *416/242–9888. 215 suites. Restaurant, minibars, exercise room. AE, DC, MC, V.*

$$$ ▦ **Sheraton Gateway Hotel.** The Sheraton, connected to the airport's brand-new, cathedral-like Terminal Three, is the most convenient of the city's airport hotels. Still unsure of its target market, the Sheraton aims to attract traveling families and travelers caught in Toronto for a night, as well as business travelers. All the comfortably decorated rooms are soundproof (a necessity) and have such amenities as hair dryers. ⊠ *Terminal Three, Toronto International Airport, L5P 1C4, ☎ 905/672–7000 or 800/325–3535,* FAX *905/672–7100. 481 rooms, 7 suites. 3 restaurants, lobby lounge, indoor pool, beauty salon, sauna, health club. AE, DC, MC, V.*

$$$ ▦ **Wyndham Bristol Place Hotel.** When you've collected your luggage, ★ pick up a phone at the arrival level and call the Bristol Place; an airport bus will have you here in about two minutes. This has long been considered the ritziest of the hotels along the airport strip, and renovations have made it more attractive than ever. Bedrooms have mahogany armoires, tables, desks, and minibars; the main lobby has a small waterfall. For an airport hotel, it's fairly quiet; rooms that face east are the quietest of all. ⊠ *950 Dixon Rd., M9W 5N4, ☎ 416/675–9444 or 800/996–3426,* FAX *416/675–4426. 287 rooms, 5 suites. 2 restaurants, lobby lounge, in-room modem lines, indoor pool, sauna, health club, playground. AE, DC, MC, V.*

$$ ▦ **Holiday Inn Select.** This chain hotel, just minutes by complimentary shuttle bus from the airport, offers pleasant rooms decorated in soothing warm tones—burgundy, red, and yellow—at affordable rates. Like most hotels along the Dixon Road airport strip, it caters mostly to the business traveler and hosts a large number of conferences. The

Metro Bar & Grill provides adequate if unexciting food. ✉ *970 Dixon Rd., M5W 1J9,* ☎ *416/675–7611,* FAX *416/674–4364. 444 rooms, 8 suites. Restaurant, lobby lounge, indoor pool, outdoor pool, sauna, fitness room, business services, meeting rooms. AE, DC, MC, V.*

$$ ⊡ **Regal Constellation.** Now part of Hong Kong's Regal chain, the former Constellation continues to be one of the bright lights at the airport. It has a stunning, six-story, glass-enclosed lobby; a fully equipped health club; and impressive service. One especially nice touch: By law, airplanes cannot fly on the north side of Dixon, making this a very quiet hotel. Weekend rates are particularly attractive here. The Regal has a limited number of economy rooms with shower only that are much less expensive ($95 as opposed to $120 or more). ✉ *900 Dixon Rd., M9W 1J7,* ☎ *416/675–1500 or 800/268–4838,* FAX *416/675–1737. 710 rooms, 18 suites. 4 restaurants, lounge, indoor-outdoor pool, health club, business services. AE, DC, MC, V.*

$$ ⊡ **Toronto Airport Marriott.** The Marriott has begun to solicit the leisure traveler by offering substantial weekend discounts of up to 50%. A skylight over the indoor pool, right beside the entrance lobby and breakfast restaurant, ensures that a generous helping of sunshine suffuses the hotel—which helps compensate for the slightly gaudy pinks of the public areas. The Marriott is one of the newest hotels near the airport, eclipsed only by the Sheraton Gateway attached to Terminal Three. ✉ *901 Dixon Rd., M9W 1J5,* ☎ *416/674–9400,* FAX *416/ 674–8292. 423 rooms, 12 suites. 2 restaurants, lobby lounge, indoor pool, sauna, health club, tennis court. AE, DC, MC, V.*

$$ ⊡ **Venture Inn.** This airport hotel conforms to the chain's overall philosophy and look: Pinewood furniture, exposed brick, and a large brass fireplace in the lobby encourage you to leave Toronto's urban sprawl at the door and slip into a rustic oasis. Each room is decorated in the same country spirit. For $10, exercise equipment can be provided in some rooms. While not the most luxurious hotel near the airport, the Venture has a certain openness to its lobby that prevents it from appearing cramped and dark like many economy hotels. The hotel has no restaurant, but Pat & Mario's is accessible. ✉ *925 Dixon Rd., M9W 1J8,* ☎ *416/674–2222,* FAX *416/674–5757. 283 rooms. Lobby lounge, indoor pool, sauna, business services, meeting rooms. AE, DC, MC, V.*

$ ⊡ **Carlingview Hotel.** A family-run economy hotel just off Dixon Road caters to travelers looking for inexpensive accommodations outside the shadow of the chain hotels. There are only three floors to this modest-size place; the first floor is essentially a motel. Rooms are plain but functional and clean. A regrettably small, dark lobby might impinge upon the good spirits of travelers, but if you're looking for basic lodgings, this may be the place for you. ✉ *221 Carlingview Dr., M9W 5E8,* ☎ *416/675–3303,* FAX *416/675–6524. 112 rooms, 5 suites. Restaurant, pool. AE, DC, MC, V.*

Camping

This is a very citified area; the only location offering tent and trailer camping within metropolitan Toronto is **Glen Rouge Park** (✉ Hwy. 2, 1 km/¾ mi east of Port Union Rd., ☎ 416/392–8188 or 416/392–8092 [end of May–Labor Day]), 25 acres in the city's northeast end. Its attractions include nature trails, horseback riding, and proximity to the city's terrific zoo.

For a list of licensed private campgrounds and trailer parks, write to **Ontario Travel** (✉ Queen's Park, 900 Bay St., Toronto, Ontario M7A 2E1). A list of provincial parks is available from the **Natural Resources Information Centre** (✉ Macdonald Block, 900 Bay St., Room MI-73, Toronto, Ontario M7A 2C1).

5 Nightlife and the Arts

Everything from lowbrow to high art, offbeat to Hollywood, can be found in a growing number of cultural arenas in Toronto. The city's many theaters present a dazzling variety of performances, and music from classical to rock can be heard throughout the year. The nightlife scene has evolved to include lounges and Latin clubs along with triple-decker dance halls, ensuring that there's plenty to do after dark.

Updated by
Liza Finlay

TORONTO'S ART SCENE HAS BLOSSOMED in recent years, aided by the introduction of some dazzling new venues and the refurbishing of some magnificent old ones. The influence of the burgeoning film industry has made nightlife in this once-staid town a lot more glamorous, too.

The best places to get information on all the city's cultural events are the free, weekly *Now* and *eye* newspapers and the "What's On" section of *The Toronto Star,* all appearing on Thursday; the Saturday (weekend) *Globe and Mail,* whose entertainment section is the most critically solid; and the monthly magazine *Toronto Life.* If you have access to the Internet, *Toronto Life*'s Web site at www.torontolife.com as well as the *Toronto Star*'s at www.torstar.com both provide comprehensive and up-to-the-minute listings.

THE ARTS

Toronto is the capital of the performing arts in English-speaking Canada, but it was not always so. Before 1950, Toronto had no opera company, no ballet, and very little theater worthy of the title "professional." Then came the Massey Report on the Arts, one of those government-sponsored studies that usually helps put sensitive subjects on the back burner for several more years. In this case, however, all heaven broke loose: Money began to come from a variety of government grants; two prominent Canadian millionaires passed to their reward, and their death taxes were put toward the creation of a Canada Council, which doled out more money; the Canadian Opera Company, CBC television, and the National Ballet of Canada were born; and a number of little theaters began to pop up, culminating in an artistic explosion throughout the 1970s, in every aspect of the arts.

More than money fueled this arts explosion, though. Other factors were a massive immigration from more culturally nourished countries of Eastern and Central Europe, as well as from England; a growing sense of independence from the mother country; a recognition that if Canada did not develop its own arts, then the damned Yankees would do it for them; and, in general, a growing civic and cultural maturity.

Now Toronto is, after New York and London, the largest center for English-speaking theater in the world. The city's smaller theaters have long been filled with interesting productions of the finest in classic and contemporary Canadian, English, American, and French drama. Since the 1960s the Hummingbird (formerly the O'Keefe Centre) and Royal Alexandra theaters have provided a mix of local, West End, and Broadway productions. Now that Toronto has gained four new performing spaces by restoration (Elgin/Winter Garden complex and the Pantages) and new construction (the Ford Centre and Princess of Wales), it can truly be called "Broadway North"—for better or for worse.

Because of the many movies that have been shot here in recent years, Toronto has also garnered the nickname "Hollywood North." The availability of excellent crews, the variety of locations (Toronto has posed for everything from Paris to Vietnam), and the savings from the exchange rate between U.S. and Canadian dollars are all contributing factors. In 1996, nearly one-quarter of a billion dollars was spent here. Films and series made in Toronto include *Mrs. Winterbourne, Extreme Measures, The Year of the Dragon, Canadian Bacon, The Ref, Moonstruck, Goosebumps, The Road to Avonlea, Due South,* and *Star Trek: The Next Generation* episodes.

Among hundreds of name actors passing through in one recent year were the likes of John Cusack, Hugh Grant, and Holly Hunter. Locals generally let the stars have their privacy, even when spotted in public, which is another reason they like working here. For information about productions in town during your visit, phone the **Toronto Film and Television Office** (☎ 416/392–7570).

Tickets

Full-price theater tickets run from as low as $20 to as high as $95. Tickets for pop concerts are usually $35 to $40, although at smaller venues the cost may drop as low as $20. Tickets for almost any event in the city can be obtained through **Ticketmaster** (☎ 416/870–8000). Tickets can be picked up at the door on the night of the event or at any Ticketmaster location; note that a service charge applies to all orders.

To obtain half-price tickets on the day of a performance, visit the **Five Star Tickets booth,** on Yonge Street at Dundas Street, open—in good weather—Monday through Saturday noon–7:30 and Sunday 11–3. All sales are final, credit cards are accepted, and a small service charge is added to the price of each ticket. The booth also gives out piles of superb brochures and pamphlets on the city. You can also call the **Toronto Theatre Alliance** (☎ 416/536–6468) for half-price tickets to certain shows.

Concert Halls and Theaters

In addition to the following, there are major concert/theater halls in Stratford and Niagara-on-the-Lake (☞ Chapter 8). Some of the most entertaining theater in Toronto is free, though donations are always welcome. **Dream in High Park,** now about 10 years old, presents quality productions of Shakespeare each July in the heart of Toronto's glorious High Park. The productions are usually a knockout. Check newspaper listings.

The **Elgin and Winter Garden Theatres** (✉ 189 Yonge St., ☎ 416/872–5555 for tickets, 416/314–2901 for tours) are two jewels in the crown of the Toronto arts scene. Two former vaudeville halls are the last operating double-decker theater in the world: The Elgin, downstairs, has about 1,500 seats, and is more suited for musicals; the Winter Garden, upstairs, is somewhat more intimate, with about 1,000 seats. The theaters have put on everything from comedy concerts and jazz to a Mozart opera festival and the Renaissance Theatre Company's productions of *King Lear* and *A Midsummer Night's Dream,* directed by Kenneth Branagh and including Emma Thompson. A $30 million restoration in 1989 showcased the building's Edwardian charm: original 1913–14 details include a nickelodeon, damask wall coverings, gilt cherubs, and, at the Winter Garden, a ceiling canopy with real beech leaves. Both theaters are wheelchair accessible, and both have excellent sight lines. The best Winter Garden seats are mezzanine row A, seats 208–209, or orchestra rows E and F, seats 31–33. At the Elgin, try for orchestra row N, seats 13–14 or 41–42; row J, seats 27–29; or mezzanine row A, seats 207–209. Guided tours are given Thursday at 5 PM and Saturday at 11 AM (☎ 416/363–5353); cost is $4.

The **Ford Centre for the Performing Arts** (✉ 5040 Yonge St., ☎ 416/872–2222 or 416/733–9388) often hosts franchised megamusicals (past favorites have included *Ragtime*) and classical music concerts. It opened in 1993 as the North York Performing Arts Centre but was quickly renamed in honor of a large donation by the auto company. This impressive complex, less than a half-hour drive north of the waterfront, close to the North York subway stop, has a 1,850-seat main theater (called the Apotex); a 1,025-seat recital hall; a 250-seat studio theater; and a two-story, 5,000-square-ft art gallery. The best seats in the Apotex are center orchestra, especially row H, seats 128–130, and mezzanine row A, seats 230–231.

The **Hummingbird Centre for the Performing Arts** (⊠ 1 Front St. E, ☎ 416/872–2262), owned and operated by the city government, was known for 36 years as the O'Keefe Centre but was renamed in 1996 after the Hummingbird Communications software company donated money for renovations and refurbishing. It has long been the home of the Canadian Opera Company and the National Ballet of Canada; at press time plans for a new opera house that would open in 2000 were being discussed. The Hummingbird is also home to visiting comedians and rock stars, and shows trying out before a Broadway opening or touring after a successful one; almost anything but the most lavish opera or musical can be accommodated in the cavernous 3,223-seat hall. The acoustics leave much to be desired. Try for seats close to A47–48 and avoid very front rows, such as AA, BB.

The **MacMillan Theatre** (⊠ Edward Johnson Building, Philosopher's Walk, University of Toronto, ☎ 416/978–3744) is an important place to hear avant-garde artists and the stars of the future; it's usually referred to by its location, the Edward Johnson Building. Because it's run by the faculty of music of the University of Toronto, serious jazz trios and baroque chamber orchestras are often presented during the academic year—at little or no cost. The U of T student newspaper, *The Varsity,* found all around the campus, lists concerts. The acoustics at this small theater are good, as are all the sight lines.

Massey Hall (⊠ 178 Victoria St., ☎ 416/872–4255) has always been cramped, but its near-perfect acoustics and its handsome, U-shape tiers sloping down to the stage have made it a happy place to hear music for nearly a century. The nearly 2,800 seats are not terribly comfortable, and a small number are blocked by pillars that hold up the ancient structure, but Massey Hall remains a venerable place to catch the greats and near-greats of the music world. Best seats are in rows G–M, center, and in rows 32–50 in the balcony.

The **Pantages** (⊠ 263 Yonge St., ☎ 416/872–2222), a 1920 vaudeville theater that was turned into a movie complex, is now one of the most architecturally and acoustically exciting live theaters. In 1988–89, the Cineplex Odeon people refurbished the magnificent theater in preparation for the Canadian debut of *The Phantom of the Opera.* The show seems destined to run through the millennium. The production is first-class, with a wonderful set, fabulous costumes, and superior singing. The theater itself is one of the most beautiful in the world: Designed by world-renowned theater architect Thomas Lamb, it has the three styles of Greek columns, a grand staircase, gold leaf detailing, crystal chandeliers, and working gas lamps. Most sight lines are better than might be expected from a theater with 2,250 seats; the best are, typically, in the middle of the orchestra and the front of the mezzanine.

The **Princess of Wales** (⊠ 300 King St. W., ☎ 416/872–1212 or 800/461–3333) claims state-of-the-art sound and technical facilities and wonderful wall and ceiling murals by American artist Frank Stella. The producers—father-and-son team Ed and David Mirvish—built this exquisite 2,000-seat theater to accommodate the technically demanding musical *Miss Saigon* when no other venue was available. All levels are accessible to people using wheelchairs and those with mobility problems. If you can, book Row A, seats 29–30 in the dress circle (mezzanine), or Row B, seats 35–36 in the stalls (orchestra).

Roy Thomson Hall (⊠ 60 Simcoe St., ☎ 416/872–4255), since 1982 the most important concert hall in Toronto, was named for the billionaire newspaper magnate known as Lord Thomson of Fleet after his family donated $4.5 million in his memory (a drop in the bucket—the hall cost a total of $43 million). The beautifully designed hall, with sensitive acoustics, is the home of the Toronto Symphony Orchestra and the Toronto Mendelssohn Choir, and also hosts visiting orchestras and popular entertainers. The best seats are rows H and J in the orchestra and row L upstairs. You can call the volunteer office (☎ 416/593–4822) to arrange a tour ($4) that highlights the acoustic and architectural features of the striking round structure with hanging fabric artwork.

The **Royal Alexandra** (✉ 260 King St. W, ☎ 416/872–3333 or 800/461–3333) has been the place to be seen in Toronto since 1907. The 1,500 plush red seats, gold brocade, and baroque swirls and curlicues all make theatergoing a refined experience. All this magnificence was about to be torn down in the 1960s and the space turned into a parking lot, when it was rescued by "Honest Ed" Mirvish, of bargain store fame and profits. (This first foray into drama and theater production was followed in the 1980s by Mirvish's purchase of London's Old Vic and by his 1990s building of the Princess of Wales; ☞ *above*). Recent programming is a mix of blockbuster musicals and a variety of dramatic productions, some touring before or after West End and Broadway appearances. The theater is wheelchair-accessible on the first floor only. Avoid rows A and B; try for rows C–L center. For musicals, aim for the front rows of the first balcony.

The **St. Lawrence Centre for the Arts** (✉ 27 Front St. E, ☎ 416/366–7723) has been presenting theater, music, dance, opera, film, and forums on public issues since 1970. The two main halls are the luxuriously appointed Bluma Appel Theatre and the Jane Mallett Theatre, often a venue for recitals and performances by companies like the Toronto Operetta and the Hannaford Street Silver Band. At the Bluma Appel Theatre, try for rows E–N, seats 1–10; the Jane Mallett is sufficiently small for all seats to be pretty good.

Dance

Dancemakers, an important modern-dance company, performs at the Premiere Dance Theatre (✉ 207 Queens Quay W, ☎ 416/973–4000), part of the lakeside Harbourfront Centre, and in a studio (✉ 927 Dupont Ave., ☎ 416/535–8880).

The **National Ballet of Canada** (✉ Hummingbird Centre, 1 Front St. E, ☎ 416/345–9686 for information, 416/872–2262 for tickets), Canada's homegrown and internationally recognized classical ballet company, was founded in 1951 by Celia Franca, an English dancer from the Sadler's Wells tradition, and is supported by infusions of dancers trained at its own school. The season runs from November to May. A series of outstanding productions, like Kenneth MacMillan's *Manon,* John Cranko's *Taming of the Shrew* and *Romeo and Juliet,* Glen Tetley's *Alice,* and James Kudelka's *The Actress and The Nutcracker,* have been mounted by the company, and many have moved into the permanent repertory. Mr. Kudelka, a Canadian choreographer, is the company's artistic director. Tickets run $15–$75. Rush tickets at about $15 are available on the same day: For students and seniors, this will buy any unsold seat in the house; for others, it will get a place in the last row on the main floor.

The **Premiere Dance Theatre** (✉ Harbourfront Centre, 235 Queen's Quay W, ☎ 416/973–4000) is a venue for dance performances by local companies as well as visiting groups.

Toronto Dance Theatre, with roots in the Martha Graham tradition, is the oldest contemporary dance company in the city. Since its beginnings in the 1960s, it has created close to 100 works, more than a third using original scores commissioned from Canadian composers. It tours Canada and has played major festivals in England, Europe, and the United States. Most performances are in the Premiere Dance Theatre (⊠ Harbourfront Centre, 235 Queen's Quay W, ☎ 416/973–4000) or at the Winchester Street Theatre (⊠ 80 Winchester St., ☎ 416/967–1365).

Film

Toronto has a devoted film audience. The result is a feast of riches: commercial first- and second-run showings, festivals, lecture series for every taste. Most first-run Toronto movie theaters change their programs on Friday. There are discounts all day Tuesday, weekdays except holidays before 5 PM; senior citizens, students, and children can get reduced rates at all times. A loosely associated group of independent movie theaters—including the Fox, Bloor, Revue, Kingsway, and Paradise—offers lower-priced screenings of independent productions, old classics, cult films, and new commercial releases; call 416/690–2600 for schedules at all five theaters.

The **Toronto International Film Festival** (☎ 416/967–7371 or 416/968–3456), held early in September since 1976, is important both to the city and to the international film business. The festival, the third largest of its kind in the world, attracts Hollywood's brightest stars to view the latest of the greats as well as to showcase lesser-known directors from around the world. Audience members, a knowledgeable crew, vote for their favorite film of the festival, often bringing the work of new directors and actors to wider acclaim. Since the early '90s, **Cinematheque Ontario** has presented several year-round film programs at the Art Gallery of Ontario (⊠ 317 Dundas St. W, ☎ 416/968–3456 or 416/977–0414).

Carlton Cinemas (⊠ 20 Carlton St., ☎ 416/598–2309) screens rare, important films from around the world in nine rooms. Foreign language films are regularly shown in the original, with subtitles.

The Cinesphere (⊠ Ontario Place, 955 Lakeshore Blvd. W, ☎ 416/965–7711) offers 70-mm films, both those especially made for the IMAX screen system and popular films that benefit from the large format and 24-track sound.

Festival Cinema's Royal Cinema (⊠ 606 College St., ☎ 416/516–4845) is a brand-new repertory cinema on a hip street in Little Italy. It plays some popular and some obscure films and will be the new flagship theater for the Toronto International Film Festival.

Harbourfront Centre (⊠ 235 Queen's Quay W, ☎ 416/973–4000) has interesting retrospectives; one might be devoted to, say, early 20th-century classics of Japanese film.

Music

Classical

Glenn Gould Studio (⊠ 250 Front St. W, ☎ 416/205–5555) hosts a variety of classical music companies; the box office is open Tuesday to Thursday.

Tafelmusik (⊠ Trinity-St. Paul's United Church, 427 Bloor St. W, ☎ 416/964–6337)—the name means "table music"—goes for baroque music on original instruments.

The Toronto Mendelssohn Choir (☎ 416/598–0422 for program information; 416/598–0422 or 416/872–4255, Roy Thomson Hall, for tickets) often guests with the Toronto Symphony. This 180-singer group, started in 1894 by Elmer Isler, has been applauded worldwide, and its *Messiah* is "handeled" well every Christmas (no, we couldn't resist that). Some of the beautiful and heartbreaking music heard in the Academy Award–winning *Schindler's List* was sung by this choir.

The Toronto Symphony Orchestra (✉ 60 Simcoe St., ☎ 416/872–4255 or 416/593–4828), now more than seven decades old, doesn't rest on its laurels. Since 1922, with conductors of the quality of Seiji Ozawa, Sir Thomas Beecham, and Andrew Davis, it has achieved world acclaim. Its director since 1994 has been the young and impressive Jukka-Pekka Saraste, who is doing wonders rejuvenating an already world-class orchestra. When the TSO is home, it presents about three concerts weekly from September to May in Roy Thomson Hall (☞ Concert Halls and Theaters, *above*).

Opera
The Canadian Opera Company (☎ 416/363–8231, 416/363–7469, or 800/250–4653), founded in 1950, has grown to be the largest producer of opera in Canada and the fifth-largest company on the continent. From the most popular operas, such as *Carmen* and *Madame Butterfly,* usually performed in the original language, to more modern or rare works, such as *The Cunning Little Vixen* and *Hansel and Gretel,* the COC has proven trustworthy and often daring. The COC often hosts world-class performers, and it pioneered the use of subtitles, which allow the audience to follow the libretto in English in a capsulized translation. Regular performances are at the Hummingbird Centre for the Performing Arts (☞ Concert Halls and Theaters, *above*). A number of free performances are held at Harbourfornt, by Queen's Quay, usually during the last week of August; seating is first-come, first-seated.

Pop and Rock
Most major international recording companies have offices in Toronto, so the city is a regular stop for top musical performers, ranging from the Rolling Stones to Janet Jackson and Madonna. Tickets can usually be booked through **Ticketmaster** (☎ 416/870–8000).

FESTIVAL
NorthbyNortheast (✉ 185A Danforth Ave., 2nd floor, Toronto, Ontario M4K 1N2, ☎ 416/469–0986, ℻ 416/469–0576), also known as N×NE, an annual conference and celebration of rock, new music, and more, brings top-notch talent into town each June. Affiliated with the similar S×SW festival in Austin, Texas, it provides a good opportunity to track new groups, artists, and trends.

VENUES
Major venues include the **SkyDome** (✉ One Blue Jays Way, ☎ 416/341–3663); **Maple Leaf Gardens** (✉ 60 Carlton St., ☎ 416/977–1641);the **Hummingbird Centre for the Performing Arts** (☞ Concert Halls and Theaters, *above*).

Kingswood Music Theatre (✉ Paramount Canada's Wonderland, 9580 Jane St., Vaughn, ☎ 905/832–8131 or 905/832–7000) hosts major rock and pop concerts during the warmer months.

The **Music Gallery** (✉ 179 Richmond St. W, ☎ 416/204–1080) offers an eclectic selection—new music, world music, atonal, classical, avant-garde jazz—in a relaxed atmosphere. The 150-seat concert hall has an industrial feel, with exposed brick walls and lighting grids; the lobby is lighter, with lots of glass and reflective surfaces.

The **Molson Amphitheatre** (✉ Ontario Place, 955 Lakeshore Blvd. W, ☎ 416/314–9900) has pop, rock, and jazz concerts by the lake throughout its summer season at modest prices. The view of the skyline and the summer breezes make this one of the loveliest places to hear music in Toronto.

The **Phoenix Concert Theatre** (✉ 410 Sherbourne St., ☎ 416/323–1251) has a wide variety of music, with DJs from local radio stations broadcasting live on Saturday (alternative music) and with sporadic live cut-ins on Monday (classic rock). On Sunday night, the Planet Vibe (techno and dance music) show goes live to air on radio station Energy 108.

Theater

The most prominent performing spaces are detailed in the Concert Halls and Theaters section (☞ *above*). Other smaller but important venues follow.

Bathurst Street Theatre (✉ 736 Bathurst St., ☎ 416/533–5561) was converted from a church, but the gods have remained. The pews aren't terribly comfortable, but at least no one passes the plate during intermission. The premises are used by dance groups and many of the more interesting theater groups in the city.

Factory Theatre (✉ 125 Bathurst St., ☎ 416/504–9971) is an alternative theater devoted to original and experimental work.

Hart House Theatre (✉ 7 Hart House Circle, ☎ 416/978–8668) is the main theater space of the University of Toronto. Amateur, student, and occasional professional productions have been presented here since 1919.

The Rivoli (✉ 332 Queen St. W, ☎ 416/596–1908 or 416/597–0794), along the Queen Street strip, has long been a major showcase for the more daring arts in Toronto. Upstairs is a pool hall. The downstairs is divided into three areas. A dining room, serving Asian-influenced cuisine (and good steaks) is lined with the works (all for sale) of not-yet-established local artists. Dinner for two, without alcohol, runs about $25. There's also a bar and a back room that functions as a performance space, with theater happenings, "new music" (progressive rock and jazz), improvisational comedy troupes, and more. Try to catch the "Poetry Sweatshop" every fourth Wednesday, in which local, non-literary personalities judge various poets. The cover charge is $5–$10.

The **Tarragon Theatre** (✉ 30 Bridgman Ave., ☎ 416/531–1827), in an old warehouse and railroad district, is the natural habitat for indigenous Canadian theater. Almost anything worthwhile in this country's drama first saw the light of day here.

Le Théâtre Français de Toronto (✉ 26 Berkeley St., upstairs, ☎ 416/534–6604, FAX 416/534–9087) has been providing French-language drama of high quality for many years. Its repertoire has ranged from classical to contemporary, from both France and French Canada.

Théâtre Passe Muraille (✉ 16 Ryerson Ave., ☎ 416/504–7529, FAX 416/504–8980), in the unfashionable area of Bathurst and Queen streets, has long been the home of fine Canadian collaborative theater.

The **Young People's Theatre** (✉ 165 Front St. E, ☎ 416/862–2222) is devoted solely to children, but unlike many purveyors of traditional children's fare, this place does not condescend or compromise its dramatic integrity.

NIGHTLIFE

Toronto has all kinds of music clubs, as well as lots of places to hang out or dance; some of these places are hard to characterize, so read the descriptions as well as the headings. Many have the life span of a butterfly, so call before you set out to make sure they're still open and still offering the kind of evening you're searching for. Adelaide Street West from University Avenue to Peter Street has spawned numerous clubs of the loud, techno variety. Few places have cover charges anymore; the few that do (mostly after-hours and private clubs) ask about $10.

Bars and Pubs

Have a good time in Toronto, but be aware of the strict drinking (minimum age 19) and driving laws: Police regularly stop cars to check sobriety with a Breathalyzer. If you have a blood alcohol level of higher than .08%, it's the judge and/or jail, no matter where you're from. Under the city's liquor laws, last call in bars is 2 AM; closing is 3 AM.

Allen's (⊠ 143 Danforth Ave., ☎ 416/463–3086), an anomaly on the mostly Greek Danforth Avenue, is a quintessential Irish pub, complete with Irish brews on tap and a dartboard. It's a great place to go for a quick drink or for an entire evening, as the food is better than most pub fare.

Atlas (⊠ 129 Peter St., ☎ 416/977–7544) is currently the busiest pickup bar in town. The hot spot for sight-seeing is the second-floor balcony, where polished professionals of both sexes line up to view the action on the main floor below. Order a martini—Atlas is renowned for them.

Brunswick House (⊠ 481 Bloor St. W, ☎ 416/964–2242) attracts mostly students from the nearby University of Toronto. The saloon atmosphere here is loud, raucous, and fun.

Gypsy Co-Op (⊠ 815 Queen St. W, ☎ 416/703–5069), formerly the Squeeze Club, has expanded to two floors to accommodate the artsy crowd of musicians and new bohemians (graphic artists) who hang there. The decor, resembling that of a general store complete with dry goods and lollipops, sets the tone—relaxed, easy, and inexpensive. While you can order good old-fashioned spaghetti and meatballs for under $5, brisk business is done at the bar, where good, cheap wine is served up in juice glasses.

Hemingway's (⊠ 142 Cumberland St., ☎ 416/968–2828), one of the most crowded singles' bars in Toronto, is homier and less tense than other Yorkville watering holes. The bar has comfortable high-back chairs, mirrors, artsy posters, and real, live books lining one wall (they're there, we suspect, as conversation starters). Thursday, Friday, and Saturday evenings the music is live rock and Top 40s. Three-quarters of the middle- to upper-class professionals who frequent this place are regulars.

Madison Avenue Pub (⊠ 14–18 Madison Ave., ☎ 416/927–1722), on the edge of the U of T campus, offers six floors of good food and drink with an English pub atmosphere—lots of brass, exposed brick, and dartboards. Sixteen brands of beer are on tap, and there's a large selection of bottled imports. VIP and billiards rooms and a boutique are also part of the scene. The patios are lovely in the summer.

Milano Billiards, Lounge, and Bistro (⊠ 325 King St. W, ☎ 416/599–9909), in the heart of the theater district, is resplendent with plush velvet booths in jewel tones. The wait for the pool tables is a long one, so consider ordering some tapas and cocktails while enjoying the scenery.

Myth (✉ 417 Danforth Ave., ☎ 416/461–8383), on the Danforth in the middle of the city's Greek area, serves up great Greek food (☞ Chapter 3), but the real action starts *après diner* and centers around the bar and chic rosewood pool tables. The big screens mounted in the vaulted corners play mostly movie classics, but the young trendy crowd is watching each other, not the films.

Wayne Gretzky's (✉ 99 Blue Jays Way, ☎ 416/979–7825), a sports bar and restaurant, is owned by the hockey superstar.

The **Whistling Oyster** (✉ 14–18 Madison Ave., ☎ 416/927–1722) is almost always packed with regulars who crowd around the bar and flirt with the waitstaff. Famed for its seafood, the Oyster really rocks during happy hour (between 4 and 7), when the martinis flow and dim sum and other delicacies are offered at invitingly low prices. The crowd is mainly professionals, and a good deal of pick-up business takes place every night. In fact, rumor has it the owner met his wife at the Oyster's bar.

Gay

Woody's (✉ 467 Church St., ☎ 416/972–0887) caters to a predominantly upscale crowd, including lots of professional types. It's friendly yet neighborly.

Comedy Clubs

The Laugh Resort (✉ 26 Lombard St., ☎ 416/364–5233) offers stand-up solo acts and sometimes improvisations, Tuesday through Saturday night. The cover is $7–$15 for the show only, $23–$31 for dinner and show.

Second City (✉ 56 Blue Jays Way, ☎ 416/343–0011 or 800/263–4485), in new quarters in the entertainment district, has been providing some of the best comedy in Toronto since it opened in 1973. Many alumni of this troupe have become well known through *Saturday Night Live* and the *SCTV* series. Among those who have cut their teeth on the Toronto stage are Dan Aykroyd, Martin Short, Andrea Martin, Catherine O'Hara, the late John Candy and Gilda Radner, and the very live Mike Myers. Visitors can test their knowledge of Canadian comics by trying to identify the celebrities in the large photographs that decorate the lobby. Sundays the troupe performs a "Best of Second City" program. The cost is $11–$20 for shows only, $33–$40 for dinner and show.

Yuk-Yuk's Komedy Kabaret (✉ 2335 Yonge St.; ✉ 5165 Dixie Rd., Mississauga; ☎ 416/967–6425 for tickets for both locations) has always been a major place to see comedy in Toronto. This is where Jim Carrey got his start and where George Carlin and Robin Williams presented their best routines. Crash and Burn Amateur Night, every Monday beginning at 8:30 PM, is as tough, uneven, and occasionally inspired as it sounds. There's a $5–$15 cover, occasionally more for a huge name act; dinner-show packages run $17–$38. The Mississauga location is open Thursday–Sunday; the Toronto Kabaret is open daily.

Dance Clubs

Al Frisco's (✉ 133 John St., ☎ 416/595–8201) draws mostly the over-25 downtown professional crowd. The upstairs bar offers dancing to DJ rock from Tuesday to Saturday. This friendly, casual spot, with a restaurant and patio dining in summer, also offers billiards.

Berlin (✉ 2335 Yonge St., ☎ 416/489–7777) became one of the most popular—and exclusive—spots in Toronto within a year of its open-

BONUS MILES MAKE GREAT SOUVENIRS.

Earn Miles With Your MCI Card.

Take the MCI Card along on this trip and start earning miles for the next one. You'll earn frequent flyer miles on all your calls and save with the low rates you've come to expect from MCI. Before you know it, you'll be on your way to some other international destination.

Sign up for MCI by calling 1-800-FLY-FREE

Is this a great time, or what? :-)

Earn Frequent Flyer Miles.

HAWAIIAN AIRLINES.

MIDWEST EXPRESS AIRLINES

NORTHWEST AIRLINES WORLDPERKS®

ing back in 1987, quickly attracting a rich, young (25–35) crowd. It remains the hot/cool place to be. Tuesday there's live Spanish music; Friday and Saturday feature a Top 40s band, playing mostly '70s and '80s sounds. The Saturday dress code bans jeans, T-shirts, and athletic clothes; other days neat and clean jeans are okay, but everything else is still verboten.

The Courthouse (✉ 57 Adelaide St. E, ☎ 416/214–9379), with its 12-ft ceilings, plush couches, and roaring fireplaces, more closely approximates a 1940s Hollywood mansion than a courthouse. The upscale cocktail crowd, however, is very modern. The dance floor is tucked away in the basement, leaving the main floor free for lounging and posing.

The Guvernment (✉ 132 Queen's Quay E, ☎ 416/869–1462) plays techno dance and underground music. A new rooftop patio, heated for chilly fall and spring nights, gives the crowded club breathing room—at least for eight months of the year.

The Joker (✉ 318 Richmond St. W., ☎ 416/598–1313), a three-story dance emporium of brooding and ominous proportions, has a cave-like atmosphere, thanks to its dark decor. Each floor plays different music, but expect high-energy dance. Friday night is the most popular night; lines start to form as early as 9.

Limelight (✉ 250 Adelaide St. W, ☎ 416/593–6126) is in the vortex of the club scene. It always has a lineup, starting at 10 PM and continuing well past midnight. This is the spot du jour for university types and suburbanites, who drive in for an evening of rave-ish dancing and drinking.

The Living Room (✉ 330 Adelaide St. W, ☎ 416/979–3168) may not have strobe lights or dry ice, but it's one of the city's latest hot spots for nighthawks who like a little privacy with their Perrier. A large dance floor, occupying about a third of the club/lounge's space, is surrounded by small cafeteria tables. This is where the cool chill.

The Velvet Underground (✉ 508 Queen St. W, ☎ 416/504–6688) is the most alternative of Toronto's alternative clubs. The dungeon-esque decor and techno music make it popular among the goth set, especially on Monday nights.

Whiskey Saigon (✉ 250 Richmond St. W, ☎ 416/593–4646) has three gigantic floors, with DJs, laser shows, and everything from rock to funk. One of the most popular clubs of the '90s, it's a very attractive option for the hip crowd. Sunday nights are retro nights, and '80s music fans line up around the block to get in.

Gay and Lesbian

Kremlin (✉ 504 Jarvis St., ☎ 416/462–7540), just on the edge of one of the largest gay communities in North America, is one of the city's major gay bars–cum–dance clubs. There are exclusively gay and lesbian nights, but on many other nights, there's disco for all, with straights welcome to visit, drink, and dance.

Pope Joan (✉ 547 Parliament St., ☎ 416/928–1495) is a late-night lesbian gathering place with live music, dancing, DJs, and karaoke.

Entertainment Center

The Docks (✉ 11 Polson St., ☎ 416/469–5655), an enormous new center on the lake, provides complete entertainment for party goers: video games, two basketball courts, a swimming pool, 22 outdoor billiard tables, indoor and outdoor dance floors, and even a bungee-jumping platform. There are plenty of places to drink at night. The Docks' terrace has spectacular views of Toronto's skyline.

Latin Dance Clubs

What disco was to the '70s, salsa is to the '90s, as Latin dance joints become the hangouts of choice for the club cognoscenti.

Ba-Ba-Lu'U (✉ 136 Yorkville Ave., ☎ 416/515–0587), in the chichi Yorkville area, truly is the best of both worlds, with the luxe of a tony lounge replete with gem-color stools and polished tables, and the sizzle born of the sexy Latin rhythms. The club also offers lessons for novices; call for times.

ChaChaCha (✉ 11 Duncan St., ☎ 416/598–3538) is the place to drag out those red stilettos and ruffled shirts hidden in the back of the closet. Here, dress the part and dance the dance—after all, this is the Copacabana of the '90s. The sleek bar and stainless-steel dance floor surrounded by marble columns ooze rich Havana. Prime time is 9 to 11, after which funk and disco take over.

El Convento Rico Club (✉ 750 College St., ☎ 416/588–7800) creates a slice of Cuba in the heart of downtown. It's seedy, it's steamy, it's sticky, and it's the real thing. Toronto's Latin community comes here to play, as do many of the city's drag queens and gays.

Lounges

The **Big Easy** (✉ 225 Richmond St. W, ☎ 416/979–3000) is what you get when you cross a New York–style loft with a disco. The dark floors, white walls, and high ceilings give the place height, and the crowd of young professionals dressed to the nines in Armani suits and Versace dresses give it sights. Couches tucked into corners create cozy conversation areas, while the empty spaces are quickly converted into dance space. The Easy is busiest Thursday through Saturday nights. Go early.

Canoe (✉ 66 Wellington St. W, ☎ 416/364–0054), a stellar restaurant (☞ Chapter 3) on the 54th floor of the Toronto Dominion Centre, has a magnificent bar with a panoramic view of the lake and Toronto Islands. The crowd is mostly made up of brokers and financial wizards from the neighboring towers, who suit the swank surroundings.

La Serre (✉ 21 Avenue Rd., ☎ 416/964–0411), the Four Seasons Hotel's classy lounge, looks like a library in a mansion: plush and green, with lots of brass and dark wood. It has a stand-up piano bar and a pianist worth standing for. Drinks, coffees, and teas are all pricey, but what can you expect in one of the poshest hotels in the country? Weekdays attract a business crowd; weekends bring out the couples.

The **Roof Lounge** (✉ Grand Bay Hotel, Avenue Rd. and Bloor St., ☎ 416/924–5471) has been used as a setting in the writings of such Canadian literary luminaries as Margaret Atwood and Mordecai Richler. Indoors, a clubby bar and marble topped tables are surrounded by books and pictures of Canadian writers. In summer, an adjoining patio affords lovely views of the downtown skyline and lake. This remains an important hangout for the upper-middle class, businesspeople, professionals, and, *bien sûr*, literary types.

Music Venues

Eclectic

Free Times Cafe (✉ 320 College St., ☎ 416/967–1078) is a relatively small space where you'll find, every night of the week, blues and folk singers, along with New Age, jazz, fusion, and other musical forms. A lot of acoustic performers love to put on quality shows here, especially singers/songwriters. This is the place to see the next stars of the Mariposa folk music festival (☞ Festivals and Seasonal Events *in* Chapter 1) and other happenings.

Jazz

C'est what? (✉ 67 Front St. E, ☎ 416/867–9499) offers rotating bands almost every night, along with its own beers, 25 other Ontario microbrews, and plain good cooking. The name—"Say what"—is punning Franglais.

The Jack Russell (✉ 27 Wellesley St. E, ☎ 416/967–9442) offers jazz Saturday nights from 8 PM to midnight in an English-style pub.

The **Pilot Tavern** (✉ 22 Cumberland St., ☎ 416/923–5716) serves up modern mainstream jazz Saturday afternoons—as well as good burgers.

Top O' The Senator (✉ 249 Victoria St., ☎ 416/364–7517), the city's first club devoted exclusively to jazz, sits atop the Senator diner. With its long wooden bar and dark-blue, towering ceilings, this fabulous room exudes a between-the-wars jazz lounge atmosphere.

Rock

The **Cameron Public House** (✉ 408 Queen St. W, ☎ 416/703–0811), a small, eclectic kind of place, showcases "alternative" music that ranges from jazz to hard rock and new wave. Because it's close to the Ontario College of Art, the Cameron draws a creative bunch during the week. The suburbanite scene gets heavy on weekends, as do the crowds.

Chick 'n Deli (✉ 744 Mount Pleasant Rd., ☎ 416/489–3363), long one of the great jazz places in Toronto, now plays top-40 music, with cover bands every night. There's a dance floor and dark wood everywhere, and the casual friendliness gives a neighborhood bar–type atmosphere.

Hard Rock Cafe at Dundas Square (✉ 283 Yonge St., across from the Eaton Centre, ☎ 416/362–3636; ✉ SkyDome, Gate 1, 1 Blue Jays Way, ☎ 416/341–2388) features recorded rock most nights and live rock on Sunday. The trademark rock-and-roll memorabilia of this chain decorates the walls. This is a busy hangout for people in their early 20s and those in their 30s who obviously want to hang out with 20-year-olds. Another branch, the Hard Rock SkyDome, has a DJ on weekends and live rock occasionally; there's a $3.50 cover charge during game events.

Horseshoe Tavern (✉ 370 Queen St. W, ☎ 416/598–4753) was known across the city for more than four decades as the tavern with entertainment, especially country music; Charlie Pride, Tex Ritter, Hank Williams, Loretta Lynn all played here. Now the music is mostly rock, along with some live roots, blues, and rockabilly. Good bands perform here six nights a week. No food is served, but there's plenty of booze. The place draws lots of flannel-shirt and blue-collar types. Rock memorabilia lines the walls, and far more men than women line the bar. On weeknights, the ages range from 25 to 40; weekends, the crowd is younger.

Lee's Palace (✉ 529 Bloor St. W, ☎ 416/532–7383), on the edge of the University of Toronto campus, is where rock-and-roll and blues are delivered by local talent. Jams go from 8 PM on. And dig that crazy decor!

The Opera House (⊠ 735 Queen Street E, ☎ 416/466–0313 for club and concert line), a venue for live, largely alternative acts, is also a dance club. It's a hot place for ravers.

The **Ultrasound Showbar** (⊠ 269 Queen St. W, ☎ 416/593–0540) is that rarest of things, a showcase room for bands and even songwriters. The intimate space is long, narrow, and dark, dark, dark. The cover is usually under $10, and the more-often-than-not capacity crowd of 100 cannot help but enjoy itself. After all, its booker advertises: "Local, original talent, must be good, no bloody rubbish."

Rhythm and Blues
Chicago's (⊠ 335 Queen St. W, ☎ 416/598–3301), on the Queen Street West strip that heads west from University Avenue, is a real charmer. Downstairs is a cowboyish bar and good hamburgers; upstairs, you can see and hear (every night) the blues stars of tomorrow—and the day after. Check out the red neon sign in the shape of a beer cap.

Grossman's Tavern (⊠ 379 Spadina Ave., ☎ 416/977–7000), old and raunchy, was described by one writer as "long established, but never entirely reputable"—which makes it ideal for the blues. There are R&B bands nightly and jazz on Saturday afternoon.

Reggae, Caribbean, and African
BamBoo (⊠ 312 Queen St. W, ☎ 416/593–5771), a onetime commercial laundry hidden behind the popular Queen Street strip, serves reasonably priced Thai/Caribbean food along with reggae and world beat music Monday to Saturday evenings (an occasional group plays acid jazz). The sight lines can be terrible, and this is no place for quiet conversation, but it's still popular for its great food and great sounds.

Supper Clubs
The past few years have witnessed the rebirth of the supper club in Toronto. Fine cuisine can be followed by a night of dancing in an atmosphere more sophisticated than that in most clubs. The places listed below also have active bars, for those who prefer to limit the evening to drinks and dancing.

ChaChaCha (⊠ 11 Duncan St., ☎ 416/598–3538) is a sophisticated supper club that turns into a dance club (☞ Latin Dance Clubs, *above*) as diners finish their meals and the late-night crowd arrives.

Rosewater Supper Club (⊠ 19 Toronto St., ☎ 416/214–5888), with blue velvet banquettes for two, is a lovely place for a festive night on the town (☞ Contemporary *in* Chapter 3). One lounge has a baby grand and a torch singer.

6 Outdoor Activities and Sports

Having a lake at its doorstep does a lot for Toronto's outdoor life all year: Summer brings out joggers, boaters, and beach lovers, while winter is great for fans of ice-skating, skiing, and tobogganing. For those who prefer to watch the fun, the city is home to baseball's Blue Jays, basketball's Raptors, and Canadian football's Argonauts. The toughest ticket in town, of course, is for hockey's Maple Leafs.

PARTICIPANT SPORTS

Updated by
Shawna Richer

From Lake Ontario to the hills outside the city and the lakes and parks beyond, a wide range of sport and recreational activities are available for year-round pleasure. As a supplement to the suggestions below, contact the **Ministry of Tourism and Recreation** (✉ Queen's Park, Toronto, Ontario M7A 2R2) for pamphlets on various activities. **Tourism Toronto** (☎ 416/203–2500 or 800/363–1990) can provide information on sports and outdoor recreation.

A number of fine **conservation areas,** including the Kortright Centre (☞ Northwest Toronto *in* Chapter 2), circle the metropolitan Toronto area, many less than a half hour from downtown. Most have large swimming areas, sledding, and cross-country skiing, as well as skating, fishing, and boating. Contact the **Metro Conservation Authority** (☎ 416/661–6600) and ask for their pamphlet.

Bicycling

More than 29 km (18 mi) of street bike routes cut across the city, and dozens more follow safer paths through Toronto's many parks. Bikes can be rented on the Toronto Islands. The **Martin Goodman Trail** is a 19-km (12-mi) strip that runs along the waterfront all the way from the Balmy Beach Club in the east end, out past the western beaches southwest of High Park. Phone the *Toronto Star* (☎ 416/367–2000) for a map.

Toronto Parks and Recreation (✉ 55 John St., ☎ 416/392–8186) has maps that show bike (and jogging) routes that run through Toronto parkland. **Ontario Cycling** (✉ 1185 Eglinton Ave. E, ☎ 416/426–7242) offers booklets and information as well as maps.

Boardsailing

Equipment for boardsailing (windsurfing) can be rented in various areas of the waterfront. Try along Bloor Street West, near the High Park subway station.

Boating

Grenadier Pond in High Park, Centre Island, Ontario Place, Harbourfront Centre, and most of the conservation areas surrounding Toronto rent canoes, punts, and/or sailboats.

Bowling

Toronto has five-pin bowling, a marvelous tradition unknown to most Americans. This sport of rolling a tiny ball down an alley at five fat pins—each with a different numerical value, for a possible (impossible) score of 450—is perfect for children, even as young as three or four, and for everyone on a rainy day. **Bowlerama** (✉ 2788 Bathurst, just south of Lawrence Ave. W, ☎ 416/782–1841; ✉ Newtonbrook Plaza, 5837 Yonge St., just south of Steeles, ☎ 416/222–4657; ✉ 115 Rexdale Blvd., near Kipling, ☎ 416/743–8388) has lanes all over the city. The Newtonbrook Plaza and Rexdale Boulevard locations are open 24 hours a day.

Golf

The season lasts only from April to late October. For information about courses, contact **Toronto Parks and Recreation** (☎ 416/392–8186) or **Travelinx Ontario** (☎ 416/314–0944 or 800/668–2746). The top course and a real beauty is the 18-hole, par 73 **Glen Abbey** (✉ 133 Dorval Dr., Oakville, ☎ 905/844–1800), where the Canadian Open Championship is held. Cart and greens fees run around $75 on weekends.

Less challenging courses—and much closer to the heart of the city—include the **Don Valley Golf Course** (✉ 4200 Yonge St., just south of

Highway 401, ☎ 416/392–2465); and the **Flemingdon Park Golf Club** (✉ 155 St. Denis Dr., near Don Mills Rd. and Eglinton Ave., ☎ 416/ 429–1740).

Health and Fitness Facilities

Nearly every major hotel in metropolitan Toronto has a health club or an exercise room, with a track, weight equipment, and some sort of swimming pool. Many private clubs and/or hotel fitness facilities will sell passes to visitors who want short-term use. The YMCA may honor your membership from another city at one its local fitness centers.

Horseback Riding

Within the city limits, **Central Don Riding Academy** (✉ Park Leslie St. and Eglinton Ave., in Sunnybrook Park, ☎ 416/444–4044) has an indoor arena, an outdoor ring, and nearly 19 km (12 mi) of bridle trails through the Don Valley.

Just north of the city, in Richmond Hill, the **Rocking Horse Ranch** (☎ 905/884–3292) offers scenic western trail rides year-round. For booklets detailing riding establishments across the province, call the **Ontario Equestrian Federation** (☎ 416/426–7232).

Ice-Skating

Toronto operates some 30 outdoor artificial rinks and 100 natural-ice rinks—and all are free. Among the most popular are in Nathan Phillips Square, in front of the New City Hall, at Queen and Bay streets; down at Harbourfront Centre (Canada's largest outdoor artificial ice rink); College Park, at Yonge and College streets; Grenadier Pond, within High Park, at Bloor and Keele streets; and inside Hazelton Lanes, the classy shopping mall on the edge of Yorkville, on Avenue Road, just above Bloor Street. For details on city rinks, call 416/392–1111.

Jogging

Good places to jog are the boardwalk of The Beaches in the city's east end; High Park in the west end; the Toronto Islands; and the ravines or other public parks, many of which have jogging paths and trails. The Martin Goodman Trail (☞ Bicycling, *above*) is ideal. Many hotels now provide printed copies of interesting routes nearby. Toronto is generally safer than most American cities, but it is still wise to use normal prudence and avoid isolated spots; check with local people on specific parks or routes.

Sailing

Sailing on Lake Ontario is especially nice between May and September, but die-hard sailors push the season at both ends. The **Ontario Sailing Association** (✉ 65 Guise St. E., Hamilton L8L 8B4, ☎ 416/ 425–7245 or 416/426–7271) is a good resource. The **Royal Canadian Yacht Club** (✉ 141 St. George St., ☎ 416/967–7245) has its summer headquarters in a beautiful Victorian mansion on Centre Island.

Skiing

CROSS-COUNTRY

Try Toronto's parks and ravines, especially Earl Bales Park; High Park; the lakefront along the southern edge of the city; Tommy Thompson Park; and best of all, Toronto Islands. The Kortright Centre (☞ Northwest Toronto *in* Chapter 2), just outside Toronto, has hiking trails, some of which are used for skiing in winter. Most of these places are free. Check the Yellow Pages for ski-equipment rentals.

DOWNHILL

Within metropolitan Toronto it's possible to ski in **Earl Bales Park** (☎ 416/395–7873 or 416/395–7902), on Bathurst Street, just south of Sheppard Avenue; and **Centennial Park Ski Hill** (☎ 416/394–8754) in

Etobicoke. Better hills are some 30 to 90 minutes north of the city, including **Blue Mountain Resorts** (☎ 905/869–3799) in Collingwood, Ontario; the **Caledon Ski Club** (☎ 905/453–7404) in Caledon; **Glen Eden Ski Area** (☎ 905/878–5011) in Milton; **Hidden Valley** (☎ 705/789–2301) in Huntsville; **Hockley Valley Resort** (☎ 519/942–0754) in Orangeville; and **Horseshoe Valley** (☎ 705/835–2790). Call 416/314–0998 for **lift and surface conditions** in the Toronto area.

Sleigh Riding and Tobogganing

The best parks for tobogganing include High Park, in the west end, and a local favorite, Winston Churchill Park, at Spadina Avenue and St. Clair Avenue, just two blocks from Casa Loma. It is sheer terror.

Swimming

Lake Ontario is rarely warm enough for sustained swimming, except in late August, and often too polluted for any kind of dip. Still, it's fun to relax or take a stroll on one of the city's beaches. In the east end, **Beaches Park,** south of Queen Street and east of Coxwell Avenue, is lovely, thanks to the lengthy boardwalk, local canoe club, and public washrooms. A 20-minute streetcar ride east of downtown, along Queen Street, are **Woodbine Beach Park** and **Ashbridges Bay Park,** both fine for sunbathing and boat-watching. To the west of downtown, a fine area, **Sunnyside Beach,** has a pool, snack bar, Jungle Gym, and washrooms. The city's most pleasing beaches—and certainly the ones with the best views—are on the **Toronto Islands** (☞ The Waterfront *in* Chapter 2).

Public swimming is available in 16 indoor pools, 12 outdoor pools, and 15 community recreation centers; call the **Toronto Department of Parks and Recreation** (☎ 416/392–7259). For the latest information on **city pools**, call 416/392–7838. For information about **late-night, outdoor swimming**, call 416/392–1899.

Ontario Place (✉ 955 Lakeshore Blvd. W, ☎ 416/314–9900; ☞ The Waterfront *in* Chapter 2) has an outstanding water park and slide. This lakefront amusement park has enough other activities and rides, as well as the Cinesphere movie theater, to amuse kids for hours once they tire of the water.

Tennis

The city provides dozens of courts, all free, many of them floodlighted. Parks with courts open from 7 AM to 11 PM, in season, include High Park in the west end; Stanley Park, on King Street West, three blocks west of Bathurst Street; and Eglinton Park, on Eglinton Avenue West, just east of Avenue Road. Call the **Ontario Tennis Association** (☎ 416/426–7135).

SPECTATOR SPORTS

The city of Toronto has traditionally enjoyed a love-hate relationship with its professional sports teams, even the Toronto Blue Jays, who won back-to-back World Series championships in 1992 and 1993. Fans can sometimes be accused of being fairweather—except when it comes to hockey. In Toronto the national sport, in typically Canadian fashion, attracts rabid, sellout crowds, whether the Maple Leafs win, lose, or draw.

Auto Racing

For the past several years, the **Molson Indy** (☎ 416/872–INDY, FAX 416/351–8560) has been roaring around the Canadian National Exhibition grounds, including the major thoroughfare of Lakeshore Boulevard; local traffic is diverted for those three days in mid-July. You can book tickets from late February or early March. You'll pay around $100 for a three-day "red" reserved seat, but general admission for the qualification rounds, the practice rounds, and the Indy itself, can be considerably less expensive.

Motorcycle and formula racing are held at **Mosport** (☎ 416/665–6665), about 96 km (60 mi) northeast of Toronto. Take Highway 401 east to Exit 75, then drive north.

Baseball

The **Toronto Blue Jays** (☎ 416/341–1111 or 416/341–1234 for ticket information), who play in the downtown SkyDome (✉ 1 Blue Jays Way) from April through September, were one of baseball's most dynamic teams until they lost many players to free agency in 1994–95. Crowds fell off after the strike-shortened season of 1994, but fans are beginning to come back to the ballpark in droves. The team has acquired a few new free agents, such as heavy hitter Jose Canseco, and a mid-season winning streak in 1998 has everyone talking about the Blue Jays again. Still, tickets are not tough to come by. It's not legal, but dozens of scalpers unload tickets at a fraction of what they have paid to people who wait until the second or third inning to buy. Regular prices range from $4 (for the cheap seats near heaven) to $28.

Basketball

The city's NBA franchise, the **Toronto Raptors,** opened its first season under former Detroit Pistons hero Isiah Thomas in 1995. The Raptors have played their 41 annual home games (November to April) in the SkyDome but expect to be in a new home, the Air Canada Centre (✉ 40 Bay St., near Lake Shore Blvd.), in February 1999. Tickets for each season, which run from $5 to $102.50 per game, are available beginning in July. The Raptors had a miserable 16–66 record in 1997–98 but have acquired Charles Oakley, an intimidating power forward from the New York Knicks, and center Kevin Willis, another NBA veteran. Call 416/872–5000 for tickets while the Raptors are still in the SkyDome; the team's head office, at 416/214–2255, will provide ticket information when the Raptors move to their new venue.

Canoeing and Rowing

Canoe Ontario (☎ 416/426–7170) has information about one of the world's largest canoeing and rowing regattas, held every July 1 on Toronto Island's Long Pond.

Cricket

The British and Commonwealth influence, though waning, is strong enough to support local teams who play in their pristine whites and make moves that those brought up on baseball may find mysterious but fascinating. The **Cricket Association of Ontario** (☎ 416/426–7160) has information about finding a game.

Football

The Canadian Football League (CFL) is back from the financial brink, and attendance is up across the country. The two-time defending Grey Cup champion **Toronto Argonauts** (☎ 416/341–5151 for tickets) draw smaller crowds than most, since plenty of other teams compete for sports fans' attention. Tickets for home games, which are played in the SkyDome, are a cinch to get a hold of. Regular prices range from $12 to $38. The season runs from mid-June to late November, and American fans who attend a CFL game will find the 110-yard-field, three-down game quicker, less predictable, and much more exciting than the NFL version. Quarterbacks in the CFL have to run around and throw on the fly a lot more than their NFL peers. Trust us.

Golf

The permanent site of the **Canadian Open** golf championship is the Jack Nicklaus–designed Glen Abbey (✉ 133 Dorval Dr., Oakville, ☎ 905/844–1800), less than 45 minutes west of the city, along the Queen Elizabeth Way (QEW). This tournament is one of golf's Big Five and is always played in late summer.

Hockey

The **Toronto Maple Leafs** will begin their 1998–99 season in October in the venerable Maple Leaf Gardens (✉ 60 Carlton St., ☎ 416/977–1641) but will move to the flashy, new Air Canada Centre (✉ 40 Bay St., near Lake Shore Blvd.) in February 1999 and share space with basketball's Toronto Raptors. The Leafs missed the playoffs in 1998, winning just 30 games, but this is still the toughest ticket to get in the National Hockey League. It's not legal, but scalpers hawk tickets on Carlton Street, a half block east of the corner of Yonge and College Streets. Another option is to show up at the office (☎ 416/977–1641) at 9 AM sharp on the day of the game for rush seats. Tickets run from $25 to $100, and scalpers often get twice the face value. The Leafs, under new coach Pat Quinn, signed free-agent goaltender Curtis Joseph to a four-year deal, so they should be a much better team. The Ticketmaster number for hockey tickets is 416/870–8000.

Horse Racing

RACETRACKS

The **Ontario Jockey Club** (☎ 416/675–7223 or 888/675–7223) operates two major racetracks, Woodbine and Mohawk. **Woodbine Race Track** (✉ Hwy. 427 and Rexdale Blvd., ☎ 416/675–7223 or 888/675–7223), 30 minutes northwest of downtown Toronto, near the airport, is the showplace of Thoroughbred and harness racing in Canada. Horses run late April–late October. **Mohawk** (✉ Hwy. 401, Campbellville, ☎ 416/675–7223 or 888/675–7223), a 30-minute drive west of Toronto, is in the heart of Ontario's standardbred breeding country. It features a glass-enclosed, climate-controlled grandstand and other attractive facilities.

Nordic Gaming operates **Fort Erie** (✉ 230 Catherine St., Queen Elizabeth Way/Bertie St. exit, Fort Erie, ☎ 905/871–3200 from Toronto, 716/856–0293 from Buffalo), in the Niagara tourist region. This is one of the most picturesque racetracks in the world, with willows, manicured hedges, and flower-bordered infield lakes. It has racing on the dirt as well as on grass, with the year's highlight being the Prince of Wales Stakes, the second jewel in Canada's Triple Crown of Racing.

ROYAL HORSE SHOW

The Royal Horse Horse Show, a highlight of Canada's equestrian season, is part of the **Royal Winter Fair** each November. It's held at the CNE grounds (✉ Dufferin St., by the waterfront, ☎ 416/393–6400).

Ice Canoe Racing

Every January, five-man/woman teams haul canoes across the ice floes off Harbourfront Centre.

Soccer

Although Toronto keeps getting and losing a professional soccer team, you can catch this exciting sport, at university and semi-pro levels, in the centrally located **Varsity Stadium** (✉ Bloor St. W at Bedford, a block west of Royal Ontario Museum and University Ave., ☎ 416/978–7388). The **Soccer Association of Ontario** (☎ 416/426–7300) can provide information about games.

Tennis

The finest players in the world gather each summer at the tennis complex on the York University campus, near Finch Avenue and Keele Street, for the **Player's International Canadian Open**; for tickets, phone Tennis Canada (☎ 416/665–9777) or Ticketron (☎ 416/872–1212).

Wrestling

Exhibitions are sometimes held at **Maple Leaf Gardens** (✉ 60 Carlton St., one block east of Yonge and College Sts., ☎ 416/977–1641).

7 Shopping

With designer boutiques peppered liberally across the city, a thriving community of funky street-wear stores, and a growing vintage and antiques scene, Toronto has something for everyone. The city's network of malls and galleries tempt one-stop shoppers, while walkers can delight in knowing that the trek from the posh Bloor Street strip to funky Queen Street West, or from upscale Yorkville to downtown's Kensington Market, is a matter of a mere mile or so. In other words, Toronto is shopping central.

By Liza Finlay

TORONTO PRIDES ITSELF on having some of the finest shopping in North America; and, indeed, most of the world's name boutiques can be found here, especially along the Bloor Street strip (between Yonge Street and Avenue Road) and in the Yorkville area, which covers the three streets immediately north of and parallel to the Bloor Street strip.

For those a little leaner of wallet, rest assured that you have come to the right place. In Toronto, bargain hunting is a sport of Olympic proportions, and locals wear those discount threads like badges of honor. Because of the weakness of the Canadian dollar, too, visitors obtain what amounts to an immediate discount on any purchase.

Toronto has a large artistic and crafts community, with many art galleries, custom jewelers, clothing designers, and artisans. From sophisticated glass sculpture to native and Inuit art, the many beautiful objects you'll find are ideal for gifts or for your own home.

Politically incorrect as they may be, fur coats and hats are popular purchases with visitors from outside Canada. You can buy from a high-fashion outlet or directly from a furrier in the Spadina Avenue garment district. Distinctive Hudson Bay wool blankets, available only at The Bay, are an enduring Canadian tradition. The unique Tilley hat, sold by mail order or in the Tilley Endurables boutique at Queen's Quay Terminal, is an ideal present for sailors and adventurers: It's advertised as having been retrieved intact after being eaten by an elephant, and comes with a lifetime guarantee and owner's manual.

The opening of the mammoth HMV Music store on Yonge Street, which has listening stations for your prepurchase pleasure and live, in-store performances, has made CD shopping great entertainment here. Canadians are proud of their own, and most record stores dedicate shelves to homegrown talent like Celine Dion, Alanis Morissette, The Tragically Hip, Bryan Adams, and Shania Twain, along with a host of smaller pop, rap, hip hop, folk, opera, and country artists. In a similar bigger-is-better vein, bookstores such as Chapters now have lounge areas where you can read while sipping a coffee from the Starbucks within the store, and offer frequent readings by Canadian authors like Carole Shields, Ann-Marie McDonald, and Rohinton Mistry.

When it comes to department stores, all roads lead from Holt Renfrew on Bloor Street West, the epicenter of Toronto's designer mecca. Within a few blocks of this high-end store are virtually all the designer boutiques from Prada to Chanel. A mere block east is the more mid-priced department store The Bay, where you'll find designer collections offset with bridge lines and The Bay's own clothing and houseware lines. The other big name is Eaton's, in the Eaton Centre at Yonge and Dundas streets.

Most stores accept MasterCard and Visa without minimums, though if you charge a purchase under $5 you won't be too popular. Major stores also accept American Express. You'll find American cash generally accepted, although not always at the most favorable rate of exchange. On Thursday and Friday most stores downtown stay open until 9 PM; on Sunday many downtown stores open at noon.

The biggest sale day of the year is Boxing Day, the first business day after Christmas, when nearly everything in the city, including furs, is half price. In fact, clothing prices tend to drop even further as winter fades. Summer sales start in late June and continue through August.

Bear in mind that the much-hated national 7% Goods and Services Tax (alias the GST, or Grab and Soak Tax) will be added to the cost of your purchases at the cash register, as will the 8% Ontario sales tax. Visitors should save receipts from hotel bills and any major purchases and inquire about rebates on the GST. Ask for the latest refund regulations and forms at Lester B. Pearson International Airport, at visitor information booths like the one outside the Eaton Centre, or at stores. For further instructions on how to claim a refund, *see* Taxes *in* the Gold Guide.

Shopping Districts

The Beaches

Queen Street East, starting at Woodbine Avenue, is a great spot for casual clothing stores, gift and antiques shops, and bars and restaurants, all with a resort atmosphere: A boardwalk along the lake is just to the south. Kew Beach Park, on the south side of Queen Street a few blocks east of Woodbine, plays host to a jazz festival every July. To get to The Beaches, take the Queen Street streetcar to Woodbine and walk east; parking can be a hassle.

Bloor Street West

Bloor Street West, from Yonge Street to Avenue Road, is a virtual runway for fashion mavens. Two city blocks play host to a world of fashion, with the haute Holt Renfrew department store at the nucleus and the more moderately priced The Bay, Canada's oldest department store, and Club Monaco's flagship store acting as bookends. The cornucopia of couture starts with Emporio Armani to the east; proceeding west, Bloor Street is handily split, with the north side offering more mainstream fare like Gap, Gap Kids, Banana Republic, and the Body Shop, and the south serving up fantasy fashion, starting with Versus, Tiffany & Co., Gianni Versace, MAC, Aveda, and Roots, and finishing with Cartier, Royal De Versailles Jewelers, Chanel, Hermès, and Corbò—a scaled-down department store carrying only upscale merchandise. The Prada store is a must, if only for the inspired interior design. Ladies should consider parking the guys at Bay Bloor Radio in the Manulife Centre; it's stereo mecca and only steps from male fashion bastions like Eddie Bauer for active wear and Harry Rosen for more professional attire. The jolts of java served up at Starbucks in Chapters, a three-story bookstore with lounge areas for adults and a play center for kids, may be just what you'll need after this shopping experience.

Farther west on Bloor Street, between Bathurst Street and Spadina Avenue, near the University of Toronto, is a vibrant mix of cafés, Hungarian restaurants, pubs, specialty groceries, casual-clothing boutiques, and discount bookstores.

Chinatown

The Chinese have made Spadina Avenue, from King Street north to College Street, their own, but Spadina's basic bill of fare is still "bargains galore." The street, and the Kensington Market area tucked behind Spadina west to Bathurst Street, between Dundas and College streets, remains a collection of inexpensive vintage clothing stores, Chinese clothing stores, Chinese restaurants, ethnic food and fruit stores, and eateries that give you your money's worth. You'll find gourmet cheeses at gourmet prices, fresh ocean fish, yards of fabric remnants piled high in bins, and designer clothes minus the labels. Start at the southern end of Spadina (south of King Street) where Winners, a discount clothing and home accessories store, offers designer brands minus the designer prices. Be warned: This area can be extraordinarily crowded on weekends, when smart suburbanites head here for bargains. Park your car at the lot just west of Spadina Avenue on St. Andrew's Street (a long block north of Dundas Street), or take the College or Queen streetcar to Spadina Avenue.

Mirvish Village

Mirvish Village, a one-block assortment of bookstores, antiques shops, and boutiques on Markham Street south of Bloor Street, has an interesting history. Ed Mirvish is an inspired capitalist who, since 1948, has run the truly silly deep-discount store called Honest Ed's that financed the revival of London's Old Vic theater. When Mirvish tried to tear down all the houses on the block behind his store to build a parking lot, he was prevented by zoning bylaws. No problem: He thought up Mirvish Village. Memory Lane sells vintage movie posters and old comic books and magazines.

Queen Street East

Queen Street East from Pape Street east to Jones Avenue is a bustling young thoroughfare now noted for its antiques and "previously loved" junk shops. With a particular fondness for fifties memorabilia, Vavoom and Ethel (and the Kitsch Cafe) start the stroll down memory lane. Yes-Ter-Year Interior Accents was the best-kept secret of locals who are now being forced to endure the crowds who come here for the exceptional assortment of quality reproduction armoires, bureaus, tables, and garden furnishings. The Tango Palace at the end of antique alley is the hot spot for gourmet coffees and decadent desserts. Parking is at a premium, but the neighborhood is easily accessible via the "Red Rocket"—the Queen Street streetcar, which passes through every 20 minutes or so.

Queen Street West

If it's funky or fun, it's found on Queen West. The best shops are concentrated on both sides of Queen Street West from University Avenue to Spadina Avenue, with some fashionable stores as far west as Bathurst Street. With its collection of vintage stores, Canadian designer boutiques, and bistros, this strip sets the pace of Toronto's street style. Citytv's headquarters at the corner of Queen and John streets, with Speaker's Corner (where you can videotape your views to be aired on the station's *Speaker's Corner* show later) is a landmark. On Queen West, the retro stylings of vintage stores like Noise and Zinc comfortably coexist with Parade, Venni, Fashion Crimes, and Sunde, which all stock Canadian designs with a bent for the street beat. To really get into the downtown groove, grab a paper or magazine at Pages and then head into the Second Cup across the street for coffee. Home decor types won't be disappointed on this strip, either, with the opening of the recently renovated UpCountry and Du Verre. In summer, the stalls of T-shirts and silver jewelry at the Soho Market (at Queen and Soho streets) yield great inexpensive gifts. Finish with a drink on the rooftop patio of Bam-Boo (☞ Nightlife *in* Chapter 5), a Toronto legend and a likely place to spot the city's Who's Who and any visiting celebrities.

Underground City

Downtown Toronto has a vast underground maze of shopping warrens that burrow in between and underneath the office towers. The tenants of the Underground City are mostly the usual assortment of chain stores, with an occasional surprise. Directions and way-finding have improved somewhat with the introduction of marked PATH walkways. The network runs roughly from the Royal York Hotel near Union Station north to the Atrium on Bay, and from Park Road, east of Bloor and Yonge, to Bellair Street and the ManuLife Centre.

Uptown

Yonge Street, the longest road in Canada, begins life at Lake Ontario and takes on a multitude of faces before exiting the city. Uptown is a

114

Toronto Shopping

Lowther Ave.

London St.

Prince Arthur Ave.

Bloor St. W.

Howland Ave.

Brunswick Ave.

Walmer Rd.

St. George St.

Devonshire Pl.

Croft St.

Washington St.

Sussex Ave.

Lennox St.

Sussex Mews

Hoskin Ave.

Tower Rd.

Herrick St.

Spadina Ave.

Huron St.

Harbord St.

Willcocks St.

College

Ulster St.

Russell St.

Markham St.

Bathurst St.

Croft St.

Borden St.

Lippincott St.

Major St.

Robert St.

Bury

College St.

Bellevue Ave.

Oxford St.

Glasgow St.

Ross St.

Henry St.

McCaul St.

Nassau St.

Huron St.

Cecil St.

Leonard Ave.

Nassau Ave.

Baldwin St.

Wales Ave.

Kensington Ave.

D'Arcy St.

Dundas St. W.

SEE QUEEN STREET WEST MAP

Alexandra Park

Bathurst St.

Ryerson Ave.

Denison St.

Augusta Ave.

Cameron St.

Grange Pl.

Beverley St.

Grange Rd.

Sullivan St.

Robinson St.

Carr St.
Eden Pl.

Wolseley St.

McDougall Sq.

Phoebe St.

Soho St.

Stephanie St.

Willis St.

Bulwer St.

Renfrew Pl.

Queen St. W.

Richmond St. W.

Rush Ln.

Spadina Ave.

Peter St.

Widmer St.

Nelson St.

Duncan St.

Maud St.

Brant St.

Camden St.

Portland St.

Adelaide St. W.

Charlotte St.

John St.

Pearl St.

King St. W.

KEY

AE American Express Office

0   440 yards

0   400 meters

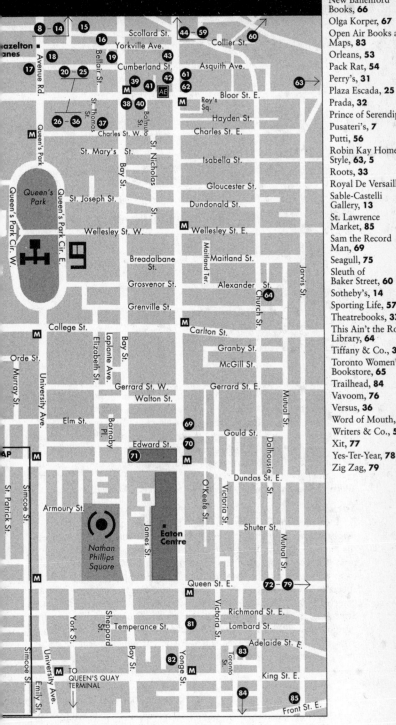

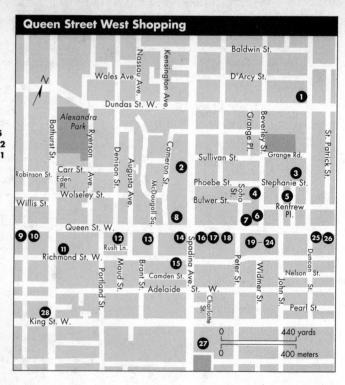

five-minute walk north of the corner of Yonge and Bloor. The stretch
of Yonge Street that runs from the Rosedale subway stop (at Yonge
and Crescent streets) north to just past the Summerhill stop (at Yonge
and Shaftesbury streets) is the best place to find the most upscale antiques and interiors shops. From the cottage chic of Pack Rat right up
to the French Provincial treasures of Absolutely, this area delights. If
the thought of freight charges dissuades you from serious spending,
you can check out the trinkets at tiny shops like French Country and
Word of Mouth, which carries every imaginable kitchen device.

Yorkville

Back in the 1960s, Yorkville was Canada's hippie headquarters, a
mecca for potheads, runaways, and folk musicians. Now this area is
the place to find the big fashion names (including about 200 shops for
men's and women's designer clothing), fine leather goods, upscale
shoe stores, important jewelers, some of the top private art galleries,
specialty bookstores, and crafts and home decor shops, as well as
eateries from coffee shops to elegant northern Italian restaurants.
Streets to explore include Yorkville Avenue and Cumberland Street, running parallel to Bloor Street, and Scollard Street, running north from
Yorkville Avenue, east of Avenue Road. These are among the most chichi
shopping streets in Canada.

Blitz Tours

Get yourself ready to move around the city by subway and streetcar,
and save enough strength to lug all your packages home from these
shopping itineraries. They're arranged by special theme; addresses, if
not included here, can be found in the store listings below.

Antiques

While Queen Street East from Pape Street to Jones Avenue is for those who enjoy trinkets and kitsch (☞ Queen Street Express, *below*), you have to go elsewhere for the more upscale antiques. Begin near the lake at the **Harbourfront Antiques Market** (⌧ 390 Queen's Quay W), easily accessible via the LRT from Union Station. Get off at Queen's Quay and walk a block west. About 50 stalls hold everything from big-ticket items like Persian carpets and armoires to smaller finds such as jewelry and china. Take the LRT back to Union Station and pick up the Yonge-University subway. Yonge Street, from the Rosedale subway stop at Crescent Street north to just past the Summerhill stop at Shaftesbury Street, is where you'll find the best pieces, though not at bargain prices. Begin your tour at **Pack Rat** (⌧ 1062 Yonge St.), across from the Rosedale subway, for items that, while not antiques, will look at home in country farms and cottages. From **Belle Époque** (⌧ 1062 Yonge St.) north to **Absolutely** (⌧ 1132 Yonge St.) are sandwiched a handful of exclusive antiques stores catering to those with a penchant for French provincial style. French bistros punctuate the trip north and make great stops for coffee and a croissant.

Queen Street Express

One of Toronto's most charming and utilitarian traditions is its streetcars. The Queen Street car, referred to by Torontonians as the Red Rocket, traverses the city from The Beaches in the east end, through antiques alley on Queen Street East, and on to the trendy Queen Street West. Start the day by scouring the one-of-a-kind gift stores like **Seagull** (⌧ 1972½ Queen St. E) and wind your way east past clothing stores like **Freeway** (⌧ 1978 Queen St. E). You can grab a latte at a coffee shop or bakery and walk through Kew Beach Park, on the south side of Queen Street, right down to the lake, where a boardwalk winds along the beach. Hop on the streetcar and continue west to Jones Avenue, where a string of quaint antiques stores begins. Be sure to stop at **Yes-Ter-Year** (⌧ 1142 Queen St. E) for the serious stuff and **Eye Spy** (⌧ 5 Coady Ave.) and **Neat Things** (⌧ 1126 Queen St. E) for whimsical '50s nostalgia pieces. Take the streetcar again to Queen St. West, where fashion and funk meet between Simcoe Street (on the east) and Spadina Avenue. It all starts at **Price Roman** (⌧ 267 Queen St. W) and **Noise** (⌧ 275 Queen St. W, at Simcoe St.) and stretches west with groovy vintage and homespun designer shops. For the home, don't miss **UpCountry** (⌧ 12 Beverly St.), a few steps north of Queen on Beverly, which carries the trendiest home decor items. Finish your day at any one of the strip's cafés, bistros, or bars.

Department Stores and Shopping Centers

The Bay (⌧ 44 Bloor St. E, ☎ 416/972–3333; ⌧ 160–184 Yonge St., ☎ 416/861–9111) carries mid-price clothing, furnishings, housewares, and cosmetics, including designer names as well as The Bay's own house lines. The Yonge Street store connects with Eaton Centre (☞ *below*). The Bloor Street store has a huge toy department, with a wide assortment of merchandise including CD-ROMs for kids.

Eaton Centre (☎ 416/598–2322), a block-long complex done in an exposed industrial style similar to that of Paris's Beaubourg Center, is anchored at its northern (Dundas Street) end by the nine-floor main branch of Eaton's (☞ *below*), one of Canada's classic department stores. The seven-floor The Bay (☞ *above*), connected by a covered skywalk over Queen Street at the southern end, is the modern descendant of the Hudson's Bay Company, charted in 1670 to explore and trade in furs. Prices at Eaton Centre increase with altitude: Level 1 contains fast-food courts, popularly priced fashions, electronics and record stores, and other useful merchandise; Level 2 is directed to the middle-income shopper; and Level 3 offers more expensive fashion and luxury goods. Well-lighted parking garages are sprinkled around the center, with spaces for some 1,800 cars. The complex is bordered by Yonge Street on the east, and James Street and Trinity Square on the west.

Eaton's (⊠ 290 Yonge St., ☎ 416/343–2111) in Eaton Centre (☞ *above*) carries low- to mid-price merchandise including clothing, housewares, furnishings, and cosmetics.

Hazelton Lanes (⊠ 99 Avenue Rd., ☎ 416/968–8600) is a paean to capitalism. This luxury shopping center's 90 stores offer everything from Teuscher's divine Swiss chocolates to Hermés silks and Giorgio Armani's latest fashions. In winter, the central courtyard café becomes a delightful skating rink.

Holt Renfrew (⊠ 50 Bloor St. W, ☎ 416/922–2333) is filled with high-end clothing and housewares, including couture lines not carried elsewhere in the city; the store sings with élan and quality.

Queen's Quay Terminal (⊠ Queen's Quay W and York St., ☎ 416/203–0510), a renovated warehouse, hosts a collection of unique boutiques, crafts stalls, patisseries, and more; it's a great place to buy gifts. A free shuttle bus runs from Union Station, as does the LRT line, but it's a fairly easy walk. Parking is expensive.

Specialty Shops

Antiques and Interiors

Absolutely (⊠ 1132 Yonge St., ☎ 416/324–8351) provides a mixture of solid French antique pieces and whimsical trinkets like stuffed and mounted animals. This store is a famed interiors destination.

Belle Époque (⊠ 1066 Yonge St., ☎ 416/925–0066) sells very French, very *cher*, antique and reproduction furnishings from sleigh beds that look as if they came direct from Versailles to accents like flirtatious ceramic lamps and candleholders.

Eye Spy (⊠ 5 Coady Ave., near Queen St. E, ☎ 416/461–4061) serves up '50s collectibles and furnishings, including the best collection of colorful '50s tableware in the city.

French Country (⊠ 6 Roxborough St., ☎ 416/944–2204) is a quaint shop that stocks mostly French treasures and trinkets, from crystal vases to vintage candelabras. If you need a hostess gift, this is the place to pick up something unique and affordable.

Harbourfront Antiques Market (⊠ 390 Queen's Quay W, ☎ 416/260–2626), Canada's largest, provides the widest choices for browsers and shoppers, including about 100 to 200 dealers in furniture, dishes, jewelry, art, and carpets. The whole area hops on Sunday, but the market is also open the rest of the week, although some stalls will be closed for hours at a time.

Neat Things (⊠ 1126 Queen St. E, ☎ 416/778–9453) is the destination for kitsch and collectibles from the '50s and '60s. Have a burning desire for a velvet Elvis painting? It can be found here.

Orleans (⊠ 1106 Yonge St., ☎ 416/925–7875) stocks antiques with a Mission twist—solid pieces reminiscent of Frank Lloyd Wright. Most items are mid- to high-priced.

Prince of Serendip (⊠ 1073 Yonge St., ☎ 416/925–3760) is a virtual visit to Versailles, with plenty of gilt goodies. The merchandise is pricey, but the pieces are great quality.

Putti (✉ 1104 Yonge St., ☎ 416/972–7652) sells treasures large and small, from France and elsewhere in Europe, for home and summer home. It's high priced but worth the visit for the beauty of the store alone.

Quasi Modo (✉ 789 Queen St. W, ☎ 416/703–8300) has a quirky collection of 20th-century furniture and design. You never know what will be on display: vintage bicycles, Noguchi lamps, a corrugated cardboard table by Frank Gehry. They will order any (available) lamp for you.

Vavoom (✉ 1114 Queen St. E, ☎ 416/465–2770) takes shoppers on a trip through time, with retro styles from soda-fountain stools to bean-bag chairs.

Xit (✉ 1124 Queen St. E, ☎ 416/778–0823) displays high-end, post-modern interior decor from polished chrome chairs to sleek vases.

Zig Zag (✉ 1107 Queen St. E, ☎ 416/778–6495) captures the feeling of Grandmother's attic, with antiques and trinkets large and small from $20 to $2,000. Shoppers can unearth vintage linens and larger items like turn-of-the-century iron beds.

Art and Crafts Galleries

Toronto is a cosmopolitan art center, with more than 200 commercial art galleries listed in the Yellow Pages, offering every kind of art for viewing and sale, from representational to abstract, from Inuit to Indian. The following is a list of some of the best and most-respected galleries. The entertainment section of the Saturday *Globe and Mail* has several pages of listings and reviews of current shows, as does *NOW*, a free city newspaper that comes out every Thursday and can be picked up at most restaurants, bars, and hotels. Gallery strolls are fun in either of two major districts—the Yorkville area, and the Queen Street area, west of University Avenue. You can also check out some of the commercial art galleries on the north side of Dundas Street, across from the Art Gallery of Ontario, many of which display classical and contemporary Chinese paintings. Most galleries are open Tuesday through Saturday, 10 AM–5 or 6 PM, but call to be sure.

Bau-Xi Gallery (✉ 40 Dundas St. W, ☎ 416/977–0600), across the street from the Art Gallery of Ontario, was founded by Paul Wong, an artist and dealer from Vancouver. It provides a window on contemporary Canadian West Coast art (some from Ontario, as well), much of it affordable.

Drabinsky Friedland Gallery (✉ 122 Scollard St., ☎ 416/324–5766), with attractive, rosy-maple floors, represents such major artists as Harold Town and Alex Colville.

Feheley Fine Arts (✉ 14 Hazelton Ave. in Hazelton Lanes, ☎ 416/323–1373) deals exclusively in Canadian Inuit art with a special emphasis on the contemporary period.

Gallery One (✉ 121 Scollard St., ☎ 416/929–3103) is one of the mainstays for large-format abstract expressionists in Canada and the United States, as well as for representational landscape art from western Ontario and Inuit art. Color-field painters, from Larry Poons to Jules Olitski, are exhibited here.

Gallery Moos (✉ 622 Richmond St. W, ☎ 416/504–5445) was opened by German-born Walter Moos more than 30 years ago to promote Canadian art. He is a discerning, reliable dealer, whose gallery has Picassos, Chagalls, Miros, and Dufys, as well as such internationally admired Canadians as Gershon Iskowitz, Ken Danby, Sorel Etrog, and Jean-Paul Riopelle.

Glass Art Gallery (✉ 21 Hazelton Ave., ☎ 416/968–1823) is a delightful showroom of stained glass, laminated and crystal sculpture, and other avant-garde work.

Guild Shop (✉ 118 Cumberland St., ☎ 416/921–1721) is an outlet for a variety of Canadian artists. Soapstone carvings from Inuit communities in the Arctic, aboriginal paintings from British Columbia and Ontario, and even woolen ties from Nova Scotia are among the items for sale.

Isaacs/Inuit Gallery (✉ 9 Prince Arthur Ave., ☎ 416/921–9985) was started by the respected Av Isaacs to showcase fine art and crafts produced in the Canadian Arctic. It is the finest gallery of its kind anywhere. Prints, drawings, sculpture, wall hangings, and antiquities are all beautifully displayed.

Jane Corkin Photographic Gallery (✉ 179 John St., ☎ 416/979–1980) has proven that photography is a major art form. Featuring everyone from André Kertesz to Richard Avedon, this gallery is one of the most fascinating in town, showing hand-painted photos, documentary photos, and fashion photography.

Maslak McLeod (✉ 25 Prince Arthur Ave., ☎ 416/944–2577) offers an assortment of Canadian native and Inuit art.

Mira Godard Gallery (✉ 22 Hazelton Ave., ☎ 416/964–8197), which came from Montréal to Toronto in 1972, carries such major French-Canadian artists as Borduas and Riopelle, as well as established Canadian artists like Alex Colville, Kenneth Lochhead, David Milne, Jean-Paul Lemieux, and Christopher Pratt.

Miriam Shiell Fine Art Ltd. (✉ 16A Hazelton Ave., ☎ 416/925–2461) is a wittily designed space for displaying 20th-century modern and contemporary fine art.

Nancy Poole's Studio (✉ 16 Hazelton Ave., ☎ 416/964–9050) is a small, intimate space, almost exclusively exhibiting Canadian contemporary painting and sculpture, generally representational. The artists include Jack Chambers, the astonishing Canadian Indian stone carver Joe Jacobs, and the fine contemporary painter John Boyle.

Olga Korper (✉ 17 Morrow Ave. N, ☎ 416/538–8220), showing art from the 1960s on, is one of the most accessible and knowledgeable dealers in Toronto, and she is a trailblazer who has discovered many important artists. This is a fine place for beginning collectors to visit.

Prime Gallery (✉ 52 McCaul St., ☎ 416/593–5750) has crafts from across Canada, including avant-garde ceramics, functional teapots, wall sculpture, and jewelry.

Sable–Castelli Gallery (✉ 33 Hazelton Ave., ☎ 416/961–0011) is the result of the Jared Sable gallery's amalgamation in 1974 with the renowned Castelli galleries of Manhattan. Since then, he has exhibited established American artists such as Warhol, Oldenburg, Johns, and Rosenquist, as well as innovative young Canadian artists who use strong expressive imagery.

S. L. Simpson Gallery (✉ 515 Queen St. W, ☎ 416/504–3738) has new Canadian paintings and mixed media.

Wynick/Tuck Gallery (✉ 80 Spadina Ave., ☎ 416/364–8716) represents contemporary Canadian artists whose work expresses a wide range of untrendy, often imagistic concerns. Many of them have become well established, attesting to the gallery's influence.

Ydessa Hendeles Art Foundation (⊠ 778 King St., ☎ 416/413–9400) is a major showcase for contemporary international art.

YYZ (⊠ 1087 Queen St. W, ☎ 416/531–7869) features performance art, films, and videos, as well as two- and three-dimensional paintings and sculptures. Graduates of the Ontario College of Art frequently have debut exhibitions here.

Auctions

Sotheby's (Canada) Inc. (⊠ 9 Hazelton Ave., ☎ 416/926–1774) auctions the rare finds and treasures of past and present, including furnishings, jewels, and art twice a year—in the spring and fall—at the nearby Design Exchange building.

Books

Toronto is rich in stores selling every sort of new and used books.

Book City (⊠ 208 Bloor St. W, ☎ 416/921–5686; ⊠ 501 Bloor St. W, ☎ 416/961–4496) provides good discounts, even on recently published books and best-sellers, has a knowledgeable staff, and offers a fine choice of magazines. It is usually open late.

Chapters (⊠ 110 Bloor St. W, ☎ 416/920–9299) is the gold standard of chain bookstores. This one is a three-story book lovers' mecca complete with coffee shop and lounge areas for reading. If you are into multimedia, Chapters also has the biggest selection of CD-ROMs in Toronto.

David Mirvish Books/Books on Art (⊠ Mirvish Village, 596 Markham St., ☎ 416/531–9975) overflows with quality books and many remainders; it has the best price in town for the Sunday *New York Times*.

Lichtman's News and Books (⊠ 144 Yonge St., ☎ 416/368–7390; ⊠ the Atrium on Bay St., north of Dundas, ☎ 416/591–1617; ⊠ 842 Yonge St., ☎ 416/924–4186) has a good selection of books, but is best known for its selection of magazines and its newspapers from around the world, often only a day old.

Pages Books and Magazines (⊠ 256 Queen St. W, ☎ 416/598–1447) has a wide selection of international and small-press literature; fashion and design books and magazines; and books on film, art, and literary criticism.

This Ain't the Rosedale Library (⊠ 483 Church St., ☎ 416/929–9912) stocks a general selection of magazines and books as well as a number of gay and lesbian titles.

Writers & Co. (⊠ 2005 Yonge St., ☎ 416/481–8432) is arguably Canada's finest literary bookstore, with hard-to-find poets, essayists, and novelists. If you have been looking for a rare Caribbean poetry collection, a Swedish play in translation, or an Asian novella, this is the store to visit. The staff will be happy to order any book for you that's not in stock.

SPECIAL-INTEREST BOOKSTORES

Children's Bookstore (⊠ 2532 Yonge St., ☎ 416/480–0233), in a 1930s YMCA building, is simply magical. It frequently holds, especially during March school break and October to December, storytelling sessions and author appearances for new books. The staff knows and loves children and the literature they long for. The store also has a superior collection of children's records, many of them Canadian.

The Cookbook Store (⊠ 850 Yonge St., ☎ 416/920–2665 or 800/268–6018) has the city's largest selection of books and magazines on cooking and wine; book signings are frequently held here.

Israel's Judaica Centre (⌧ 897 Eglinton Ave. W, ☎ 416/256–1010 or 800/449–5918) offers the city's best selection of adult and children's books relating to Judaism in English, Hebrew, and Yiddish. Service is excellent.

New Ballenford Books (⌧ 600 Markham St., ☎ 416/588–0800) has Canada's largest selection of architecture titles and a gallery with usually interesting exhibits of architectural drawings and related work.

Open Air Books and Maps (⌧ 25 Toronto St., ☎ 416/363–0719) offers more than 10,000 travel guides, oodles of atlases and road maps, specialized travel books, and titles on nature and food.

Sleuth of Baker Street (⌧ 1600 Bayview Ave., ☎ 416/483–3111) is the best place for mysteries and detective fiction.

Theatrebooks (⌧ 11 St. Thomas St., ☎ 416/922–7175 or 800/361–3414, FAX 416/922–0739) has an astounding collection of performance arts books: theater, film, opera, jazz, television, and media studies.

Toronto Women's Bookstore (⌧ 73 Harbord St., ☎ 416/922–8744) carries the latest feminist works on women's political and legal issues, divorce, childbirth, lesbian topics, and more. A reading lounge is upstairs.

Clothing

CHILDREN'S CLOTHING

Gap Kids (⌧ 80 Bloor St. W, ☎ 416/515–0668) has plenty of pint-size basics in one of few freestanding Gap Kids stores in Canada.

MEN'S CLOTHING

Boomer (⌧ 309 Queen St. W, ☎ 416/598–0013), one of the best-kept secrets of Toronto men, brings together tasteful yet trendy suitings and separates.

Eddie Bauer (⌧ 50 Bloor St. W, ☎ 416/961–2525) offers casual wear and clothes for sports along with accessories like Swiss Army knives and watches.

Harry Rosen (⌧ 82 Bloor St. W, ☎ 416/972–0556) is a department store in miniature, dedicated to men's fashion. Rosen brings together the finest menswear designers from Abboud to Boss.

Moore's, the Suit People (⌧ 100 Yonge St., ☎ 416/363–5442, 416/736–7520 for other locations) stocks thousands of Canadian-made men's dress pants, sport coats, and suits, including many famous labels and sizes ranging from extra tall to extra short and oversize, at low prices (e.g., all-wool suits that usually cost about $500 may sell for about half that). You'll find solid quality and good service.

Perry's (⌧ 131 Bloor St. W, ☎ 416/923–7397) maintains a collection of some of the finest accessories and suitings. This is also one of the best places in town to have a suit custom made from a broad range of fabrics.

MEN'S AND WOMEN'S CLOTHING

Banana Republic (⌧ 80 Bloor St. W, ☎ 416/515–0018) serves up basic separates, suitings, and casual wear at middling to high prices. This two-story flagship store also stocks men's styles.

Club Monaco (⌧ 157 Bloor St. W, ☎ 416/591–8837), along with Roots (☞ *below*), is a Canadian fashion success story. An old gymnasium provides the Canadian flagship store with a spacious shopping environment for homegrown design basics—mid-priced sportswear and career clothes.

Roots (✉ 95-A Bloor St. W, ☎ 416/323–3289) is the manufacturer famous for the Canadian Olympic team's winning uniforms. The flagship store offers the city's favorite leather jackets, bags, and basics.

Angi Venni (✉ 274 Queen St. W, ☎ 416/597–9360) sells funked-up office attire (sort of Armani meets Lacroix). A Canadian designer and retailer, she has done well with young professionals without the budget for more upscale basics.

Chanel (✉ 131 Bloor St. W, ☎ 416/925–2577) is a boutique Coco would have loved. The lush surroundings showcase most of Karl Lagerfeld's creations for the Chanel line, including the double-C'd bags and accessories.

Corbò Boutique (✉ 110 Bloor St. W, ☎ 416/928–0954) gathers clothes by some of the most tasteful designers under one roof, along with some of the finest footwear in town. It's upscale one-stop shopping.

Fashion Crimes (✉ 395 Queen St. W, ☎ 416/592–9001) sells fashion inspired by the medieval and Victorian ages. The clothes are dramatic but still wearable.

Fetoun (✉ 162 Cumberland St., ☎ 416/923–3434) offers high-fashion gowns and evening clothes. If you go to a lot of charity balls, this is the place to shop.

Freeway (✉ 1978 Queen St. E, ☎ 416/693–6670) presents casual clothing much in keeping with Coney Island atmosphere of the store's locale in the Beaches district. Freeway is the place to find lines like Mexx and Dex Bros.—lines that are both sporty and sexy.

F/X (✉ 383 Queen St. W, ☎ 416/585–9568) embraces the philosophy of fashion as costuming. Some call the crinolined skirts, wild colors, and short skirts masquerade, but the clothes are undeniably fun, especially for evening wear.

Gianni Versace (✉ 83 Bloor St. W, ☎ 416/920–8300) is a testament to the late designer, whose sister, Donatella Versace, is designing both the Versus and Versace lines. This magnificent store carries both colorful couture creations and some home-decor items from stemware to throw cushions.

Hermès (✉ 131 Bloor St. W, ☎ 416/968–8626), a tony boutique, caters to the horse- and hound-loving set with the house's trademark casual wear, accessories, handbags, and luggage.

Linda Lundstrom (✉ 2507 Yonge St., ☎ 416/480–1602; ✉ 136 Cumberland St., ☎ 416/927–9009) is an award-winning designer of high-fashion winter clothing. This is the place to buy an eye-catching parka.

Mendocino (✉ 365 Queen St. W, ☎ 416/593–1011) carries the best of the mid-price lines, from InWear to Powerline. Mendocino is a great stop if you have limited time and want to pack a lot in, since you can peruse the day and evening designs of a number of lines here.

Parade (✉ 315 Queen St. W, ☎ 416/971–7767) specializes in whimsical and flirtatious female fashion. Parade is known for Betsey Johnson–esque dresses.

Plaza Escada (✉ 110 Bloor St. W, ☎ 416/964–2265) is a spacious new store carrying the Italian designer's line.

Prada (✉ 131 Bloor St. W, Unit 5, ☎ 416/513–0400) is a much heralded addition to Bloor Street. The avant-garde designs are overshadowed only by the brilliant celadon interior of the store.

Price Roman (⊠ 267 Queen St. W, ☎ 416/979–7363) sells edgy career wear and separates for women. Think Jil Sander minimalism combined with Alexander McQueen's sexy cutouts and surprising fabric choices; you'll find it here.

Sunde (⊠ 355 Queen St. W, ☎ 416/977–8834) showcases smart and sexy little suits that put a new spin on office wear. If a lavender miniskirted Versace suit is out of your price range, Sunde offers the next-best thing.

Versus (⊠ 77 Bloor St. W, ☎ 416/929–5966) is Versace's more moderately priced ready-to-wear line, designed by the late designer's sister Donatella Versace. This austere boutique carries most of the Versus line, including the signature suits in outrageous colors and the trademark daringly bare dresses for evening.

VINTAGE CLOTHING

Black Market (⊠ 323-A Queen St. W., ☎ 416/591–7945), tucked on the second floor overlooking Queen Street, sells vintage for real aficionados. You have to hunt through racks and bins—very thrift shop—but the bargains are here.

Noise (⊠ 275 Queen St. W, ☎ 416/971–6479), a favorite with Toronto teens, stock staples like vintage furs, sweaters, and '50s garb.

Preloved (⊠ 611 Queen St. W, ☎ 416/504–8704) was created by former models and fashion insiders who have combed the vintage market for couture pieces from the '50s to be offered at vintage prices. If you want a piece of fashion history, this is the place to find it.

Zinc (⊠ 471 Richmond St. W, ☎ 416/504–6013) typifies a growing number of upscale vintage shops. Its pristine surroundings and cleaned and pressed '50s stock bestows a boutique feel to vintage merchandise.

Discount Clothing and Housewares

Winners (⊠ 57 Spadina Ave., ☎ 416/585–2052) offers designer lines at rock-bottom prices. This is Toronto's best bargain outlet.

Food Markets

Kensington Market (⊠ northwest of Dundas St. and Spadina Ave., ☎ no phone) is an outdoor market with a vibrant ethnic mix. This is where you'll find delightful and exotic Caribbean foods; great cheese, coffee, nuts, and spices; natural foods; South American delicacies; Portuguese bakeries; and charming restaurants. Vintage clothing lovers will delight in the trove of shops tucked into houses lining the streets. Saturday is the best day to go, preferably by public transit, as parking is difficult.

St. Lawrence Market (⊠ Front St. and Jarvis St., ☎ 416/392–7219) is best early (from 5 AM) on Saturday, when, in addition to the permanent indoor market on the south side of Front Street, there's a farmer's market in the building on the north side. The historic south market was once Toronto's city hall, and it fronted the lake before extensive landfill projects were undertaken; it's open all week except Monday and has good selections in everything from produce to equipment for make-your-own wine and beer.

Food Shops

All the Best Fine Foods (⊠ 1099 Yonge St., ☎ 416/928–3330) provides imported cheeses and good local breads as well as high-quality prepared foods and condiments.

The Big Carrot (⊠ 348 Danforth Ave., ☎ 416/466–2129), a large and adventurous health-food supermarket, carries large selections of organic produce, health and beauty aids, and vitamins; there's a café on site and fresh prepared foods for takeout.

Pusateri's (✉ 1739 Avenue Rd., ☎ 416/785–9100) started as a produce stand in Little Italy and today is Toronto's deluxe supermarket, with a wide range of in-house prepared foods, local and imported delicacies, and desserts and breads from the city's best bakers. It's great for putting together a picnic.

Fur
Fur central is Spadina Avenue, from Queen Street north to Dundas Street.

Magder Furs (✉ 202 Spadina Ave., ☎ 416/504–6077), run by fur king Paul Magder, is where the ladies who lunch have bought coats and jackets for more than two decades.

Home Decor and Furnishings
Brendan's Bedding (✉ 60 Bloor St. W, ☎ 416/921–8997) sells high-end accessories for the bedroom and bathroom, including some of the best linens in Toronto.

Demarco Perpich (✉ 1116 Yonge St., ☎ 416/967–0893) is a floral bounty with adorable arrangements and garden-inspired accents for the home.

Du Verre (✉ 280 Queen St. W, ☎ 416/593–0182) started as a glass company and has expanded to include some of the trendiest pieces for the home (tables, sofas, and more) Toronto has to offer.

Hollace Cluny (✉ 1070 Yonge St., ☎ 416/968–7894) sells mainly modern furnishings and accents from chrome pieces to letter holders.

Pack Rat (✉ 1062 Yonge St., ☎ 416/924–5613) stocks home furnishings for a chic cottage or for cottage chic in the city.

Robin Kay Home and Style (✉ 276 Queen St. W, ☎ 416/585–7731; ✉ 348 Danforth Ave., ☎ 416/466–1211; ✉ 394 Spadina Rd., ☎ 416/932–2833; ✉ 2599 Yonge St., ☎ 416/485–5097), this country's answer to Martha Stewart, carries homespun, eco-friendly clothing in hemp and linen, and products to enliven any interior.

Seagull (✉ 1972½ Queen St. E, ☎ 416/690–5224) specializes in unusual lamps, including Art Deco–inspired brass bases sculpted in female forms and Tiffany-style light fixtures.

UpCountry (✉ 12 Beverly St., ☎ 416/586–1370) is an expansive, loft-inspired space filled with a wide array of modern and reproduction furnishings.

Urban Mode (✉ 389 Queen St. W, ☎ 416/591–8834) carries modern and trend-oriented home accessories from chenille leopard throws to funky wine racks and CD stands.

Yes-Ter-Year (✉ 1142 Queen St. E, ☎ 416/778–6888) is the place for quality reproduction pieces with an Indonesian flair.

Jewelry
Cartier (✉ 101 Bloor St. W, ☎ 416/967–1785) caters to Toronto's elite. The store has the best of the famed jewelry designer's creations.

Royal De Versailles (✉ 101 Bloor St. W, ☎ 416/967–7201) is well guarded, but don't let the security at the front door scare you away. Royal De Versailles is noted for having some of the most innovatively classic jewelry designs in town.

Tiffany & Co. (✉ 85 Bloor St. W, ☎ 416/921–3900) makes the grade for breakfast or anytime. Tiffany's is still the ultimate for variety and quality in classic jewelry.

Kitchenware and Tabletop

Ashley China (✉ 55 Bloor St. W, ☎ 416/964–2900) has a computer system capable of tracking virtually any china pattern ever made. Crystal and china are beautifully displayed, and prices are decent on expensive names such as Waterford. If Ashley's doesn't stock a pattern, the staff can find it for you.

Word Of Mouth (✉ 1134 Yonge St., ☎ 416/929–6885) sells kitchen appliances, accessories, and tools at very competitive prices.

Music and Stereo Equipment

Bay Bloor Radio (✉ 55 Bloor St. W, ☎ 416/967–1122), a stereo haven, has the latest equipment and has sound-sealed listening rooms that allow the connoisseur to test-drive equipment.

HMV (✉ 50 Bloor St. W, ☎ 416/324–9979; ✉ 333 Yonge St., ☎ 416/596–0333) has the largest selection of CDs of all categories in the city. In-store listening stations allow consumers to sample any CD prior to purchase.

Sam the Record Man (✉ 347 Yonge St., ☎ 416/977–4650) is a Toronto institution, having occupied the corner of Yonge and Gould streets for over three decades. A wide assortment of music is stocked, and the bargain bins are always overflowing.

Shoes

Brown's (✉ Eaton Centre, ☎ 416/979–9270; ✉ 50 Bloor St. W, in Holt Renfrew, ☎ 416/960–4925) has an excellent selection of shoes, including the latest designer models from Manolo Blahnik to Steve Madden. Brown's also carries a broad range of handbags and boots.

David's (✉ 66 Bloor St. W, ☎ 416/920–1000) has a somewhat subdued but always elegant collection.

Mephisto Boutique (✉ 1177 Yonge St., ☎ 416/968–7026) has been making its fine walking shoes since the 1960s—and all from natural materials. Passionate walkers swear by these shoes, and claim they never, ever wear out—even in cross-Europe treks.

Sporting Goods

Sporting Life (✉ 2665 Yonge St., ☎ 416/485–1611), in Toronto's north end, has become the ultimate place for sports equipment and apparel. The first off the mark with the latest sports trends, this is the place to get rad snowboard gear and advice on where to go to use it.

Trailhead (✉ 61 Front St. E, ☎ 416/862–0881) started life catering to camp and canoe enthusiasts but has grown to include sporting equipment for activities from racquetball to rock climbing. Still, this store's specialty is rugged outdoor sports, and the staff are real experts who can offer great advice on the best gear.

8 Side Trips

Of course there's no question of leaving the vicinity without seeing the Falls—you know the ones we mean—but there's more to the Toronto environs than a huge water rush. Two major theater events (the Stratford Festival and the Shaw Festival) and the pleasures of lovely Niagara-on-the-Lake are additional reasons to stray from the metropolis.

ACOMBINATION OF RURAL PLEASURES and sophisticated theater draw people to the town of
Stratford and to the Niagara area. Stratford, a
small industrial city, made a name for itself with its Shakespeare festival, while the Niagara Peninsula has both the famous falls and the
Shaw festival. Once you're in these areas, you'll also discover other
lures—parks, gardens, wineries, and country trails.

Updated by
Mike Filey and
Sara Waxman
(dining)

Pleasures and Pastimes

Dining

There's more to Stratford than its theatrical performances. The creation of the Stratford Chef's School in 1983, with 100% employment
for its yearly graduating class, has made an enormous difference in the
quality of restaurant dining in the area. Though there is a something-
for-everyone range of eateries in this small town, they all have one thing
in common: They'll get you to the show on time. During the festival,
from early May through October, even the restaurants get into the act
with culinary tableaux.

George Bernard Shaw once said "No greater love hath man than the
love of food," so it's only proper that Niagara-on-the-Lake, home to
a festival devoted to the playwright, should have a wealth of good restaurants. Many of them serve fine wines and produce from the verdant
Niagara Peninsula. Though the town seems to have changed little
from its turn-of-the-century style, new restaurants proliferate, including Italian, Chinese, and glitzy North American fusion.

Most people go to Niagara Falls for the view and fall for the food. Just
a few years ago, you would have been hard pressed to find anything
other than steaks, chops, and chicken here, but lately this small town
with big ideas has clued into the fact that the collective palate demands
excitement. These days it's easy to find Japanese, Greek, and Italian
cuisine, as well as copious Canadian-style breakfasts and brunches.

For approximate costs, *see* the dining price chart *in* Chapter 3.

Fruit-Picking

Many fruit farms on the Niagara Peninsula offer roadside stands
and/or pick-your-own options (☎ 800/263–2988 for a guide to the
latter as well as for information on other Niagara attractions). Here
and around Stratford you'll find an abundant choice of such fruit as
blueberries, peaches, and cherries, as well as late summer vegetables
like corn and field tomatoes; don't miss the fresh juice drinks, either.

Hiking

The Bruce Trail, a posted hiking path, starts in the Niagara region and
follows the Niagara Escarpment north about 240 km (150 mi) to Lake
Huron. The Niagara Parkway, which runs 56 km (35 mi) along the
Niagara River, has easy walks and great water views. Many pleasant
hiking trails can be found outside Stratford proper.

Lodging

Stratford has a range of comfortable accommodations but no luxury
hotels. Still, in Stratford the term "bed-and-breakfast" often refers to
an establishment more like a small luxury inn (with prices to match),
while "guest home" is more like a bare-bones European-style bed-and-
breakfast. The surrounding towns have some lovely old country inns.

In Niagara Falls, you can take your pick from almost any price range,
services, or facilities. Heart-shape bathtubs, water beds, heated pools,

Jacuzzis, baby-sitting services—the choice is yours. Prices fall between mid-September and mid-May, and less expensive packages for families, honeymooners, and others are usually available. Although Niagara-on-the-Lake has few accommodations, the ones here possess unusual charm. For those on a tight budget, remember that Niagara Falls, with its abundance of low-priced motels, is less than 20 minutes away.

If you want to stay in a bed-and-breakfast in the area, contact the **Niagara Region Bed & Breakfast Service** (✉ 2631 Dorchester Rd., Niagara Falls L2J 2Y9, ☎ 905/358–8988) or the **Niagara-on-the-Lake Chamber of Commerce Visitor and Convention Bureau** (☞ Visitor Information *in* Niagara Peninsula A to Z, *below*), which lists more than 60 guest homes.

For approximate costs, *see* the lodging price chart *in* Chapter 4.

Theater

Who says there's no money in the arts? A couple of long-dead British playwrights have managed to make two Ontario towns boom from May through October. The Shakespeare festival in Stratford and the Shaw festival in Niagara-on-the-Lake both enjoy great popular success as well as critical acclaim.

Wineries

One of the three best regions for wine production in Canada (Point Pelee, also in Ontario, and British Columbia are the others), the Niagara Peninsula has an unusually good microclimate for growing grapes. More than 20 small, quality vineyards produce fine wines in the area; most of them offer tastings and tours.

STRATFORD

Ever since July 1953, when one of the world's greatest actors, Alec Guinness, joined with probably the world's greatest Shakespearean director, Tyrone Guthrie, beneath a hot, stuffy tent in a backward little town about 145 km (90 mi) and 90 minutes from Toronto, the Stratford Festival has been one of the most successful, most widely admired theaters of its kind in the world—and the town has been ensured a place on the map of Canada.

The origins of Ontario's Stratford are modest. After the War of 1812, the British government granted a million acres of land along Lake Huron to the Canada Company, headed by a Scottish businessman. When the surveyors came to a marshy creek surrounded by a thick forest, they named it "Little Thames" and noted that it might make "a good millsite." It was Thomas Mercer Jones, a director of the Canada Company, who decided to rename the river the Avon, and the town Stratford. The year was 1832, 121 years before the concept of a theater festival would take flight and change Canadian culture.

For many years Stratford was considered a backwoods hamlet. Although it had the highest elevation of any town in Ontario—1,150 ft above sea level—it was too swampy to grow anything. In 1871, "Muddy Stratford" was made a division point for a major railway, attracting both industry and population. Though the river was now named Avon, it was a stump-filled, filthy disaster, bordered by a livery stable, a junkyard, and the city dump.

Then came the first of two saviors of the city, both of them (undoubting) Thomases. In 1904, an insurance broker named Tom Orr transformed Stratford's riverfront into a park. He also built a formal English garden, where every flower mentioned in the plays of Shakespeare—monkshood to sneezewort, bee balm to bachelor's button—blooms grandly to this day. When Tyrone Guthrie compared an aerial photograph of Stratford's park with a photo of the park in Stratford-upon-Avon, England, he was stunned to find the two nearly identical.

Next, Tom Patterson, a fourth-generation Stratfordian born in 1920, looked around; saw that the town wards and schools had names like Hamlet, Falstaff, and Romeo; and felt that some kind of drama festival might save his community from becoming a ghost town. (The diesel was coming in, and all the steam-engine repair shops that had kept Stratford alive for generations were soon to close down.)

The astonishing story of how he began in 1952 with $125 (a "generous" grant from the Stratford City Council), tracked down the directorial genius Tyrone Guthrie and the inspired stage and screen star Alec Guinness, obtained the services of the brilliant stage designer Tanya Moiseiwitsch, and somehow pasted together a world-class theater festival in a little over one year is recounted in Patterson's memoirs, *First Stage—The Making of the Stratford Festival.*

The festival is now moving into middle age and it has had its ups and downs. Soon after it opened and wowed critics from around the world with its professionalism, costumes, and daring thrust stage, the air was filled with superlatives that had not been heard in Canada since the Great Blondin walked across Niagara Falls on a tightrope.

The early years also brought giants of world theater to the tiny town of some 20,000: James Mason, Siobhan McKenna, Alan Bates, Christopher Plummer, Jason Robards Jr., and Maggie Smith. But the years also saw an unevenness in productions, a dreadful tendency to go for flash and glitter over substance, and a focus on costumes and furniture rather than on the ability to speak Shakespeare's words with clarity and intelligence. Many never lost faith in the festival; others, such as Canada's greatest theater critic, the late Nathan Cohen of the *Toronto Star,* once bemoaned that "Stratford has become Canada's most sacred cow."

Sacred or not, Stratford's offerings are still among the best of their kind in the world, with at least a handful of productions every year that put most other summer arts festivals to shame. The secret, of course, is to try to catch the reviews of the plays, which have their debuts in May, June, July, and August in the festival's three theaters, and then book as early as you can. (The *New York Times* always runs major write-ups, as do newspapers and magazines in many American and Canadian cities. And many of these papers now make their reviews available on the Internet.) For details about obtaining tickets, *see* Nightlife and the Arts, *below.*

There are many quieter things to do in Stratford when the theaters close. Art galleries remain open throughout winter. Shopping is great off-season, and those who love quiet walks will appreciate a quiet walk along the Avon. Many concerts are scheduled in the off-season, too.

Gallery Stratford has regular exhibits of Canadian visual art in a variety of media (some for sale) and, in summer, of theater arts. ✉ *54 Romeo St.,* ☎ *519/271–5271.* ☜ *$5.* ☽ *July–Aug., Mon. noon–4, Tues.–Sun. 9–6; June and Sept.–Oct., Tues.–Sun. 10–5; Nov.–May Tues.–Sun. 1–4.*

The **Stratford Perth Museum** interprets the history of Stratford and Perth County with displays that cover everything from the settlement of the area in the early 1800s to some of Canada's firsts, including the story of Dr. Jenny Trout, Canada's first female physician. Hockey in Stratford, Stratford's railroad history, children's activities, and a working printing press are other exhibits. ✉ *270 Water St.,* ☎ *519/271–5311.* ✉ *$3.* ⊙ *May–early Oct., Tues.–Sat. 10–4, Sun. noon–7; early Oct.– Apr., Thurs.–Sat. 10–4, Sun. noon–4.*

Dining and Lodging

$$$$ ✕ **Church Restaurant.** It was constructed in 1873 as a Congregational
★ church, but today white cloths gleam in the afternoon light that pours through the stained-glass windows, and greenery thrives. If your plan is to run in for a quick bite, you're in the wrong pew. Fixed price or à la carte, the meals here are production numbers. Tea-smoked salmon comes with sea scallops and shrimp; warm salad of spiced veal sweetbreads is lively with a cherry-tomato compote. The roast Ontario lamb with garlic custard and eggplant flan is outstanding. ✉ *70 Brunswick St.,* ☎ *519/273–3424. Reservations essential. AE, DC, MC, V. Closed Mon. and Dec.–May. No lunch Sun., Tues., Thurs., Fri.*

$$$$ ✕ **Rundles Restaurant.** The look here is Venetian, in a theatrical Stratford way. Flowing white silk scarves hang from a series of primitive stone masks in this sophisticated, calm restaurant. Several set menus with three courses each and a wine-with-dinner menu still leave plenty of choices. Seared fois gras with caramelized endive on garlic fried potatoes; marinated mushroom salad strewn with fresh nasturtium blossoms and a scattering of asparagus and just-picked peas; and crisp, potato-wrapped duck ravioli are worthy of applause. Chicken is roasted with a whole range of vegetables, and the peppered rib-eye steak is set on goose-fat-fried potatoes. ✉ *9 Cobourg St.,* ☎ *519/271–6442. AE, DC, MC, V. Closed Nov.–Apr. No lunch Mon.–Tues. and Thurs.–Fri.*

$$$–$$$$ ✕ **Old Prune.** A converted Victorian house holds a number of charm-
★ ing dining rooms and a glass-enclosed conservatory surrounded by a tidy sunken garden. The kitchen coaxes fresh local ingredients into innovative dishes: smoked rainbow trout with apple radish and curry oil; vegetable lasagna with roasted tomato sauce; or, with a nod to the East, chicken seasoned with coriander and cumin. Desserts are baked fresh for each meal and come straight from the oven. ✉ *151 Albert St.,* ☎ *519/271–5052. AE, MC, V. Closed Mon. and Nov.–Apr. No lunch Tues.*

$$–$$$ ✕ **Belfry at the Church Restaurant.** The upstairs level of the Church
★ Restaurant (☞ *above*) uses the same excellent kitchen, but you'll find a more casual ambience here and some lighter dishes. Typical dishes may include crab cakes with a zippy tequila and orange salsa; appetizer-size pasta with olive oil herbs and garlic; and medallions of Perth country pork, partnered with black linguine that is sauced with caper-flecked goat cheese cream. Forget your vows of prudence and go for the raspberry crème brûlée with orange. ✉ *70 Brunswick St.,* ☎ *519/ 273–3424. AE, DC, MC, V. Closed Mon. May–Oct. and Sun.–Mon. Nov.–Dec. No lunch Sun.*

$–$$ ✕ **Down the Street Bar and Café.** Funky and informal, this bistro with live jazz and food by Stratford Chefs School graduates is the hottest place in town. Thrilling grills of chicken, salmon, and rib eye, as well as grilled stacked tomato salad and herb-crusted pizza, make for delicious casual dining. An inspirational late-night menu includes everything from spicy spring rolls and steamed Prince Edward Island mussels to a classic cheeseburger with the works. ✉ *30 Ontario St.,* ☎ *519/ 273–5886. AE, MC, V. No lunch Mon.*

$ ✕ **Anna Banana's Cheesecakes and Cones.** The beautiful garden patio is a fine place to indulge in frozen yogurt, ice cream, cheesecakes, muffins, and a gourmet barbecue with four different kinds of natural 100% all-beef hot dogs. Nothing costs over $5. ✉ *39 George St.,* ☎ *519/272– 0065. Reservations not accepted. No credit cards. Closed mid-Oct.–Mar.*

$ ✕ **Bentley's Inn.** At this long and narrow British-style pub that is part
★ of an inn, the well-stocked bar divides the room into two equal halves.
There's an unspoken tradition here: The actors have claimed one side,
and the locals the other. Darts are played here, seriously, and getting a
bull's-eye is the norm. The menu consists of pub fare such as good fish-
and-chips, grilled steak and fries, and steak-and-mushroom pie. The ultimate club sandwich on homemade multigrain bread hits the spot for
lunch or dinner, while the sturdy dessert of fruit crumble and ice cream
is big enough for two. The regulars say they come for the imported, domestic, and microdraft beers—the easygoing ambience and camaraderie
are bonuses. ⊠ *99 Ontario St.,* ☎ *519/271–1121. AE, MC, V.*

$ ✕ **Movable Feast.** You can enjoy a special picnic prepared by the chefs
★ of the green room (where the actors eat) at the Festival Theatre. Dine
on the banks of the Avon or the Festival Theatre terraces. The Molière
picnic consists of marinated goat cheese, salad niçoise, and pudding,
while the Cyrano includes fresh asparagus vinaigrette, grilled chicken
breast with Thai rice-noodle salad, and lemon cheesecake. You can order
your picnics in advance up to 8 PM the day before a performance from
May 31 to October 2. ⊠ *Festival Theatre, 55 Queen St.,* ☎ *519/273–
1600. Reservations essential. AE, MC, V. Closed Nov.–Apr.*

$$$$ ✕🏠 **Langdon Hall and Country House Hotel.** Eugene Langdon Wilkes,
a descendant of John Jacob Astor, built Langdon Hall in 1898. It was
restored into a gracious country hotel in 1989 by William Bennett and
Mary Beaton. Rooms are luxuriously appointed; some have refrigerators and/or wood-burning fireplaces. All the civilized pleasures—tennis, croquet, and walking trails, for example—abound. The kitchen
dazzles with vivacious cooking that marries the nuances of classic
French cuisine with fresh Ontario meats and produce. Chicken, lamb,
and fish are roasted with vegetables and herbs from the garden. A trained
contingent of attentive servers are ever-vigilant. This charmer is just
35 minutes from Stratford. ⊠ *R.R. 33, Cambridge N3H 4R8,* ☎ *519/
740–2100 or 800/268–1898,* ℻ *519/740–8161. 41 rooms with bath.
Restaurant, bar, pool, hot tub, sauna, spa, steam room, tennis court,
croquet, exercise room. AE, DC, MC, V.*

$$–$$$ 🏠 **Stone Maiden Inn.** This beautiful place near the city center is furnished
with a Victorian theme. It's now totally nonsmoking. Rates include a
full buffet breakfast and afternoon refreshments. ⊠ *123 Church St., N5A
2R3,* ☎ *519/271–7129. 14 rooms with bath. Lobby lounge. MC, V.*

$$–$$$ 🏠 **Woods Villa Bed and Breakfast.** This elegant 1875 home once be-
longed to a wealthy magistrate; it has since been restored to its 19th-
century grandeur. The public rooms hold an astonishing collection of
restored vintage jukeboxes, music boxes, and player pianos. Start the
day on the right foot with a grand breakfast accompanied by full table
service. Five of the six rooms have fireplaces. Woods Villa does not accept children or pets; the latter might ruffle the feathers of the owner's
five tropical birds. Note that while the credit cards listed below are accepted, cash is preferred. ⊠ *62 John St. N, N5A 6K7,* ☎ *519/271–
4576. 6 rooms. Pool. MC, V.*

$$ 🏠 **Queen's Inn.** Large, curved windows and cheerful furnishing are part
of this country-style inn that stands in the heart of Stratford. The
Boar's Head is a popular pub-lounge with light snacks and a great va-
riety of brews. ⊠ *161 Ontario St., N5A 3H3,* ☎ *519/271–1400. 31
rooms with bath. Restaurant, lobby lounge. AE, MC, V.*

$–$$ 🏠 **23 Albert Place.** Since this three-story, brick-fronted building was
opened in 1876 as the Windsor Arms hotel, it has been refurbished a
few times; no elevator was ever installed, however, so you'll have to
walk up one or two flights to your room. The hotel is conveniently located in the heart of the downtown shopping area, just a few hundred
yards from the Avon Theatre. Some of the suites offer mini-refrigera-

tors and VCRs. ⊠ *23 Albert St., N5A 3K2,* ☎ *519/273–5800,* ⨎ *519/ 273–5008. 29 rooms with bath, 5 suites. Restaurant, lobby lounge. AE, MC, V.*

$–$$ 🏨 **Festival Inn.** An old-English atmosphere has survived modernization of this hotel on the eastern outskirts of town, only a short drive from the theaters. A building opened in 1996 added 40 rooms. All rooms have refrigerators, some have coffeemakers, and four rooms have double whirlpools. ⊠ *1144 Ontario St., Box 811, N5A 6W1,* ☎ *519/273– 1150,* ⨎ *519/273–2111. 183 rooms with bath. Restaurant, lobby lounge, indoor pool, hot tub, sauna, exercise room. AE, MC, V.*

$–$$ 🏨 **Swan Motel.** This unassuming brick motel, some 3 km (2 mi) south of the Avon Theatre, is known for the flower beds set on its generous grounds. Free coffee and muffins await guests in the morning. The Swan is happy to book guests at nearby public and private golf courses. ⊠ *959 Downie St., Stratford N5A 6S3,* ☎ *519/271–6376,* ⨎ *519/271– 0682. 24 rooms with bath. Refrigerators, pool. MC, V.*

$ 🏨 **Stratford General Hospital Residence.** Those traveling on a tight budget will like this modern, bright residence, rented out to tourists in the summer like a university residence. Rates include a full, cooked breakfast. ⊠ *Brenda Smellie, Housekeeping Supervisor, Stratford General Hospital Residence, 130 Youngs St., N5A 1J7,* ☎ *519/271–5084. 167 rooms with shared baths. Cafeteria, pool, coin laundry. No credit cards.*

Nightlife and the Arts

Theaters

The **Stratford Festival** offerings, now a mix of Shakespeare, works by other dramatists, and popular musicals, take place in three theaters, each in its own building and each with particular physical aspects (size, stage configuration, technical support) that favor different types of productions. This also means that at the height of the season you may have the flexibility of choosing among three simultaneous performances, and a weekend menu including up to 10 different productions.

The Festival Theatre, the original and, with nearly 1,850 seats, the largest, has a thrust stage that brings the action deep into the audience space. The theater has recently undergone an extensive renovation that included improved seating, installation of an elevator to improve access, and additional rest-room facilities. A new acoustical dome has also been added. Be forewarned: Due to the great fidelity of the stage to its Shakespearean original, and despite the new acoustical dome, it is recommended that fairly central seats be selected; otherwise, words and even whole speeches can be lost. The Avon has about 1,100 seats and a traditional proscenium stage. The Tom Patterson Theatre (formerly The Third Stage), with about 500 seats, is the most intimate. It has a modified thrust stage.

The Festival and the Avon theaters are open from early May to late October, the Tom Patterson Theatre and the Festival Fringe (a variety of special events and performance) start up in early June, with the Patterson productions going through September and the Fringe's continuing into October. There are matinee and evening performances Tuesday through Saturday, matinees only on Sunday; the theaters are dark on Monday.

Tickets

For tickets and information, contact the **Stratford Festival** (⊠ Box Office, Box 520, Stratford, Ontario N5A 6V2, ☎ 416/364–8355 in Toronto, 519/273–1600, or 800/567–1600). Regular tickets are $37–$67, but many special plans are available. If you order tickets, the festival has an accommodations department that can help you book a room, too. Special plans include the "Family Experience" plan, which allows the purchase of up to two seats at $25 for children 18 or younger with each regular-price ticket. Rush seats, when available, may be bought the day of the performance in person at the Stratford box office at 55 Queen Street, beginning at 9 AM, or by telephone beginning at 10 AM; prices range from $19.50 to $40. Students can get seats for $26. "Two for One" tickets are available for selected performances during June, September, October, and November at both the Festival and Avon theaters.

Wheelchair seating is available at all three theaters, but needs to be booked when ordering tickets. The two larger theaters also offer infrared receivers for people with hearing impairments at a nominal fee; again, you need to reserve when ordering tickets.

Events surrounding the plays include "Meet the Festival," a free series of informal discussions with members of the company, held at the Tom Patterson Theatre from July through August on Wednesday and Friday mornings 9:30 AM–10:30 AM. At the same time and place on Thursday mornings, Stratford Festival personnel host discussions about production issues and that season's themes. On designated Thursday nights from late June through late August there are also post-performance half-hour question-and-answer sessions with the actors. Meet the usher at Aisle 2, Orchestra Level, immediately after the performance. Contact the theater for confirmation of events.

Shopping

There are many tasteful shops in the downtown area, including antiques stores, arts-and-crafts studios, galleries, and bookshops.

Stratford A to Z

Arriving and Departing
BY BUS
Buses depart regularly from Toronto's main bus terminal at the corner of Dundas and Bay streets (☎ 416/594–3310). The trip takes up to three hours.

BY CAR
Take Highway 401 west to interchange 278 at Kitchener, follow Highway 8 through Kitchener, then join Highway 7/8 west to Stratford. Watch for the blue trailblazing signs along Highways 8 and 7/8. The drive takes about 1½ hours.

BY TRAIN
The trip from Toronto's Union Station takes about two hours. For tickets and schedules, call **Via Rail** (☎ 416/366–8411) or, from the United States, **Amtrak** (☎ 800/872–7245).

Guided Tours
The **Avon Historical Society** (☎ 519/271–5140) conducts charming one-hour tours of the city from July 1 to Labor Day, Monday through Saturday at 9:30 AM. Meet at the tourist information booth at Lakeside Drive and Ontario Street.

From June to October, **Backstage Tours** offers a fascinating look behind-the-scenes at the physical business that makes the plays work. On Sunday, between 9:15 and 10:30 AM, they depart every 15 minutes from the Festival Theatre lobby. Tickets are $5. Book in advance through the Festival Box Office.

Costume Warehouse Tours provide 45-minutes of views and explanations about making and using costumes and props. From June through October the tours are run every Wednesday and Saturday morning on the half hour from 9:30 to 11:30. They depart from the warehouse, on 359 Burritt Street; pay $4 at the Festival Box Office.

Visitor Information

Tourism Stratford (✉ 88 Wellington St., Stratford, Ontario N5A 2L2, ☎ 800/561–SWAN).

THE NIAGARA PENINSULA

The two most visited towns on the Niagara peninsula have very different flavors. Home to a wildly popular natural attraction, Niagara Falls has, shall we say, a certain energetic quality, while Niagara-on-the-Lake, which draws theatergoers to its annual Shaw festival, epitomizes ye olde British tastefulness. Because they are in such close proximity to each other, however, there's no need to choose; just decide on the day's mood.

Niagara Falls

130 km (81 mi) southeast of Toronto.

★ Cynics have had a field day with **Niagara Falls,** calling it everything from "water on the rocks" to "the second major disappointment of American married life" (Oscar Wilde). Others have been far more glowing. Missionary and explorer Louis Hennepin, whose books were widely read across Europe, first described the Falls in 1678 as "an incredible Cataract or Waterfall which has no equal." Nearly two centuries later, Charles Dickens wrote, "I seemed to be lifted from the earth and to be looking into Heaven. Niagara was at once stamped upon my heart, an image of beauty, to remain there changeless and indelible." Henry James recorded in 1883 how one stands there "gazing your fill at the most beautiful object in the world."

Understandably, all these rave reviews began to bring out professional daredevils, as well as self-destructive amateurs. In 1859, the French tightrope walker Blondin walked across the Niagara Gorge, from the American to the Canadian side, on a 3-inch-thick rope. On his shoulders was his (reluctant, terrified) manager; on both shores stood some 100,000 spectators. "Thank God it is over!" exclaimed one of the onlookers after the completion of the walk. The future King Edward VII of England was even more emphatic when he pleaded with Blondin, "Please never attempt it again."

From the early 18th century, dozens went over in boats, rubber balls, and those famous barrels. Not a single one survived, until 1901, when schoolteacher Annie Taylor made the attempt. Emerging from her barrel, she asked, "Did I go over the Falls yet?" The endless stunts were finally outlawed in 1912, but not before the province of Ontario created the first provincial park in all of Canada—Queen Victoria Park—in 1887.

The Falls alone—with a combined flow of close to 800,000 gallons per second—are obviously worth the 75-minute drive from Toronto, the 30-minute drive from Buffalo, New York, or whatever time it takes to come from anywhere else. They are, after all, the greatest waterfalls in the world, by volume.

The story of Niagara Falls started more than 10,000 years ago, when a group of glaciers receded, diverting the waters of Lake Erie northward into Lake Ontario. (Before that time, they had drained south; such are the fickle ways of nature.) The force and volume of the water as it flowed over the Niagara Escarpment caused the phenomenon we know as the Falls.

Considerable erosion has occurred since that time: More than 11 km (7 mi) in all, as the soft shale and sandstone of the escarpment have been washed away. Wisely, there have been major water diversions for a generating station (in 1954) and other machinations (1954–63), which have spread the flow more evenly over the entire crestline of the Horseshoe Falls. The erosion is now down to as little as 1 ft every decade, so you needn't rush your visit.

The area's human history is fairly interesting, too. The War of 1812 had settlers on both sides of the river killing one another, with the greatest battle taking place in Niagara Falls itself, at Lundy's Lane (today, the name of a major street, with a Historical Museum on the site of the battle). Soon after, at the Treaty of Ghent, two modest cities of the same name arose on each side of the river—one in the United States, the other in Canada.

The Niagara Parks Commission (NPC) was formed in 1885 to preserve the area around the falls. Beginning with a small block of land, the NPC has gradually acquired most of the land fronting on the Canadian side of the Niagara River, from Niagara-on-the-Lake to Fort Erie. The Niagara Parkway, a 56-km (35-mi) riverside drive, is a 3,000-acre ribbon of parkland lined with parking overlooks, picnic tables, and barbecue pits; the public is welcome to use the facilities at no charge.

Only some 76,000 people actually live in Niagara Falls, Ontario, and when one considers that close to 15 million visitors come and see the Falls every year, you can get an idea of just how central tourism is to the area.

Niagara Falls has something for everyone. For the children, there's Marineland, water slides, wax museums, haunted houses; for newly-weds, there's a Honeymoon Certificate and free admission for the bride to such sights as to the Ripley's Believe It or Not Museum. Sure, many of the motels and attractions are tacky, but that's part of the charm. A more recent draw is the Niagara Casino, a tremendous success.

Don't allow winter to put you off from coming. The **Winter Festival of Lights** is a real stunner. Seventy trees are illuminated with 34,000 lights in the parklands near the Rainbow Bridge, and "The Enchantment of Disney" consists of lighted displays based on cartoon characters and movies. The Falls are illuminated nightly from 5 to 10 PM, mid-November through mid-January. For additional information, call 800/563–2557 in Canada, 800/461–5373 in the United States.

Exploring Niagara Falls

The city of Niagara Falls is quite easy to picture: To the west, running north–south (and eventually east, around Lake Ontario and up to Toronto), is Queen Elizabeth Way; nearby are Lundy's Lane Historical Museum and a group of economical motels.

To the east lie the Niagara River and the glorious Falls, as well as the more expensive hotels. One of the best ways to get a sense of the layout is to go up the Skylon Tower, which has breathtaking views. Clifton Hill, right near the Falls and northeast of the Skylon Tower, is where most bus and boat tours begin and where many of the classic tourist attractions are.

To the north, near Whirpool Rapids Bridge, the Via Rail trains pull in; here you'll find The Spanish Aerocar, the helicopter tours, and the Great Gorge Adventure. For the latter, take an elevator down to the river's edge and walk along a boardwalk beside whirlpool rapids.

To the south and east of the Falls is Marineland. Along the river is the very beautiful Queen Victoria Park, which features an attractive greenhouse and a modest-size golf course. If you're visiting during the busy spring to fall period, consider the Explorer's Passport Plus (☞ Getting Around *in* Niagara Peninsula A to Z, *below*), which combines special admissions to some attractions and transportation.

Numbers in the margin correspond to points of interest on the Niagara Falls, Ontario map.

❶ The **Niagara Parks Botanical Gardens and School of Horticulture** has been graduating professional gardeners since 1936, and the art of horticulture is celebrated by its students with 80 acres of immaculately maintained gardens. Within the Botanical Gardens is the **Niagara Parks Butterfly Conservatory** (☎ 905/356–8119), home to one of North America's largest collections of free-flying butterflies—at least 2,000 are protected in a lush rain-forest setting by a glass-enclosed conservatory. The climate-controlled conservatory operates year-round and contains 50 species from around the world, each with its own colorful markings. In 1997, an outdoor butterfly garden was added with 120 domestic species. ⊠ *2565 North Niagara Pkwy.,* ☎ *905/356–8554.* ☜ *Botanical Gardens free, Butterfly Conservatory $7.* ☉ *Botanical Gardens, daily dawn–dusk; Butterfly Conservatory, daily 9–9.*

❷ Nearly 20,000 plants that bloom from earliest spring to late autumn make up the 40-ft **Floral Clock,** one of the world's biggest bloomin' timepieces. Chimes ring every quarter-hour, and its "living" face is designed by the Niagara Parks Commission and planted in a different design twice every season. It's on River Road (Niagara Parkway), less than 9½ km (6 mi) north of the Falls and a short distance south of the Botanical Gardens and School of Horticulture (☞ *above*) on the Niagara Parkway; watch for the signs.

❸ At the **Niagara Glen Nature Area,** on Niagara Parkway, some 6 km (4 mi) north of the Falls, you can actually work your way down to the gorge, observing the plant life. There's also access to a bicycle trail that parallels the Niagara Parkway from Fort Erie to Niagara-on-the-Lake. It winds between beautiful homes on one side and the river, with its abundant bird life, on the other.

❹ The **Niagara Spanish Aero Car,** in operation since 1916, is a cable car that crosses the Whirlpool Basin in the Niagara Gorge. This trip on a 1,800-ft-long cable is not for the fainthearted; when you're high above the roiling whirlpool, those cables seem awfully thin. ⊠ *Niagara Pkwy., 4½ km (3 mi) north of the falls,* ☎ *905/354–5711.* ☜ *$5.* ☉ *Mid-May–Labor Day, daily 9–9; Labor Day–mid-Oct., shorter hrs, weather permitting.*

❺ The **Great Gorge Adventure** involves taking an elevator to the bottom of the Niagara Gorge, where you can walk a boardwalk beside the torrent of the Niagara River. There the gorge is rimmed by sheer cliffs as it enters the giant whirlpool. ⊠ *Niagara Pkwy., 3 km (2 mi) north of the falls,* ☎ *905/354–5711.* ☜ *$4.75.* ☉ *Mid-May–Labor Day, daily 9–9; Labor Day–mid-Oct., call for hours.*

❻ The **Niagara Falls Museum,** founded in 1827, claims to be North America's oldest museum. It contains both shlock and quality—everything from stuffed birds, dinosaur remains, and Egyptian mummies to the **Daredevil Hall of Fame,** where the barrels and other contraptions in which people have gone over the falls pay tribute to two centuries of Niagara Falls rebels. There are 26 galleries on four floors and 700,000 exhibits, so gauge your time accordingly—this museum is well worth two hours of browsing. ⊠ *5651 River Rd., at the Rainbow Bridge,*

Niagara Falls, Ontario

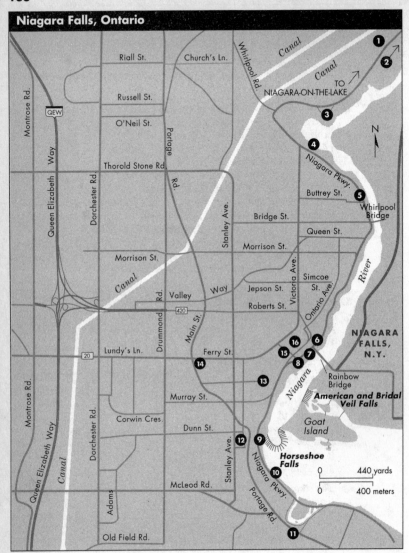

Casino Niagara, **16**

Clifton Hill, **15**

Floral Clock, **2**

Great Gorge
Adventure, **5**

Greenhouse and Plant
Conservatory, **10**

Journey Behind the
Falls, **9**

Lundy's Lane
Historical
Museum, **14**

Maid of the Mist, **8**

Marineland, **11**

Minolta Tower-
Centre, **12**

Niagara Falls
Museum, **6**

Niagara Glen Nature
Area, **3**

Niagara Parks
Botanical Gardens
And School of
Horticulture, **1**

Niagara Spanish
Aero Car, **4**

Ride Niagara, **7**

Skylon Tower, **13**

☎ *905/356–2151.* ✎ *$6.75.* ☉ *June–early Oct., daily 8:30 AM–11 PM; mid-Oct.–May, daily 10–5.*

7 **Ride Niagara** is divided into three portions: a theater presentation, an elevator ride down to the tunnel, and the shuttle that simulates plunging over the falls and down the rapids in a barrel. The entire event takes about 20–25 minutes. Children under three are not admitted. ✉ *5755 River Rd.,* ☎ *905/374–7433.* ✎ *$7.95.* ☉ *Daily 11:45–6.*

8 *Maid of the Mist* boats are surely an unforgettable experience; they sail right to the foot of the Falls. The boats have been operating since 1846, when they were wooden-hulled, coal-fired steamboats. Today, they tow fun-loving passengers on 30-minute journeys to the Falls, where the spray is so heavy that raincoats must be distributed. ✉ *Boats leave from foot of Clifton Hill,* ☎ *905/358–5781.* ✎ *$10.10.* ☉ *Apr. and Sept.– Oct., weekdays 10–5, weekends 10–6; May–Aug. hrs vary, sometimes opening as early as 9:15 AM, closing as late as 8 PM.*

9 At **Journey Behind the Falls,** an elevator will take you to an observation deck, which allows a fish's-eye view of the Canadian Horseshoe Falls and the Niagara River. From there a walk through three tunnels cut into the rock takes you behind the wall of crashing water. Your admission ticket includes use of a hooded rain slicker. ✉ *Tours begin at Table Rock House, Queen Victoria Park,* ☎ *905/354–1551.* ✎ *$6.* ☉ *Mid-June–Labor Day, 9 AM–10:30 PM; 9–5 rest of yr. Closed Dec. 25.*

10 The NPC's enormous **Greenhouse and Plant Conservatory,** just south of Horseshoe Falls, is open daily. Here you can see myriad plants and flowers year-round. ✉ *Niagara Pkwy.,* ☎ *905/356–4699.* ✎ *Free; parking $3 per hr.* ☉ *Sun.–Thurs. 9:30–6; Fri.–Sat. 9:30–8.*

11 **Marineland,** a theme park with a marine show, wildlife displays, and rides, is, after the Falls themselves, the highest-quality attraction in the area. The 4,000-seat aqua theater has the world's largest troupe of performing sea lions and dolphins, as well as two killer whales, Kandu and Nootka. There are rides for all ages as well, including the world's largest steel roller coaster, spread over 1½ km (1 mi) of track and traveling through 1,000 ft of tunnels, double spirals, and giant loops. The Game Farm is also a delight, with its buffalo, bears, and more than 400 deer to pet and feed. To get here, follow the Marineland signs along parkway by the Falls, or exit QEW at McLeod Road (Exit 27) and follow the signs. ✉ *7657 Portage Rd.,* ☎ *905/356–8250 or 905/356– 9565.* ✎ *$21.95; varies with season.* ☉ *Mid-Apr.–mid-May and Sept.–mid-Oct., daily 10–4; mid-May–June, daily 10–5; July–Aug., 9–6, with some activities continuing until dusk.*

12 **Minolta Tower-Centre** rises some 535 ft above the cataracts, offering an indoor observation deck and three open ones. An Incline Railway will take you to and from the brink of the Falls. Also in the tower are a variety of high-tech games: Cybermind Virtual Reality, offering precisely what its name suggests; Galaxian Adventure, a laser action game played from seated consoles; and Smash Factory Simulator, which lets you pretend you're taking part in a demolition derby. Across the street from the Minolta Tower but part of the same complex is Darkzone Laser Adventure: Participants get individual phaser weapons to arm them for a battle game set in a 5,000-square-ft maze. ✉ *6733 Oakes Dr.,* ☎ *905/356–1501 or 905/358–0980 (Laser Adventure).* ✎ *Tower $6, Cybermind Virtual Reality $6, Smash Factory Simulator $6, Galaxian Adventure $3, Darkzone Laser Adventure $9.* ☉ *9 AM until the lights go off on the Falls (as late as midnight in summer).*

❸ Rising 775 ft above the falls, **Skylon Tower** offers the best view of both the great Niagara and the entire city. An indoor-outdoor observation deck facilitates the view. Amusements for children plus a revolving dining room (☞ *Dining and Lodging, below*) are other reasons to visit. ✉ *5200 Robinson St.,* ☎ *905/356–2651.* 🎫 *$7.50.* ☻ *Mid-June–Labor Day, daily 8 AM–1 AM; Labor Day–early June, daily 10–9.*

At the **Niagara Falls IMAX Theatre/The Daredevil Adventure Gallery**, you can see the wonder of the falls up close and travel back in time for a glimpse of its 12,000-year-old history with *Niagara: Miracles, Myths and Magic.* The movie screen, Canada's largest, is more than six stories high. The Daredevil Adventure Gallery chronicles the brave expeditions of those who have tackled the falls. The theater is near the Skylon Tower (☞ *above*). ✉ *6170 Buchanan Ave.,* ☎ *905/358–3611.* 🎫 *$7.50.* ☻ *Sept.–Oct. and late Apr.–June, daily 11–8; Nov.–late Apr., weekdays and Sun. 11–4, Sat. 11–7; movies run every hr on the hr.*

❹ **Lundy's Lane Historical Museum,** dating to 1874, is on the site of a savage battle in the War of 1812. There are displays of the lives of settlers of that era, as well as military artifacts. ✉ *5810 Ferry St.,* ☎ *905/358–5082.* 🎫 *$1.60.* ☻ *May–Canadian Thanksgiving (about Oct. 10), daily 9–4; off-season, weekdays noon–4.*

❺ Children—and adults with great patience—will get a kick out of **Clifton Hill,** which hosts an array of ultratouristy attractions sometimes referred to as "Museum Alley." Attractions include **The Guinness Museum of World Records** (✉ 4943 Clifton Hill, ☎ 905/356–2299); **The Haunted House and The Funhouse** (✉ 4943 Clifton Hill, ☎ 905/357–4330); **Louis Tussaud's Waxworks** (✉ 4915 Clifton Hill, ☎ 905/374–6601); **Movieland Wax Museum** (✉ 4950 Clifton Hill, ☎ 905/358–3061); and **Ripley's Believe It or Not Museum** (✉ 4960 Clifton Hill, ☎ 905/356–2238). All are between the Niagara Parkway and Victoria Avenue and all are open year-round; call ahead for hours, which change seasonally. Coming here can be a pricey proposition: The admission charge for each of these attractions runs around $6 or $7.

❻ **Casino Niagara,** set in an architectural design reminiscent of the 1920s, has a total of 3,000 slot machines and 123 gambling tables, such as blackjack, roulette, baccarat, Caribbean stud poker, Let It Ride, Pai Gow poker, and Big Six. Within the casino are five restaurants, seven lounges with live entertainment, and a clothing boutique. ✉ *5705 Falls Ave.,* ☎ *888/946–3255 or 905/374–5964.* ☻ *Daily 24 hrs.*

Dining and Lodging

$$$–$$$$ ✕ **Farfalle Restaurant.** Whether you come to the casino for baccarat or the slots, dining at this elegant restaurant is no gamble. Farfalle (Italian for butterfly) was named to honor the Niagara Parks Butterfly Conservatory (☞ *above*). Nothing flighty, however, exists on the solidly classic Mediterranean-American menu. The room, totally insulated and away from the crowds, is a great setting in which to appreciate classic shrimp cocktail or lobster lasagnetta, fresh pasta wrapped around sautéed lobster, shallots, and basil. You'd have to search far to find a more delectably grilled 20-ounce Canadian T-bone steak. ✉ *Casino Niagara, 5705 Falls Ave.,* ☎ *905/374–3598. AE, DC, MC, V.*

$$–$$$ ✕ **Casa Mia.** This off-the-tourist-track restaurant, in a pink stucco villa
★ about 10 minutes from the center of town, is airy and modern, with a comfortable piano lounge (there's live music Friday and Saturday). All the pasta is kitchen-made. Fresh-grated beets impart a shocking pink color to the gnocchi, divine with fresh Gorgonzola sauce. If you've ever wondered what real cannelloni was like, these light pasta pancakes, filled with coarse-ground veal and spinach, will tell you. The veal

chop grilled with lemon and caper juice is a thing of beauty. Heart-smart menu selections are indicated, and even the desserts, particularly cassata—a light cake with homemade ice-cream terrine—are not overly heavy. ⊠ *3518 Portage Rd., about 10 km (6 mi) from Niagara-on-the-Lake,* ☎ *905/356–5410. AE, MC, V.*

$$–$$$ ✕ **Skylon Tower.** Don't come here for surprises—this tower is owned by the same people who own the local Holiday Inn—but for the view from the Revolving Dining Room, which rotates at one revolution per hour. Traditionally prepared rack-of-lamb, baked salmon, steak, and chicken make up the list of entrées. It's an eclectic crowd, with cocktail wear and casual clothes seated side-by-side. Even with a reservation, there may be a short wait. ⊠ *5200 Robin St.,* ☎ *905/356–2651. AE, MC, V.*

$$ ✕ **Casa d'Oro.** You'll think you've stepped into a Disney version of a Venetian castle, but ornate wall sconces, fireplaces, wine casks, and huge faux-marble and bronze sculptures are somehow not out of place in Niagara Falls. The Roberto family has been serving steak, seafood, and traditional Italian specialties here for 30 years. Folks come not only for the gigantic portions of prime rib, T-bones, and fillets but also for the experience. After dinner, you can cross a painted bridge that spans a water-filled moat to the Rialto nightclub's raised dance floor. ⊠ *5875 Victoria Ave.,* ☎ *905/356–5646. AE, D, DC, MC, V.*

$–$$ ✕ **Capri.** This award-winning restaurant is not only family-owned, but—
★ a rarity in this business—it's had the same chef for 40 years. Chef Carmen continues to prepare huge, Italian-style platters such as linguine with chicken cacciatore. The three separate dining rooms, decorated in dark wood paneling, draw families daily because of the half dozen specially priced children's dishes and a something-for-everyone menu. Breakfast is served, too. ⊠ *5438 Ferry St. (Hwy. 20), about ½ mi from Falls,* ☎ *905/354–7519. AE, DC, MC, V.*

$–$$ ✕ **Table Rock.** Run by Niagara Parks, Table Rock serves inoffensive, standard U.S./Canadian fare in an amazing setting: As they love to advertise, "If you were any closer, you'd go over the Falls." The dining room, in the rear of a two-story souvenir shop, offers tourist comfort food such as Caesar salads, baked salmon, veal and chicken fettuccine, beef and chicken burritos, and shaved roast beef hoagies. ⊠ *Just above Scenic Tunnels,* ☎ *905/354–3631. AE, MC, V.*

$–$$ ✕ **Victoria Park.** What you see is what you get at this middle-of-the-road kitchen, run by Niagara Parks. A salmon is a salmon. Chicken is chicken. But who's looking at their plates when the Falls are right outside? Pass on the cake on Sunday; it's often a bit dry by the end of the week. The restaurant is open for breakfast. ⊠ *Corner of River Rd. and Murray St.,* ☎ *905/356–2217. AE, MC, V.*

$–$$ ✕ **Yukiguni.** Excellent Japanese food is served up in what might have been a country-and-western restaurant in a previous life. Among the reasons that Yukiguni is popular with locals and Japanese tourists are reasonable lunch specials, which include miso soup, fresh salad, and such entrées as juicy pepper-flavored chicken skewers. Other menu options are tempura soba, thin buckwheat noodles that come with shrimp and vegetable tempura; and steamed smoked eel, served on rice in a round stacked lacquer box. Chicken and salmon teriyaki leave an aromatic trail as they are carried aloft on sizzling iron plates. ⊠ *5980 Buchanan Ave.,* ☎ *905/354–4440. AE, DC, MC, V.*

$ ✕ **Simon's Newsstand and Restaurant.** This large, bustling room, run by the Simon family for more than 100 years, has a few Formica tables with red vinyl–and–chrome chairs—as well as decades of license plates, duck decoys, and a hodgepodge of Canadian memorabilia. You can take out such staples as bread, milk, and soda pop, or sit down at the long counter and enjoy a hearty all-day breakfast. Simon's makes super grilled-cheese sandwiches, BLTs, and tuna salads, and the meat-loaf dinner has its die-hard fans. ⊠ *4116 Bridge St.,* ☎ *905/356–5310. Reservations not accepted. No credit cards.*

$$$$ ✕⊡ **Sheraton Fallsview Hotel and Conference Centre.** Overlooking the spectacular Canadian and American falls, this modern high-rise hotel has oversize guest rooms and suites, more than half with breathtaking views of the falls and upper rapids. Business facilities are excellent; the hotel provides high-quality teleconferencing. The fine dining room has snagged the best view in town. In the evening, candlelight adds romance, and the kitchen does its part with a French Continental menu that might include tournedos with a three-peppercorn sauce. For more casual dining, the hotel's La Piazza Cafe is a cheerful Old World salad, pasta, burger, and pizza restaurant—it's more moderately priced, but minus the view. There's a two-night minimum stay on weekends. ⊠ *6755 Oakes Dr., L2G 3W7,* ☎ *905/374–1077 or 800/267–8439,* ℻ *905/374–6224. 295 rooms. 2 restaurants, lobby lounge, pool, hot tub, sauna, spa, business center, meeting rooms. AE, DC, MC, V.*

$$$–$$$$ ⊡ **Renaissance Fallsview Hotel.** Many rooms overlook the falls at this luxuriously appointed hotel, about ½ km (¼ mi) from the mighty cataracts. There are lots of recreational facilities on the premises and golf and fishing nearby. Free morning coffee is available for guests, and in summer a light breakfast is also included in the room rate. ⊠ *6455 Buchanan Ave., L2G 3V9,* ☎ *905/357–5200,* ℻ *905/357–3422. 262 rooms. 2 restaurants, indoor pool, hot tub, sauna, exercise room, racquetball, squash, business services, meeting rooms. AE, D, DC, MC, V.*

$$–$$$ ⊡ **Fallsway Quality Inn.** Very near the Falls and not far from a golf course, the inn is on nicely landscaped grounds, which can be viewed from a pleasant patio. ⊠ *4946 Clifton Hill, Box 60, L2E 6S8,* ☎ *905/ 358–3601. 265 rooms. Restaurant, lobby lounge, 2 pools, hot tub, playground. AE, MC, V.*

$$ ⊡ **Lincoln Motor Inn.** A pleasant landscaped courtyard gives this motor inn, within walking distance of the Falls, an intimate feeling. Connecting family suites sleep up to a dozen. Facilities include an extra-large heated pool and an outdoor whirlpool heated to 102°F. A golf course is nearby. ⊠ *6417 Main St., L2G 5Y3,* ☎ *905/356–1748. 57 rooms. Restaurant, pool, hot tub. AE, MC, V.*

$–$$ ⊡ **Candlelight Motor Inn.** This two-story motel offers good, basic accommodations. Some rooms have whirlpool tubs and slightly fancier decor; the two efficiency suites have small kitchens. ⊠ *7600 Lundy's La., L2H 1H1,* ☎ *905/354–2211 (reservations) or 905/374–7010,* ℻ *905/358–0696. 50 rooms. Restaurant, pool. AE, DC, MC, V.*

Niagara-on-the-Lake

19 km (12 mi) north of Niagara Falls.

Since 1962 Niagara-on-the-Lake has been considered the southern outpost of fine summer theater in Ontario because of its acclaimed Shaw Festival. But it offers far more than Stratford, its older theatrical sister to the west: This city is a jewel of Canadian history, architectural marvels, remarkable beauty, and, of course, quality theater. Though the town of 14,000 is worth a visit at any time of the year, its most attractive period is from April to October, when both the Shaw Festival and the flowers are in full bloom.

Being located where the Niagara River enters Lake Ontario has both advantages and disadvantages. Because of its ideal placement, the area was settled by Loyalists to the British Crown, who found it a haven during the American Revolution. Soon after, it was made the capital

of Upper Canada by John Graves Simcoe, a soldier-statesman who settled here after fighting in the war. For a time the town was the site of
the provincial capital, but its proximity to the border made it subject
to easy attack. As a result, Simcoe moved the capital to a more remote
outpost, York—today's Toronto. Simcoe was also unimpressed with
the native-sounding word Niagara (roughly translated as "thundering
waters"), so he changed the town's name to Newark (it was a new ark
of safety for the Loyalists fleeing the upheaval south of the border).
Eventually the original name returned, but following years of confu-
sion with the Niagara with the Falls to the south, in 1906 it was renamed once again, to the present Niagara-on-the-Lake.

Simcoe's decision to move the capital was vindicated during the War
of 1812 when the upstart Americans came calling, but not as tourists.
They captured nearby Fort George in 1813, occupied the town itself
that summer, and burned it to the ground that December. Some of Niagara-on-the-Lake's best days were in the late 1800s to early 1900s,
when it was connected to Toronto by steamer and the town became a
prominent summer retreat for sweltering Torontonians. A passenger
boat service connecting the town with Toronto has recently been rein-
troduced.

Following the transfer of the county seat to nearby St. Catharines and
the arrival of the automobile and four-lane highways, the town slipped
into relative obscurity. It remained a sleepy town until 1962, when local
lawyer Brian Doherty organized eight weekend performances of two
George Bernard Shaw plays, *Don Juan in Hell* and *Candida*. The next
year he helped found the festival, whose mission is to perform the works
of Shaw and his contemporaries. Today Niagara-on-the-Lake is one of
the best-preserved 19th-century towns on the continent, with many neo-
classical and Georgian homes still standing proudly—and lived in, too.

The three theaters used by the Shaw Festival present quality performances, but what's also special are the abundant orchards and flower
gardens, sailboats, and the utterly charming town of Niagara-on-the-
Lake itself.

Exploring Niagara-on-the-Lake
This is a very small town that can easily be explored on foot. **Queen
Street** is the core of the commercial portion; walking east along that
single street, with Lake Ontario to your north, you'll get a glimpse of
the town's architectural history. At No. 209 is the handsome Richard-
son-Kiely House, built about 1832 for a member of Parliament, with
later additions at the turn of the century. No. 187 dates back to 1822,
with later Greek Revival improvements. A veteran of the 1814 Battle
of Lundy's Lane in Niagara Falls once occupied No. 165, an 1820 beauty.
For decades, No. 157, built in 1823, was occupied by descendants of
the Rogers-Harrison family, prominent since the early 19th century in
church and town affairs. McClelland's, a store now at No. 106, has
been in business in Niagara-on-the-Lake since the War of 1812. The
huge "T" sign means "provisioner."

Grace United Church, built in 1852, is a collage of architectural styles,
including Italianate and Norman. Stained-glass windows dedicated to
the memory of Canadians killed in World War I were installed in the
1920s. The church was originally commissioned by a congregation of
"Free Kirk" Presbyterians, but was later sold to Methodists and now
serves a congregation of the United Church (a merger of Presbyterians, Methodists, and Congregationalists). During the summer the
Shaw Festival often uses the church as a rehearsal space. ⊠ *222 Victoria St.,* ☎ *905/468–4044.*

The **Niagara Apothecary Museum** occupies a building that had been used a an apothecary (pharmacy) since 1866 and reopened as a museum in 1971. Now owned by the Ontario Heritage Foundation, the museum is operated by volunteers from the Ontario College of Pharmacists. Note the exquisite walnut and butternut fixtures, crystal pieces, and a rare collection of apothecary glasses. ⊠ *5 Queen St.,* ☎ *416/325–5015.* ⊠ *Free, donations welcome.* ☉ *Mid-May–Labor Day, Mon-Sun, noon–6.*

The **Niagara Historical Society Museum,** one of the oldest and most complete museums of its kind in Ontario, has an extensive collection relating to the often colorful history of the Niagara Peninsula from the earliest times through the 19th century. The museum has a gift shop and also offers guided tours of the town. ⊠ *43 Castlereagh St.,* ☎ *905/468–3912.* ⊠ *$3.* ☉ *Jan.–Feb., weekends 1–5; Mar.–Apr, daily 1–5; May–Oct., 10–5; Nov.–Dec., daily 1–5.*

🛦 On a wide stretch of parkland south of town, **Fort George National Historic Park** was built in the 1790s to replace Fort Niagara but was lost to the Yankees during the War of 1812. It was recaptured after the burning of the town in 1813, and largely survived the war, only to fall into ruins by the 1830s. It was reconstructed a century later, and you can explore the officers' quarters, barracks rooms of the common soldiers, the kitchen, and more. Like many other historic sites in Ontario, the town is staffed by people in period uniform who conduct tours and reenact 19th-century infantry and artillery drills. ⊠ *Queen's Parade, Niagara Pkwy.,* ☎ *905/468–4257.* ⊠ *$6, family pass $20.* ☉ *Apr.–June, daily 9:30–4:30; July–Labor Day, daily 10–5; Labor Day–Oct., daily 9:30–4:30.*

Dining and Lodging

The area has some lovely restaurants and inns, both within town and outside it; a number of wineries in the area have restaurants and inns as well.

$$$–$$$$ ✕ **Hillebrand Estates Café.** After a complimentary winery tour and tasting, you can settle down to a superb meal that focuses on the freshest local produce. Chef Tony di Luca creates dishes like grilled salmon and fennel on vegetable risotto; juicy venison burger with onion, sage, and Dijon mustard relish; and hearty pasta tossed with a luscious peppery–edged beef ragout. Tossed salad is a beautiful relationship between organic greens, sun-dried blueberries, and roasted crisp garlic. The pastry chef composes incredible desserts: bittersweet chocolate nut tart molded in a cup is filled with vanilla ice-cream and topped with candied hazelnuts. ⊠ *Hwy. 55, Niagara Stone Rd.,* ☎ *905/468–3201. AE, D, MC, V.*

$$$–$$$$ ✕ **Vineland Estates Winery.** Exquisite Italian food and award–winning wines are served by an enthusiastic staff on the wine deck or in the glassed-in restaurant, with a panoramic view of the vineyard and lake. The fresh lemon poppyseed baguette is served warm, and the pasta is homemade. Black linguine, French beans, and carrots come on a radicchio cup rakishly capped by a skewer of grilled shrimp and kumquat; Arctic char is grilled and served on organic greens, each with its own fresh flavor. The desserts are a happy marriage of local fruits and an imaginative pastry chef. ⊠ *3620 Moyer Rd., Vineland,* ☎ *905/562–7088. AE, D, MC, V.*

$$–$$$$ ✕ **Ristorante Giardino.** Italian marble combines with stainless steel and rich colors to create a contemporary Italian ambience on 19th-century Queen Street. Chefs recruited from Italy produce antipasti such as beef carpaccio with black olive paste and slivers of Parmesan, and thinly sliced marinated salmon dotted with caviar. There's always a mixed seafood grill—say, salmon, swordfish, and shrimp—and the ravioli are plump with spinach and ricotta cheese. Make time to savor each spoonful of Mandarin chocolate soufflé, or indulge in the kitchen's own ice creams and fresh Niagara fruits. The long wine list is worth a careful read. ⊠ *Gate House Hotel, 142 Queen St.,* ☎ *905/468–3263. AE, DC, MC, V. Closed Jan.–Feb.; closed Mon. Nov.–Dec., Mar.–mid-Apr; no lunch Nov.–Dec., Mar.–mid Apr.*

$$$ ✕ **Buttery Theatre Restaurant.** At Margaret Niemann's authentic British pub/café, the wood-beam ceiling, beaten copper tabletops, and china and pewter all bear the patina of age. Lively Tudor banquets and feasts are held every Friday and Saturday, and the tavern menu includes good pâtés and Cornish pasties (a beef-filled pastry envelope). The chef bakes chicken with fresh lemons and roasts leg of lamb in the manner of Henry VIII. A unique bed-and-breakfast is also available. After-theater dinners (10 PM–midnight) are offered on Friday and Saturday, and there's afternoon tea daily from 2 to 5. ⊠ *19 Queen St.,* ☎ *905/468–2564. AE, MC, V.*

$$–$$$ ✕ **Fans Court.** The Chu family serves delicate Cantonese cuisine prepared by the Chu family in a lovely, antiques-filled restaurant in a courtyard between an art gallery and a greenhouse. Mature jade trees in urns stand at the entrance. In summer, you can sit outdoors and sample such favorites as fried rice served in a pineapple, lemon chicken, and black-pepper-and-garlic beef. ⊠ *135 Queen St.,* ☎ *905/468–4511. AE, MC, V.*

$$$–$$$$ ✕🏨 **Prince of Wales.** A visit from The Prince of Wales at the turn of ★ the century prompted the name of this hotel, built in 1864. It's in the heart of town and has been tastefully restored. The Prince of Wales Court, adjacent to the main hotel, has many larger, newer rooms at higher prices, and some housekeeping units are available. The suede-walled Royals dining room offers a tree-filled patio that looks out to the street. The cuisine is comparable to that of any fine city restaurant; entrées might include roasted breast of pheasant with double smoked bacon and quince-and-pear compote, or beef tenderloin with pumpkin relish and buttermilk corn bread. The more casual Queen's Royal Lounge offers daily soup-and-sandwich, lunch, and dinner buffets, all for under $10. ⊠ *6 Picton St., L0S 1J0,* ☎ *905/468–3246 or 800/263–2452 from Toronto,* FAX *905/468–5521. 105 rooms. Restaurant, café, lobby lounge, indoor pool, saunas, health club, business services, meeting rooms. AE, MC, V.*

$$$ ✕🏨 **Queen's Landing Inn.** The views are a knockout, since Queen's ★ Landing is just across from historic Fort Niagara, at the mouth of the Niagara River. Rooms are nicely decorated with antiques, including canopy beds; many have working fireplaces and modern whirlpool baths. Unlike the other century-old country inns of this town, Queen's Landing has a superb indoor swimming pool, a lap pool, and an exercise room. The Tiara Restaurant ($$$–$$$$) is arguably the town's finest dining, in a room flattered by stained glass and a full view of the lake. The kitchen provides a blend of Asian spicing and excellent local meats and produce. Don't miss the rosemary-grilled quail with Japanese greens and Niagara peach preserves, or the pan-seared foie gras with wild raspberries. Main courses like cinnamon-roasted veal tenderloin and parsley-crusted breast of chicken with buckwheat risotto show the skill and imagination of the chef. The menu also lists vegetarian choices. ⊠ *Byron St., Box 1180, L0S 1J0,* ☎ *905/468–2195 or 800/361–6645,* FAX *905/468–2227. 137 rooms. Restaurant, lounge, indoor pool, lap pool, hot tub, sauna, exercise room. AE, DC, MC, V.*

$$$ ✕🏨 **Vintner's Inn.** The owners have added a luxurious inn to their sophisticated country restaurant On the Twenty ($$$–$$$$), named for its picturesque view of Twenty Mile Creek. The inn is part of

Leonard Pennachetti's Cave Spring Cellars winery in the village of Jordan, some 25 minutes from Niagara-on-the-Lake. All rooms have a working fireplace and whirlpool tub and are furnished with new and antique pieces, with a unifying emphasis on comfort. You are welcome to tour and sample the wines of Cave Spring Cellars across the street. Some dinner highlights are quail grilled with shiitake mushrooms; trout baked in parchment with Riesling and leeks; or Ontario rack of lamb with mashed potatoes, all from the fertile Niagara region. Breakfast is included in the room rate. The restaurant is closed some days from January through April, so call ahead. ⊠ *3836 Main St., Jordan L0R 1S0,* ☎ *905/562–5336 or 800/701–8074. 16 rooms. Restaurant, no-smoking rooms. AE, DC, MC, V.*

$$–$$$ ✕▨ **Oban Inn.** In 1992 this 1824 inn, built by a sea captain from Oban, burned to the ground, but it reopened less than a year later, finely rebuilt. The centrally located inn has broad verandas and beautifully manicured gardens. Each room is distinct, embellished with antiques in an Old World English tone; four offer gas fireplaces and overlook the lake. Even if you don't book a room with a view, you can get one while having lunch on the dining room patio, decked with fresh-cut flowers. On Sunday, a brunch of whole turkey, ham, and prime rib brings out the locals, and the fresh poached salmon is popular in the summer. The popular dining room spotlights Canadian beef favorites with a fresh twist of vegetables and fruits. Afternoon tea is served daily. Pets are allowed. ⊠ *160 Front St., Box 94, L0S 1J0,* ☎ *905/468–2165,* ℻ *905/468–4165. 22 rooms. Restaurant, pub, library, baby-sitting. AE, DC, MC, V.*

$$–$$$ ✕▨ **Pillar and Post Inn, Spa and Conference Center.** This hotel, six long blocks from the heart of town, has been a cannery, barracks, and basket factory. Most rooms have handcrafted Early American pine furniture and patchwork quilts, along with such modern amenities as hair dryers. The 100 Fountain Spa offers three different pools, including an outdoor hot spring with a waterfall, as well as a variety of soothing body treatments, relaxing classes, and massages at about triple the prices you would pay in Toronto; appointments must be made two weeks in advance. The casual Vintages Wine Bar and Lounge serves regional cuisine and wines. The dining-room menu is also inspired by what the market has to offer: four-peppercorn liver country pâté with fig-and-onion marmalade, perhaps, or stuffed chicken breast with herbed goat cheese on roasted eggplant. ⊠ *48 John St., L0S 1J0,* ☎ *905/468–2123,* ℻ *905/468–3551. 12 rooms. 2 restaurants, lobby lounge, 3 pools, sauna, spa, health club, business services. AE, MC, V.*

$$ ✕▨ **Olde Angel Inn.** The War of 1812 saw much action around this inn, a charming lemon yellow coach house with green shutters that was established circa 1779. A resident ghost—some say he's a soldier who had gone AWOL and was killed here—is believed to walk the cellar. Each room has antiques and beds with canopies. The tavern sets out pub fare like steak, Guinness, and oyster pie on antique wooden refectory tables. Entrées on the dining room menu ($$–$$$) include roast baby duckling with orange and brandy sauce or *trois amours*—shrimp, scallops, and crab baked in a supreme sauce with Swiss and Parmesan cheese. Even if you don't stay here, be sure to stop in for a meal. ⊠ *224 Regent St., L0S 1J0,* ☎ *905/468–3411. 5 rooms with bath, 2 cottages. Restaurant, pub. AE, D, DC, MC, V.*

$$–$$$ ▨ **White Oakes Inn.** Close to town, this luxury resort has a full range of activities—squash, racquetball, and tennis, as well as aerobics classes. A video arcade keeps kids occupied. ⊠ *R.R. 4, Taylor Rd., L0S 1J0,* ☎ *905/688–2550 or 800/263–5766,* ℻ *905/688–2220. 90 rooms. 2 restaurants, lobby lounge, indoor pool, hot tub, sauna, 12 tennis courts, health club, racquetball, squash, baby-sitting. AE, D, MC, V.*

$$ ⊡ **Moffat Inn.** This charmer has individually appointed rooms, some with original 1835 fireplaces, outdoor patios, brass beds, and wicker furniture. Enjoy breakfast fritters on the outdoor patio. All guest rooms and common areas except the pub are nonsmoking. ⊠ *60 Picton St., L0S 1J0,* ☎ *905/468–4116. 22 rooms. Restaurant. AE, MC, V.*

Nightlife and the Arts

The **Shaw Festival** began modestly back in the early 1960s with a single play and a premise: To perform the plays of George Bernard Shaw and his contemporaries. Shaw lived into his nineties, and his contemporaries included nearly everyone of note for nearly a century—Noel Coward, Bertolt Brecht, J. M. Barrie, and J. M. Synge, to name a few. The season now runs from April through October and includes close to a dozen plays.

The Festival operates in three buildings, within a few blocks of each other. The handsome Festival Theatre, the largest of the three with 861 seats, stands on Queen's Parade near Wellington Street and houses the box office. The 353-seat Court House, on Queen Street between King and Regent streets, served as the town's municipal offices until 1969. At the corner of Queen and Victoria streets is the slightly smaller (328-seat) Royal George Theater, the most intimate of the Festival's theaters.

For festival schedules, lists of hotels and restaurants, and a Historic Guide, contact the Shaw Festival (⊠ Box 774, Niagara-on-the-Lake, Ontario L0S 1J0, ☎ 905/468–2153 or 416/690–7301 in Toronto, FAX 905/468–3804). Phone (☎ 905/468–2172 or 800/511–7429) for ticket purchases. Standard prices for tickets run from $22 to $65, but there are a variety of discounts. Summer Sunday-night performances cost $28 to $35; lunchtime plays run $15, lunchtime readings, $7; it's $23 for senior matinees, $15 for student matinees. Family tickets offer any seat at half price for those 18 or younger accompanied by the adult holder of a full-price ticket; rush seats are sold from 9 AM the day of performance in person for 20%–50% off (maximum four per performance).

Niagara Peninsula A to Z

Arriving and Departing

BY BOAT

A new hydrofoil service, the **Hydrofoil** (☎ 800/313–3237), runs three to four times a day from Toronto to Niagara-on-the-Lake; departures are from Queen's Quay East and Sherbourne. Cost is $25 one-way; $45 round-trip.

BY BUS

Greyhound Canada (☎ 800/367–8747) has three buses leaving Toronto's Bay and Dundas streets terminal every morning for Niagara Falls; seven more depart later in the day. The trip takes about two hours and costs about $50 round-trip.

From Toronto, it's about 129 km (80 mi) to Niagara-on-the-Lake, but bus transfers are complicated (you have to go to St. Catharines and then take a cab). It's easier to go to Niagara Falls first and catch a shuttle from there. **5-0 Taxi** (☎ 800/667–0256) runs three buses daily between Niagara Falls and Niagara-on-the-Lake; the rate is $15 round-trip.

BY CAR

Niagara Falls is approximately 129 km (80 mi) southeast of Toronto, less than a 90-minute drive. From downtown, take the Gardiner Expressway west; it quickly turns into Queen Elizabeth Way (QEW) and curves south (heading west and then east) around Lake Ontario. Exit at Highway 420, which runs straight into the downtown area. The distance from Toronto to Niagara-on the Lake is also about 129 km (80 mi), and the route starts out the same, but you'll need to get off the QEW at St. Catharines/Interchange 38, drive north 4 km (2½ mi) to Highway 55, and take it to its end.

To get to Niagara-on-the-Lake from Niagara Falls, take the Niagara Parkway north about 19 km (12 mi); the trip should take under half an hour.

BY PLANE

The closest airport is **Buffalo International Airport,** served by several major carriers. Niagara Air Bus (☎ 905/374–8111) provides short flights between Buffalo and Niagara Falls.

Niagara Air Bus (☎ 905/685–8323; 716/835–8111 toll-free from Buffalo; 800/268–8111 toll-free from Toronto) provides door-to-door ground transportation to and from the Toronto and Buffalo airports to the Niagara region, including Niagara Falls and Niagara-on-the-Lake.

BY TRAIN

Via Rail (☎ 905/357–1644 or 800/361–1235) runs daily trains from Toronto to Niagara Falls.

Getting Around

From late April to mid-October, one way to explore Niagara Falls is the Niagara Parks Commission's **Explorer's Passport Plus,** a package that includes admission to the Great Gorge Adventure, Niagara Spanish Aero Car, and Journey Behind the Falls, as well as all-day transportation aboard the commission's buses, which operate frequently from south of the Falls to Queenston Heights Park. The buses are particularly useful during the busy summer season, when traffic is very heavy. ☎ 905/357–9340. ⌷ $17.95.

Guided Tours

NIAGARA FALLS

Helicopter: Niagara Helicopter Rides (⌷ 3731 Victoria Ave., at River Rd., ☎ 905/357–5672) let you see the Falls from an unforgettable vantage point. There are daily departures 9 AM–sunset (weather permitting). Call for reservations. Rates are $75.

Orientation: Double Deck Tours (☎ 905/374–7423) offers bus tours of the Falls and environs. In high season, buses operate every 30 minutes from 9:30 AM. The complete tour lasts 90 minutes, but you may get off at any stop and grab another bus later in the day. Cost is approximately $17. Tours depart from the *Maid of the Mist* building. **Executive Coach Services** (☎ 416/740–3339) has year-round guided day trips from Toronto to Niagara. These include a buffet lunch overlooking the Falls year-round; in summer, a ride on the *Maid of the Mist* boat under the Falls is added, and in winter the IMAX film *Miracles, Myths, and Magic of Niagara* is part of the package. Cost is about $100.

NIAGARA-ON-THE LAKE

Wineries: The area has more than 10 wineries; call the visitor bureau (☞ *below*) for information; the area has a wine trail, too, to make visiting easier. **Hillebrand Estates Winery** (⌷ Hwy. 55, Niagara Stone Rd., ☎ 905/468–7123) offers year-round tours, followed by a sampling of their award-winning products; both are free. The winery has a restaurant (☞ Dining and Lodging, *above*). **Inniskillin Wines** (⌷ Off Niagara River Pkwy., just south of town, ☎ 905/468–3554) runs free tours on the weekends. Numerous displays in a 19th-century barn illustrate the wine-making procedures. Samples at the wine tasting bar cost 50¢ an ounce.

Visitor Information

Niagara Falls, Canada, Visitor and Convention Bureau (✉ 5433 Victoria Ave., Niagara Falls, Ontario L2G 3L1, ☎ 800/56–FALLS). **Information Center** (✉ Corner of Hwy. 420 and Stanley Ave., ☎ 905/358–3221).

Niagara-on-the-Lake Chamber of Commerce Visitor and Convention Bureau (✉ 153 King St., Box 1043, Niagara-on-the-Lake, Ontario L0S 1J0, ☎ 905/468–4263, FAX 905/468–4930).

INDEX

X = restaurant, ⊞ = hotel

NOTES

NOTES

Fodor's Travel Publications

Available at bookstores everywhere. For descriptions of all our titles and a key to Fodor's guidebook series, visit www.fodors.com/books

Gold Guides

U.S.

Alaska

Arizona

Boston

California

Cape Cod, Martha's Vineyard, Nantucket

The Carolinas & Georgia

Chicago

Colorado

Florida

Hawai'i

Las Vegas, Reno, Tahoe

Los Angeles

Maine, Vermont, New Hampshire

Maui & Lāna'i

Miami & the Keys

New England

New Orleans

New York City

Oregon

Pacific North Coast

Philadelphia & the Pennsylvania Dutch Country

The Rockies

San Diego

San Francisco

Santa Fe, Taos, Albuquerque

Seattle & Vancouver

The South

U.S. & British Virgin Islands

USA

Virginia & Maryland

Washington, D.C.

Foreign

Australia

Austria

The Bahamas

Belize & Guatemala

Bermuda

Canada

Cancún, Cozumel, Yucatán Peninsula

Caribbean

China

Costa Rica

Cuba

The Czech Republic & Slovakia

Denmark

Eastern & Central Europe

Europe

Florence, Tuscany & Umbria

France

Germany

Great Britain

Greece

Hong Kong

India

Ireland

Israel

Italy

Japan

London

Madrid & Barcelona

Mexico

Montréal & Québec City

Moscow, St. Petersburg, Kiev

The Netherlands, Belgium & Luxembourg

New Zealand

Norway

Nova Scotia, New Brunswick, Prince Edward Island

Paris

Portugal

Provence & the Riviera

Scandinavia

Scotland

Singapore

South Africa

South America

Southeast Asia

Spain

Sweden

Switzerland

Thailand

Toronto

Turkey

Vienna & the Danube Valley

Vietnam

Special-Interest Guides

Adventures to Imagine

Alaska Ports of Call

Ballpark Vacations

The Best Cruises

Caribbean Ports of Call

The Complete Guide to America's National Parks

Europe Ports of Call

Family Adventures

Fodor's Gay Guide to the USA

Fodor's How to Pack

Great American Learning Vacations

Great American Sports & Adventure Vacations

Great American Vacations

Great American Vacations for Travelers with Disabilities

Halliday's New Orleans Food Explorer

Healthy Escapes

Kodak Guide to Shooting Great Travel Pictures

National Parks and Seashores of the East

National Parks of the West

Nights to Imagine

Orlando Like a Pro

Rock & Roll Traveler Great Britain and Ireland

Rock & Roll Traveler USA

Sunday in San Francisco

Walt Disney World for Adults

Weekends in New York

Wendy Perrin's Secrets Every Smart Traveler Should Know

Worlds to Imagine

Fodor's Special Series

Fodor's Best Bed & Breakfasts
America
California
The Mid-Atlantic
New England
The Pacific Northwest
The South
The Southwest
The Upper Great Lakes

Compass American Guides
Alaska
Arizona
Boston
Chicago
Coastal California
Colorado
Florida
Hawai'i
Hollywood
Idaho
Las Vegas
Maine
Manhattan
Minnesota
Montana
New Mexico
New Orleans
Oregon
Pacific Northwest
San Francisco
Santa Fe
South Carolina
South Dakota
Southwest
Texas
Underwater Wonders of the National Parks
Utah
Virginia
Washington
Wine Country
Wisconsin
Wyoming

Citypacks
Amsterdam
Atlanta
Berlin
Boston
Chicago
Florence
Hong Kong
London
Los Angeles
Miami
Montréal
New York City
Paris

Prague
Rome
San Francisco
Sydney
Tokyo
Toronto
Venice
Washington, D.C.

Exploring Guides
Australia
Boston & New England
Britain
California
Canada
Caribbean
China
Costa Rica
Cuba
Egypt
Florence & Tuscany
Florida
France
Germany
Greek Islands
Hawai'i
India
Ireland
Israel
Italy
Japan
London
Mexico
Moscow & St. Petersburg
New York City
Paris
Portugal
Prague
Provence
Rome
San Francisco
Scotland
Singapore & Malaysia
South Africa
Spain
Thailand
Turkey
Venice
Vietnam

Flashmaps
Boston
New York
San Francisco
Washington, D.C.

Fodor's Cityguides
Boston
New York
San Francisco

Fodor's Gay Guides
Amsterdam
Los Angeles & Southern California
New York City
Pacific Northwest
San Francisco and the Bay Area
South Florida
USA

Karen Brown Guides
Austria
California
England B&Bs
England, Wales & Scotland
France B&Bs
France Inns
Germany
Ireland
Italy B&Bs
Italy Inns
Portugal
Spain
Switzerland

Languages for Travelers (Cassette & Phrasebook)
French
German
Italian
Spanish

Mobil Travel Guides
America's Best Hotels & Restaurants
Arizona
California and the West
Florida
Great Lakes
Major Cities
Mid-Atlantic
Northeast
Northwest and Great Plains
Southeast
Southern California
Southwest and South Central

Pocket Guides
Acapulco
Aruba
Atlanta
Barbados
Beijing
Berlin
Budapest
Dublin
Honolulu
Jamaica
London

Mexico City
New York City
Paris
Prague
Puerto Rico
Rome
San Francisco
Savannah & Charleston
Shanghai
Sydney
Washington, D.C.

Rivages Guides
Bed and Breakfasts of Character and Charm in France
Hotels and Country Inns of Character and Charm in France
Hotels and Country Inns of Character and Charm in Italy
Hotels of Character and Charm in Paris
Hotels of Character and Charm in Portugal
Hotels of Character and Charm in Spain
Wines & Vineyards of Character and Charm in France

Short Escapes
Britain
France
Near New York City
New England

Fodor's Sports
Golf Digest's Places to Play (USA)
Golf Digest's Places to Play in the Southeast
Golf Digest's Places to Play in the Southwest
Skiing USA
USA Today The Complete Four Sport Stadium Guide

Fodor's upCLOSE Guides
California
Europe
France
Great Britain
Ireland
Italy
London
Los Angeles
Mexico
New York City
Paris
San Francisco

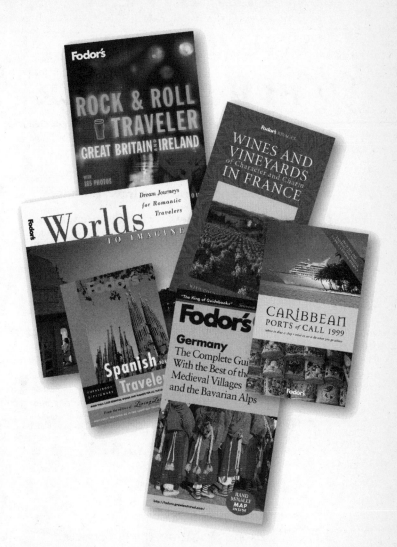

Looking for a different kind of vacation?

Fodor's makes it easy with a full line of international guidebooks to suit a variety of interests—from adventure to romance to language help.

At bookstores everywhere.
www.fodors.com

WHEREVER YOU TRAVEL, *H*ELP IS NEVER FAR AWAY.

From planning your trip to providing travel assistance along the way, American Express® Travel Service Offices are always there to help you do more.

Toronto

American Express Travel Service
Holt Renfrew Building
50 Bloor Street West
416/967-7113

American Express Travel Service
Royal York Hotel, #133-134
100 Front Street West
416/363-3883

Don Mills
American Express Vacation Travel Services
895 Don Mills Road
Two Park Center, 6th Floor
416/445-4700

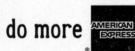

do more® AMERICAN EXPRESS
Travel
www.americanexpress.com/travel